Effective Curriculum

for Students With

Emotional
and
Behavioral
Disorders

Reaching Them Through Teaching Them

Beverley H. Johns
Garrison Alternative School
Jacksonville, Illinois

E. Paula Crowley
Illinois State University

Eleanor Guetzloe
University of South Florida

LOVE PUBLISHING COMPANY®
Denver • London • Sydney

Beverley Johns dedicates this book to Lonnie and all of her family and friends who stand with her in her advocacy for specialized instruction delivered by well-qualified special educators.

Paula Crowley dedicates this book to all the special education teachers who will use this as a reference in their classrooms, to the wonderful educators who have been a part of her own life, and to Dan and Patrick—her two inspirations.

Eleanor Guetzloe thanks her husband, Bruce, for tolerating the absence of his wife and the presence of large stacks of paper.

Published by Love Publishing Company
Denver, Colorado 80222

Library of Congress Catalog Card Number 2001096427

CONTENTS

Part Five: Focus on Partnerships   183

INTRODUCTION

"Curriculum bleakness," a description of exemplary programs across the United States serving students with emotional and behavioral disorders (E/BD), appeared in the 1990 publication titled *At the Schoolhouse Door.* The observers saw a curriculum that "hardly ever engaged the hearts and minds of teachers and students" (Steinberg, 1991, p. 7). Almost 10 years later, the Center for Effective Collaboration and Practice (1999) described programs for students with emotional and behavioral disorders: "Many special education programs for students with emotional and behavioral problems target behavioral change but place less emphasis on academic achievement" (p. 252).

Gunter and Denny (1998) note that there is a paucity of research on the topic of improving academic performance of students with emotional and behavioral disorders. Further, they comment that research indicates that effective instructional strategies may not be employed commonly in classrooms for students with E/BD. In fact, they believe, as do we, that emotional and behavioral disturbances may be "exacerbated by ineffective instruction" (p. 49).

We believe that ineffective instruction of our students must be stopped. It is time that we focus on the components of effective curriculum and instruction for students with emotional and behavioral disorders. This text is designed to assist educators in planning that effective curriculum.

The recurring theme in this book is how to create specialized instruction based on the individualized needs of the student with emotional and behavioral disorders. According to Sam Kirk, this is "what is special about special education." Minskoff (1998) credits Kirk: "He identified the use of individualized instruction in which methods and materials are adapted to a child based on a thorough diagnosis of the child's abilities and disabilities" (p. 16).

As you read this book, you will find that we stress the importance of knowing as much as possible about a child—a key component of the diagnostic-prescriptive approach. The teacher must know the strengths, deficits, interests, and behavioral functions of the child. Based on that diagnostic information, the teacher must then plan an appropriate program based on effective, direct instructional approaches. Those approaches are described in full in this work.

References

Center for Effective Collaboration and Practice (1999). Emphasizing achievement. *Reclaiming Children and Youth, 7*(4), 252–254.

Gunter, P., & Denny, R. (1998). Trends and issues in research regarding academic instruction of students with emotional and behavioral disorders. *Behavioral Disorders, 24*(1), 44–50.

Minskoff, E. (1998). Sam Kirk: The man who made special education special. *Learning Disabilities Research and Practice, 13*(1), 15–21.

Steinberg, Z. (1991). Pandora's children. *Beyond Behavior,* Spring 1991, 5–14.

PART ONE

Focus on the Teacher

1

The Teacher as a Catalyst for Change

Josh, a student who has had significant emotional and behavioral disorders, received intense intervention through a public day school for students with emotional and behavioral disorders. He was ready to graduate from high school and had held a job in a grocery store for over two years. Josh received a statewide award from the Illinois Council for Exceptional Children for his accomplishments in overcoming his disability. When he accepted the award, he stood proudly at the microphone and gave thanks to his parents, his teacher, and the principal of the school for "believing in me." That statement, which brought tears to the eyes of those individuals and many others in the audience, expressed the importance of the teacher in the life of a student. Furthermore, it expressed the importance of the roles of the teacher and the principal as catalysts for a successful change in Josh's life.

eachers of students with emotional and behavioral disorders have an opportunity to transform human lives. The students who come to their classrooms certified with such disorders have a long history of negative experiences, both as learners and in their social interactions with peers and teachers. Their observable behaviors range from withdrawing to acting out; some are clearly anxious and even frightened; some are depressed; some cannot focus their attention; and most of them consider school to be their least favorite place. Coping with the academic and social demands of school are nearly beyond the capacity of many of these students.

Special education teachers can be catalysts of effective educational outcomes for students with emotional and behavioral disorders both within and outside their classrooms. In their unique roles they have the opportunity to develop, implement, and evaluate innovative and productive academic and behavioral programs for students within the school setting. Beyond the school setting, they become partners with community agencies and other service providers who are essential to the positive growth and development of their students. In a real sense, teachers of students with behavioral disorders are catalysts for positive changes in the lives of the students they teach.

Prior to their placement in special education, students with emotional and behavioral disorders have histories of behaving in counterproductive ways that set them up for failure in the school setting. As we review the data on outcomes of students with emotional and behavioral disorders, we cannot but be seriously concerned about the current status of educational programming for these students (Knitzer, Steinberg, & Fleisch, 1990). The National Longitudinal Transition Study (Wagner, 1989) showed that students with emotional and behavioral disorders (E/BD) obtained lower grade-point averages than any other group of students with disabilities. According to data from the Chesapeake Institute (1994), only one third of students identified with emotional and behavioral disorders completed school. After school many live marginalized lives in which they become either victims or oppressors or alternate between these two roles.

Evidence abounds to support the assertion that students with emotional and behavioral disorders often require teachers' attention even at the level of an emergency. If these students do not receive the socialization and academic intervention they need, they will continue to fail academically and will continue to have difficulty in their relationships with peers and adults. Once again, a teacher can become a catalyst of more positive social and academic outcomes. In the long run, teachers of students with emotional and behavioral disorders can make the difference between a life lived in desperation or one lived with dignity.

McIntyre and Battle (1998) studied students' perceptions of the traits of "good teachers" of students with emotional and behavioral disorders. The students cited specific personality traits such as "likes kids," "is a nice person," and "is friendly" as most important. Other traits valued by students were respectful treatment of students, skillful behavior management practices, and skillful instructional procedures. Research studies on resilience conducted by Emmy Werner (1984; 1986) and Luthar and Zigler (1991) indicate that it only takes the caring, interest, warmth, support, and understanding of one person to make a critical difference in the life of a vulnerable human being. Such a person can be a teacher, parent, relative, neighbor, or librarian, among others. Therefore, we cannot overemphasize the seriousness of the professional responsibility undertaken by teachers of students with emotional and behavioral disorders.

A willingness to embrace one's potential to be a positive influence on the lives of students with emotional and behavioral disorders is essential. Many teachers do so with joy. Essential to the acceptance of this professional responsibility is an eagerness to learn how to teach these students effectively. The special education teacher, who is aware that many other teachers have made attempts that have been unsuccessful, has another chance to succeed.

In classroom settings, teachers of students with emotional and behavioral disorders design learning environments to maximize the students' opportunity to learn. Teachers have knowledge of and skill in using behavior management procedures without which learning cannot take place. They select curriculum content and instructional procedures that are relevant for each student. They spend much time and effort problem-solving: Many students bring not only emotional and behavioral disorders to the classroom but also poor study skills, poor work skills, and often specific learning disabilities (Epstein, Kinder, & Bursuck, 1989; Luebke, Epstein, & Cullinan, 1989). Teachers will often find themselves thinking: "How can I motivate John?" "How can I get Laurie to complete her work?" "Why is Brett so frightened?" They will entertain a host of other challenging questions daily. As catalysts, teachers connect students with the curriculum, instructional materials and procedures, and with the appropriate setting in order to start them on a path toward better social adjustment and scholastic achievement.

Effective teachers of students with behavioral disorders have specific competencies (Fink & Janssen, 1993). They use instruction that is individualized and specialized to meet the unique academic and behavioral needs of students with disabilities in this area. Individualized instruction is truly that. Teachers have the skills to collaborate effectively with a team of professionals and the parents/guardians of each child/adolescent to develop an individualized education plan (Bullock, Ellis, & Wilson, 1994). Together they develop legal documents that form the cornerstone of the child's special education.

Another hallmark of effective teaching of students with E/BD is the use of a diagnostic and prescriptive approach to teaching and learning. In this approach, teachers assess the knowledge and skill level of students on an ongoing basis. The outcome of such ongoing assessment guides the teacher's decision making about what the student needs to learn, how the content needs to be taught, what materials to use, and other decisions related to teaching and learning. A diagnostic and prescriptive approach guides the continual decision making that is an integral part of a teacher's day.

Educators of students with E/BD use effective teaching methods that uniquely address the behavioral and academic needs of each student in the classroom. These are data-based methods that, careful research studies indicate, bring about positive behavioral change. Effective teaching methods facilitate the academic and social development of students. This text is designed to present educators of students with E/BD with a thoughtful, up-to-date, and comprehensive data-based guide to teaching students with emotional and behavioral disorders.

In addition to being highly effective within the classroom, teachers should also play a significant role in the community of care that surrounds their students. We no longer expect that teachers can work effectively in the classroom if their roles do not extend beyond it. Today we recognize that it takes communities, partnerships, and entire systems in concert to address the academic and behavioral needs of students with emotional and behavioral disorders (Brendtro, Brokenleg, & Van Bockern, 1990).

Outside of the classroom, teachers collaborate with their general education colleagues in providing appropriate education for their students. Furthermore, within the school setting, the administrative support as well as district-level administrative support teachers receive is essential for successful work with students with behavioral disorders. Beyond the school setting, teachers collaborate with parents, guardians, and often extended family members. Furthermore, teachers often work with other professionals involved with the students. In their search for curriculum content with high "real world" relevance, teachers seek out employment opportunities for students. The role of catalyst both within and outside the classroom setting is integral to the role of the teacher of students with E/BD.

Teaching students with E/BD is a multifaceted challenge. By using existing resources and developing new ones both within and outside the classroom, and by using curriculum and instructional methods that reach students who have failed academically and socially, teachers can meet the challenge of changing human behavior.

This book is designed to focus primarily on the curriculum and instructional aspects of this endeavor. We write from the perspective that the development and use of appropriate curricula and instruction is essential for effective educational programming for students with emotional and behavioral disorders. Part One is devoted solely to communicating our understanding of the teacher's role. Part Two, containing chapters 2 through 4, presents guiding principles for teachers of students with emotional and behavioral disorders. We present the assumptions underlying quality educational programming, we discuss life skills and the transition to adulthood, and we examine the role of the individualized education program in quality educational programming. In Part Three, we focus on the curriculum specifically and present chapters examining the concept of a meaningful and relevant curriculum, the central role of social skills, and diversity education. Finally, we present a chapter on the curriculum of hope whereby the community and the arts play essential parts in the students' educational experiences.

Part Four focuses on instruction. We examine engaged time in the classroom, higher-level thinking skills, self-management skills, and learning strategies and study skills. Part Five focuses on partnerships and explores relationships with general educators and parents. We conclude with a discussion on special educators and how they engage in self-care in order to protect their personal and professional well-being.

Discussion Questions

1. In what ways do you view the role of teachers of students with emotional and behavioral disorders as catalysts? Describe what the authors mean by teachers as catalysts both within and outside the classroom environment.
2. Interview a teacher of students with emotional and behavioral disorders and find out what aspects of that teacher's professional role are most rewarding and satisfying. What aspects does the teacher find most challenging?
3. In her role as a teacher of adolescents with emotional and behavioral disorders, it is a common experience for the educator to be a catalyst both within and outside the classroom. List as many ways as you can to show how she is a catalyst.

References

Brendtro, L. K., Brokenleg, M., & Van Bockern, S. (1990). *Reclaiming youth at risk: Our hope for the future.* Bloomington, IN: National Educational Service.

Bullock, L. M., Ellis, L. L., & Wilson, M. J. (1994). Knowledge/skills needed by teachers who work with students with severe emotional/behavioral disorders: A revisitation. *Behavioral Disorders, 19,* 108–125.

Chesapeake Institute. (1994). *National agenda for achieving better results for children and youth with serious emotional disturbance.* Washington, DC: U.S. Department of Education.

Epstein, M. E., Kinder, D., & Bursuck, B. (1989). The academic status of adolescents with behavioral disorders. *Behavioral Disorders, 14,* 157–165.

Fink, A. H., & Janssen, K. N. (1993). Competencies for teaching students with emotional-behavioral disabilities. *Preventing School Failure, 37,* 11–15.

Knitzer, J., Steinberg, Z., & Fleisch, B. (1990). *At the schoolhouse door: An examination of programs and policies for children with behavioral and emotional problems.* New York: Bank Street College of Education.

Luebke, J., Epstein, M. H., & Cullinan, D. (1989). Comparison of teacher-rated achievement levels of behaviorally disordered learning disabled and nonhandicapped adolescents. *Behavioral Disorders, 15,* 1–8.

Luthar, S. S., & Zigler, E. (1991). Vulnerability and competence: A review of research on resilience in childhood. *American Journal of Orthopsychiatry, 6,* 6–22.

McIntyre, T., & Battle, J. (1998). The traits of "good teachers" as identified by African-American and White students with emotional and/or behavioral disorders. *Behavioral Disorders, 23,* 134–142.

Wagner, M. (1989). *Youth with disabilities during transition: An overview of descriptive findings from the National Longitudinal Transition Study.* Palo Alto, CA: Stanford Research Institute.

Werner, E. E. (1984). Resilient children. *Young Children, 40,* 68–72.

Werner, E. E. (1986). The concept of risk from a developmental perspective. *Advances in Special Education, 5,* 1–23.

PART TWO

Guiding Principles for Teachers of Students With Emotional and Behavioral Disorders

2

Assumptions Underlying Quality Educational Programming for Students With Emotional and Behavioral Disorders

JJ is a 13-year-old intense young man. He is tall, slender, and has blond hair and blue eyes. He is two grade levels below his peers in most academic subjects. He always looks as if he is ready to verbally or physically attack his peers and teachers. His eyes maintain an intense glare and an emotionless facial expression. He is usually quiet and withdrawn, but when he speaks, he often argues about all aspects of being a student in a public school classroom setting. Much to the surprise of his teacher, one day he put his head on his folded arms, which were resting on the desk, and cried in what seemed to be an out-of-control manner for no apparent reason.

Laurel is 11 years old, with light brown hair and blue eyes. She dresses provocatively and is often requested to button her blouses or dresses. She is generally uninterested in the academic tasks assigned to her but is very willing to help other students in the classroom. Laurel can be an enjoyable student at times, but at other times she becomes verbally aggressive to teachers and peers. When frustrated, she throws any available object. Her behavior is erratic and unpredictable from hour to hour.

J J and Laurel are just two of several children a teacher of students with emotional and behavioral disorders works with on a daily basis. Effective educators of students like JJ and Laurel must have an extensive knowledge base and possess a large repertoire of skills even before they enter the classroom. This chapter addresses the assumptions underlying quality educational programming for students with emotional and behavioral disorders (E/BD). More specifically, we will first discuss the knowledge and skills essential for special educators as described by the Council for Exceptional Children. Then we will present six guiding principles underlying quality educational programming for teachers of students with emotional and behavioral disorders.

Standards Set by the Council for Exceptional Children

When teachers of E/BD students accept the challenge of working with students like JJ and Laurel, they must have the appropriate academic preparation to meet the inherent professional challenges in this complex and multidimensional work. In the publication *What Every Special Educator Must Know: The International Standards for the Preparation and Certification of Special Education Teachers,* the Council for Exceptional Children (CEC, 1995) presents a common core of knowledge and skills special educators must possess prior to working with students with disabilities.

First, CEC expects that all special educators will uphold its Code of Ethics. This professional organization holds members of the special education profession responsible for living by and advancing these principles. The Code of Ethics comprises eight distinct requirements of special education professionals:

1. Special educators are committed to develop the highest education and quality-of-life potential of individuals with disabilities.
2. They are expected to promote and maintain a high level of competence and integrity in practicing their profession.
3. They are expected to engage in professional activities that benefit individuals with disabilities, their families, colleagues, students, and research participants.
4. The Code of Ethics also requires special educators to exercise objective professional judgment.
5. The Code requires that special educators advance their professional knowledge and skills.
6. It requires them to work within the standards of local, state, and national policies.
7. The Code of Ethics encourages special educators to be innovators and thereby seek to improve the delivery of special education and the practice of the profession when necessary (CEC, 1995).

8. Finally, special educators are expected to live lives of integrity in the practice of their profession.

Following the Code of Ethics, CEC presents a common core of knowledge and skills in eight areas that all special educators are expected to have in common. Prior to entry into the classroom, special educators are expected to have knowledge and skills in the philosophical, historical, and legal foundations of special education. They are expected to be aware of the characteristics of learners, to be able to assess, diagnose, and evaluate them. They are expected to have knowledge and skills in the areas of instructional content and practice, in planning and managing the teaching and learning environment, and in managing student behavior and social interaction skills. Furthermore, special educators are expected to have knowledge and skills in establishing communication and collaborative partnerships with individuals, parents, and school and community personnel. Finally, special educators are expected to know what constitutes professionalism and ethical practices.

Assumptions Underlying Quality Educational Programming

Criticisms of current educational programming for students with E/BD (Knitzer, Steinberg, & Fleisch, 1990; Koyanagi & Gaines, 1993) have inspired a new examination of what it takes to develop quality educational programs for those children and youth. What are the underlying assumptions and essential indicators of quality educational programming for students with emotional and behavioral disorders?

The need to develop quality educational programs for E/BD students was considered so important during the 1990s that a National Agenda (U.S. Department of Education, 1994) was developed. The Agenda included seven target areas: expanding positive learning opportunities, strengthening school and community capacity, valuing and addressing diversity, collaborating with families, promoting appropriate assessment, providing ongoing skill development and support, and creating comprehensive and collaborative systems.

A paramount consideration in the Agenda was the importance of students' engagement in useful and positive learning opportunities (Neel, Alexander, & Meadows, 1997). Knitzer et al. (1990) found educational programs across the country that were dull, uninteresting, repetitive, and unmotivating. They criticized the use of countless worksheets and work folders, which required students to work alone for hours at a time.

The National Agenda assumes the importance of fostering initiatives that strengthen the capacities of schools and communities (McLaughlin, Leone, Meisel, & Henderson, 1997). This target encourages local schools and communities to provide support to students with E/BD rather than placing them in residential or out-of-state facilities.

The Agenda encourages a renewed commitment to valuing the diversity of all individuals in society. There is concern that lack of appreciation for cultural diversity is related to academic failure and to high school drop-out rates (Singh, Ellis, Oswald, Wechsler, & Curtis, 1997; Smith & Coutinho, 1997). The Agenda brings attention to the importance of valuing and addressing diversity in the schools with the hope that this will bring about better outcomes for students with emotional and behavioral disorders.

The fourth target area addresses the importance of working effectively with families. Cheney and Osher (1997) describe some of the current barriers to effective collaboration with families of students with E/BD. They review literature that provides methods of developing positive collaborative relationships.

Target 5 of the National Agenda focuses on the appropriate assessment of students with E/BD. Wehby, Symons, and Hollo (1997) state that one of the most pressing problems in this area is the failure to identify school-age children who are at risk for developing emotional and behavioral disorders. Kauffman (1997) brings attention to the under-identification of students with emotional and behavioral disorders. Wehby et al. (1997) address the importance of assessment-based interventions and the recognition of the necessary skills and supports for successful reintegration of students with E/BD.

Providing ongoing skill development and support to teachers who work with students with emotional and behavioral disorders is the focus of Target 6. Sugai, Bullis, and Cumblad (1997) address the unique challenges faced by teachers of students with E/BD. Much hard work can be done to provide teacher education and supports that are often lacking.

Finally, Target 7 of the National Agenda focuses on the creation of coherence among agencies who serve E/BD students. Much has been written about the need for the development of partnerships, collaboration, and systems of care for these students (Epstein, Cullinan, Quinn, & Cumblad, 1995; Walker, Horner, Sugai, Bullis, Sprague, Bricker, & Kaufman, 1996). The needs of these students are so complex and so varied that schools alone cannot serve them effectively.

The seven targets of the National Agenda clearly present the complex range of assumptions that underlie quality educational programming for students with emotional and behavioral disorders. It is clear that a supportive administration and sufficient resources (Ayres, Meyer, Erevelles, & Park-Lee, 1994; Neel et al., 1997), involved parents (Cheney & Osher, 1997), and support teachers (Sugai et al., 1997), addressing diversity (Singh et al., 1997) and the need for collaboration (Epstein et al., 1995; Walker et al., 1996) are all essential elements in the development of effective education programs. We must always remember, however, that teachers themselves have central roles in this process. Knowledge and skills are the essential tools teachers must process to do the complex work of educating students with varied academic deficits and with emotional and behavioral disorders.

Teachers of E/BD students must hold the following six assumptions:

Assumption 1: Educators of students with emotional and behavioral disorders are committed to respecting the dignity of the individual child and adolescent.

An essential starting point for teachers of E/BD students is a commitment to the dignity of each individual student. Despite their students' behavioral histories, level of severity of behavioral or academic need, teachers of students with emotional and behavioral disorders must respect each student's uniqueness as a human being. Nothing can undermine this commitment.

On a daily basis, teachers of students like JJ and Laurel are faced with children who behave in ways that run counter to socially acceptable behavior and to the teachers' values. For example, teachers encounter students who are willing to use verbal or physical aggression to solve conflicts, who avoid challenging academic tasks, or who withdraw from social and emotional exchanges with peers and adults. The special educator knows that these behaviors are, in fact, communicative efforts on the students' parts. Despite these and other such behaviors, the teacher of students with E/BD maintains a sense of the dignity of each human being.

To do so, teachers can adopt thinking strategies and theories of behavior that assist them in separating the student from the behavior. The child's behavior is unacceptable but the child as a human being is to be respected. Behavioral theory, which supports the belief that all human behavior is learned, reminds a teacher that the child must simply learn a new behavior. Such thinking strategies are essential to those who desire to remain positive and productive professionals.

Assumption 2: Educators of students with emotional and behavioral disorders are committed to the individualization of instruction.

Special educators teach students one by one. No two students are alike. Teachers are reminded of this fact every time they use the student's individualized education plan (IEP). The teacher must expect to find differences among students in a classroom of those with emotional and behavioral disorders. Furthermore, rarely do students function at predictable levels across academic areas. For example, JJ functioned at grade level in the area of mathematics, but in the area of sight-word vocabulary and spelling he functioned on the third-grade level. Differences between students and within students make for a continuous challenge.

Recognition of the importance of individualization leads a teacher to use many and varied instructional methods, educational materials, and curricula. When individualizing instruction, it is essential for the teacher to be knowledgeable, flexible, and creative. Although the teacher will teach the students one by one, there will be many opportunities for grouping students and giving them the opportunity to work together. Such arrangements foster the development of critically needed social skills.

Assumption 3: Educators of students with emotional and behavioral disorders are committed to a curriculum that focuses on the behavioral as well as academic needs of students.

Not only do students with emotional and behavioral disorders need to work on their academic skills, but also it is imperative that they work on the development of their behavior. After all, it is usually due to their behavioral difficulties that they are first identified as students who need special education services. Teachers of students with E/BD have dual roles: that of academic educators and that of socializing agents. It is not sufficient to focus on one role to the exclusion of the other. Teachers of students with emotional and behavioral disorders will make a serious error if they consider that their primary responsibility is to teach the student academic skills. Just as serious an error is the idea that the teacher should focus only on the improvement of behavior. Somehow the teacher must engage in the delicate balance of giving sufficient recognition to both academic and behavioral development.

There is some controversy about how to perform these dual tasks. Should teachers focus on academic skills and behavioral skills separately? In reality, the two are often taught in conjunction. A teacher working on reading with Laurel and a peer on the same level might remind Laurel of appropriate ways to express her anger. However, it is also important for teachers to set aside time to work on social skills directly and to focus primarily on the development and use of appropriate social behaviors. It is strongly advised that teachers work on academic and social behaviors together, as well as set aside time to focus specifically on each set of skills.

Assumption 4: Educators of students with emotional and behavioral disorders are committed to data-based instruction, which involves the observation and measurement of academic and social behaviors.

Data-based instruction involves the use of assessment procedures that provide data on students' academic and social skills, which guide the focus of instruction. An example: When teaching spelling to Laurel, it is essential to know what she has already learned and from there to continue to develop her spelling skills. A gross error occurs when a teacher presents assignments to students that are either too difficult or too easy for them. Assessing students' knowledge and skills and using the data from this assessment will assure a match between the students' academic skill level and the instructional level chosen by the teacher.

When teachers fail to use data-based instruction, they run the risk of wasting the time and effort of both parties. The student may be involved in learning that is irrelevant for one reason or another. Furthermore, when instruction is not matched to the academic and social skill needs of students, teachers increase the chance that students will engage in negative behaviors (Munk & Repp, 1994). Therefore, data-based instruction will assist in maximizing the educational opportunities offered in the classroom.

Assumption 5: Educators of students with emotional and behavioral disorders are committed to the use of positive behavior management methods and refuse to participate in the use of aversive behavior-changing strategies.

A wide range of behavior management strategies exists; teachers of students with E/BD must select the most positive methods possible. In recent years much concern has been expressed about the use of aversive methods or any other methods that would undermine the dignity of students. The Council for Children with Behavioral Disorders (CCBD) has taken a stand against such methods and urges professionals not to engage in strategies that may put students at risk for abuse or neglect.

This is a critical area of concern as it is possible to use even generally accepted methods to manage behavior in an inappropriate manner. For example, when JJ uses verbally aggressive language to communicate with his peers, the teacher may use a time-out procedure. However, if JJ is placed in time-out for an undue amount of time (say, 30 minutes or more), the management strategy becomes abusive. Leaving students in time-out for lengthy periods of time is never acceptable. Time-out must be understood as time-out from reinforcement (Alberto & Troutman, 1995) and should be used in a highly structured and supervised manner.

It is imperative, then, that teachers of E/BD students engage in positive behavior management methods. Munk and Repp (1994) have much to say about the range of instructional methods that positively influence students' behavior. For example, giving students a choice of tasks (Clarke et al., 1995) and varying tasks and the pace of instruction influence behavior positively. Therefore, in addition to using positive behavior management procedures, teachers can select and use instructional procedures that reduce the amount of negative student behaviors in the classroom setting.

Assumption 6: Educators of students with emotional and behavioral disorders are committed to the use of formative and summative evaluation methods.

A final assumption is that teachers of students with E/BD will engage in ongoing evaluation to ensure that students are learning what the teacher intends. If they are not doing so, teachers will adjust the educational program variables as necessary. Data from formative and summative evaluations pinpoint a student's status in either academic or behavioral knowledge and skills. Through these data, teachers monitor the students' progress through the course of weeks, months, and years. By using these evaluation procedures, teachers can determine the effectiveness of specific interventions and make changes in accord with the IEP when they are indicated.

A teacher of students with emotional and behavioral disorders is often called upon to provide information to parents and colleagues. Data from both formative and summative methods will be crucial in monitoring and planning the program. Teachers who can provide evidence of student learning can also provide evidence of their own teaching efforts. These data provide them with evidence of their accountability. Finally, teachers who conduct formative and summative evaluations of both academic and behavioral skill development avoid false assumptions and increase the probability that the educational program will match the academic and behavioral needs of the students.

Conclusion

Students with emotional and behavioral disorders have unique educational needs. These needs present serious professional challenges for the personnel committed to students' educational development. Educational personnel undertake this challenging endeavor by first establishing a solid knowledge base of the field. They then develop a set of skills through the use of clinical experiences at the preservice level.

Today the National Agenda for Achieving Better Results for Children and Youth with Serious Emotional Disturbance (U.S. Department of Education, 1994) provides direction for personnel in the area of educating students with behavioral disorders. The seven areas targeted in the National Agenda focus attention on points of critical importance for effective educational programming. One may consider this era a time of renewed interest and concern about providing the best possible programming for students with E/BD (Landrum & Tankersley, 1999; Simpson, 1999; Smith, 1996; Walker, Zeller, Close, Webber, & Gresham, 1999). Current professionals are invited and challenged to be as creative, knowledgeable, and dedicated as possible. They are challenged to do new and brave experiments as they boldly embrace the challenge of doing their best work in the education of children who are among the nation's most needy.

Finally, underlying all efforts at preparing personnel to teach students with E/BD is the disposition to do the work. It is essential, for example, that preservice educators have profound respect and appreciation for students with behavioral disorders and that they cherish an unshakable hope in these students' potential to learn, grow, and become independent and fully functioning members of society.

Discussion Questions

1. What do you believe are the key components of a professional development plan for teachers of students with emotional and behavioral disorders?
2. If a colleague within your school building were to engage in activities that did not comply with the ethical standards established by the CEC, what would you do?

References

Alberto, P. A., & Troutman, A. C. (1999). *Applied behavior analysis for teachers* (5th ed.). Columbus, OH: Merrill.

Ayres, B. J., Meyer, L., Erevelles, N., & Park-Lee, S. (1994). Easy for you to say: Teacher perspectives on implementing most promising practices. *The Journal of the Association for Persons with Severe Handicaps, 19,* 84–93.

Cheney, D., & Osher, T. (1997). Collaborate with families. *Journal of Emotional and Behavioral Disorders, 5,* 36–44, 54.

Clarke, S., Dunlap, G., Foster-Johnson, L., Childs, K. E., Wilson, D., White, R., & Vera, A. (1995). Improving the conduct of students with behavioral disorders by incorporating student interests into curricular activities. *Behavioral Disorders, 20,* 221–237.

Council for Exceptional Children. (1995). *What every special educator must know: The international standards for the preparation and certification of special education teachers.* Reston, VA: Council for Exceptional Children.

Epstein, M. H., Cullinan, D., Quinn, K., & Cumblad, C. (1995). Personal, family, and service use characteristics of young people served by an interagency, community-based system of care. *Journal of Emotional and Behavioral Disorders, 3,* 55–64.

Kauffman, J. M. (1997). *Characteristics of behavioral disorders in children and youth* (6th ed.). New York: Merrill.

Knitzer, J., Steinberg, Z., & Fleisch, B. (1990). *At the schoolhouse door: An examination of programs and policies for children with behavioral and emotional problems.* New York: Bank Street College of Education.

Koyanagi, C., & Gaines, S. (1993). *All systems failure: An examination of the results of neglecting the needs of children with serious emotional disturbance.* Alexandria, VA: National Mental Health Association.

Landrum, T. J., & Tankersley, M. (1999). Emotional and behavioral disorders in the new millennium: The future is now. *Behavioral Disorders, 24,* 305–318.

McLaughlin, M. J., Leone, P. E., Meisel, S., & Henderson, K. (1997). Strengthen school and community capacity. *Journal of Emotional and Behavioral Disorders, 5,* 15–23.

Munk, D. D., & Repp, A. C. (1994). The relationship between instructional variables and problem behavior: A review. *Exceptional Children, 60,* 390–401.

Neel, R. S., Alexander, L., & Meadows, N. B. (1997). Expand positive learning opportunities and results. *Journal of Emotional and Behavioral Disorders, 5,* 3–14.

Simpson, R. L. (1999). Children and youth with emotional and behavioral disorders: A concerned look at the present and a hopeful eye for the future. *Behavioral Disorders, 24,* 284–292.

Singh, N. N., Ellis, C. R., Oswald, D. P., Wechsler, H. A., & Curtis, W. J. (1997). Value and address diversity. *Journal of Emotional and Behavioral Disorders, 5,* 24–35.

Smith, C. R. (1996). Advocacy for students with emotional and behavioral disorders: One call for redirected efforts. *Behavioral Disorders, 22,* 96–105.

Smith, S. W., & Coutinho, M. J. (1997). Achieving the goals of the National Agenda: Progress and prospects. *Journal of Emotional and Behavioral Disorders, 5,* 2–5, 23.

Sugai, G., Bullis, M., & Cumblad, C. (1997). Provide ongoing skill development and support. *Journal of Emotional and Behavioral Disorders, 5,* 55–64.

U.S. Department of Education. (1994). *National Agenda for achieving better results for children and youth with serious emotional disturbance.* Washington, DC: Office of Special Education Programs.

Walker, H. M., Horner, R. H., Sugai, G., Bullis, M., Sprague, J. R., Bricker, D., & Kaufman, M. J. (1996). Integrated approaches to preventing antisocial behavior patterns among school-age children and youth. *Journal of Emotional and Behavioral Disorders, 4,* 194–209.

Walker, H. M., Zeller, R. W., Close, D. W., Webber, J., & Gresham, F. (1999). The present unwrapped: Change and challenge in the field of behavioral disorders. *Behavioral Disorders, 24,* 293–304.

Wehby, J. H., Symons, F. J., & Hollo, A. (1997). Promote appropriate assessment. *Journal of Emotional and Behavioral Disorders, 5,* 45–54.

3

Life Skills and Transition to Adulthood

When she was 8 years old, Susan was identified as having a behavioral disorder and began to receive special education services. She was placed in a self-contained classroom for students with emotional and behavioral disorders. Susan had average intelligence, although her mother functioned in the range of mental retardation. When Susan was 6 years old, her mother was denied custody because of evidence of serious neglect and abuse. Susan's father was never actively involved in her life. Through the years, she was placed in one foster home after another. By the age of 14, she had been placed in 10 different foster homes.

During the tenth grade, Susan became pregnant. Mark, the father of her child, was also identified as having a behavioral disorder and was receiving special education services. They wanted to get married but state law would not permit them to do so. Susan moved in with Mark and his mother before she gave birth to their child. Shortly after, Susan became pregnant again, and this time, she had twins. She dropped out of school to care for her children full-time. By age 19, she had four children. Periodically, her name has appeared in the local newspaper for the theft of small items in local stores.

At the age of 14, Beth began to engage in bizarre behaviors such as losing her way around the city in which she grew up, failing to bathe herself regularly, and dressing herself in black and unkempt clothing. At school her behavior changed, too. She was often truant; when present she was withdrawn, would cry, and was unmotivated to do her academic assignments.

Beth's parents sought the assistance of therapists and school personnel. After she was deemed eligible to receive special education services, she was placed in a special school for students with emotional and behavioral disorders. Years of ups and downs followed, but despite every challenge, Beth's parents and extended family members remained supportive throughout. She was diagnosed with schizophrenia and was prescribed daily medication as well as weekly therapy sessions.

She dropped out of school during her senior year of high school and began to work full-time at a local nursing home. She learned how to drive and started to make plans to live independently in her own apartment. Soon she had a boyfriend, was studying for her GED, and continued to work full-time.

Today Beth is married, has a healthy teen-age son, and she and her husband work full-time. They have their own home and pay a monthly mortgage. She continues to take her medication daily and attends monthly therapy sessions. Her family lives nearby and is a constant source of support for Beth, her husband, and son.

I n the vignettes, the lives that Susan and Beth lead after their school years are quite different. Although she has the responsibility of four children, Susan continues to exhibit antisocial behaviors. Her life fails to exhibit the presence of an active and supportive network. Unlike Susan, Beth got her GED, is employed, and is living independently in her own home. She participates in family and in sporting events with her husband and son. She never lost her link to her family, community, and the professional agencies that provide her with a crucial network of support. We might well wonder why more young adults with emotional and behavioral disorders do not live independent lives and are not fully integrated into mainstream society.

Current Status of Young Adults With Emotional and Behavioral Disorders

A growing body of literature indicates that large numbers of students with disabilities, and particularly those with emotional and behavioral disorders, face a very challenging adulthood (Blackorby & Wagner, 1996; Carson, Sitlington, & Frank, 1995; Edgar, 1988; Frank, Sitlington, & Carson, 1995; Neel, Meadows, Levine, & Edgar, 1988; Phelps & Hanley-Maxwell, 1997; Sitlington, Frank, & Carson, 1993). Six to 12 months after graduation, youths with disabilities in general are employed at a rate of 58% (Edgar, 1988). Up to two years after leaving school, 25% of youths with disabilities are engaged in full-time competitive employment and 21% are engaged in part-time competitive employment (Blackorby & Wagner, 1996). Also, three to five years after they leave school 14% are engaged in part-time competitive employment and 44% are engaged in full-time competitive employment.

Overall, 60% of youths with emotional and behavioral disorders are employed either full- or part-time, and 31% are unemployed and do not attend school (Neel et al., 1988). According to Blackorby and Wagner (1996), 41% of youths with serious emotional disturbance are engaged in competitive employment less than two years after leaving school and after three to five years this number increases to 47%. These data also indicate that even among those who are employed, 36% are dissatisfied with their work.

The personal characteristics of youths with disabilities influence what adulthood holds for them (Blackorby & Wagner, 1996; Heal & Rusch, 1995). For example, Blackorby and Wagner found that males are more frequently employed than females, ethnicity influences chances of employment, and completion of secondary school is significant in their potential for postschool employment. According to employment statistics, youths from Caucasian and Hispanic ethnic backgrounds fare better than African Americans. Graduates from high school are employed at higher rates than dropouts or those who can no longer attend school because they have reached a certain age (age out of school systems). Heal and Rusch (1995) found that personal characteristics such as academic skills, life skills, individual competencies, and family networks positively influence outcomes for young adults with disabilities.

Data consistently report that youth with emotional and behavioral disorders face particular challenges during adulthood (Blackorby & Wagner, 1996; Carson et al., 1995; Maag & Katsiyannis, 1998; Malmgren, Edgar, & Neel, 1998; Neel et al., 1988). As special education professionals, we might well be concerned that, in general, the outcomes data indicate that at least 40% of youths with emotional and behavioral disorders are not engaged in either part-time or full-time work. Additionally, we must be concerned that even when they do work, only 9% earn more than $5.00 per hour in the two years following school. After three to five years, 49% earn more than $6.00 per hour, and once again, males fare better than females (Levine & Edgar, 1995; Neel et al., 1988). Caucasians fare better than Hispanics and African Americans, and graduates fare better than dropouts and those who are no longer in school because of age (Blackorby & Wagner, 1996). Carson et al. (1995) found that when youths with emotional and behavioral disorders are employed, they are involved in menial work, which is largely part-time, and fewer than half of them receive any type of benefits, such as health insurance coverage or vacation days, even three years after they leave school. Neel et al. (1988) found that only 1% of young adults with emotional and behavioral disorders avail themselves of services provided by mental health agencies.

Although employment statistics are important, we must also be concerned about other indicators of adult adjustment, such as engagement in recreational activities and living as independently as possible. Carson et al. (1995) set up criteria for "successful adult adjustment" (p. 131) for young adults with emotional and behavioral disorders. The criteria for a high level of successful adult adjustment involved engagement in competitive employment, living independently, paying some or all living expenses, and involved in more than three leisure activities. The criteria for a low level of adult adjustment involved competitive employment, a variety of living arrangement options, and involvement in at least one leisure activity. They found that one year after graduating from high school, only 3% of youths with emotional and behavioral disorders met the criterion for high adult adjustment and 0% met the criterion three years after graduation. A total of only 18% of graduates met the criterion for a low level of successful adult adjustment one year after graduation, and 25% met the criterion three years after graduation. Of the dropout population, 1% met the criteriona for high adult adjustment and 8% met this criterion following three years after exiting from school. Additionally, 23% of the dropout population met the criterion for a low level of adult adjustment one year after exiting from school, and 20% met this criterion three years after exiting from school.

We may be concerned, too, about the extent to which young adults with emotional and behavioral disorders are involved in postsecondary educational programming. Despite ever-expanding postsecondary education, training, career options, and the choices for individuals with disabilities in general (Hallahan & Kauffman, 2000), individuals with emotional and behavioral disorders were not faring well in postsecondary educational environments (Mattison, Spitznagel, & Felix, 1998). Blackorby and Wagner (1996) found that only 17% of youths with serious emotional disturbance attended a postsecondary school within two years after leaving high school and 26% attended a postsecondary school three to five years after high school. Gender differences mark these data in that 15% of males and 12% of females attend school within two years after high school. It is interesting that 29% of females and 26% of males attend a postsecondary school three to five years after high school. Caucasians are engaged in postsecondary education more often than African Americans and Hispanics, and high school graduates attend postsecondary education programs more often than high school dropouts and those who leave school because of age.

Special Education Professionals' and Legislators' Responses to the Outcomes Data

Among the most positive developments in the special education profession in the past decade is its concern about the lives of adults with disabilities. Moreover, adults with disabilities themselves are increasingly seeking choice and control over the decisions that impact their lives (Gagne, 1994; Kennedy, 1996; Wehmeyer & Schwartz, 1997).

The Individuals with Disabilities Education Act, Public Law 101-476, further affirmed concern about the lives of adults with disabilities in 1990 (Individuals with Disabilities Education Act, 1990). This law mandated an individual transition plan for students with disabilities to be implemented no later than age 16. This became a component of the IEP process. Transition planning and services involve coordinating activities for a student within an outcome-oriented process, and promoting movement from school to adulthood. Transition planning prepares students for postsecondary eduction, vocational training, integrated employment, supported employment, continuing and adult education, adult services, independent living, and community participation. Transition programming concentrates on the development of skills needed to live a responsible and independent adult life in a democratic society.

In the 1997 reauthorization of IDEA (Public Law 105-17), new transition requirements are outlined. Beginning when a child is 14, a statement of the transition needs of that child, under the applicable components of the child's IEP, is required. The statement must focus on the child's participation in courses of study, such as advanced placement courses or a vocational education program. Beginning at the age of 16 (or younger, if determined appropriate by the IEP team), a statement of needed transition services is required for the child, including, when appropriate, a statement of interagency responsibilities or needed links. At least one year before the student reaches the age of majority under state law, the IEP must contain a statement that the student has been informed of the rights that will be transferred under the law (Maag & Katsiyannis, 1998).

An important accomplishment of the transition legislation is the recognition that as professionals, we must be concerned not only about students' employment skills but also with the broader context of students' need for life skills, independent living skills, community adjustment, and their overall quality of life. Transition programming for students with emotional and behavioral disorders encompasses a range of disciplines and invites the development of bold, creative, innovative, far-reaching, and life-centered educational programming (Frank, Sitlington, & Carson, 1991).

Implications of the Outcomes Data for Elementary and Secondary School Teachers

Elementary and secondary school teachers who work with students with emotional and behavioral disorders have one of the most challenging responsibilities in the teaching profession. These teachers must recognize that graduation from high school and successful preparation for adulthood are very difficult tasks for students with emotional and behavioral disorders (Maag & Katsiyannis, 1998). In a national study, Oswald and Coutinho (1996) found that only 30% of these students graduate from high school through the regular diploma process, 8% graduate with a certificate (versus 74% in the general population), fewer than 2% become too old for educational programs, 40% drop out, and 20% are unaccounted for. We may only speculate that the 20% relocate, become ill, become involved in the justice system, or die; but we do know, however, that for one reason or another, these students discontinue attending school.

Oswald and Coutinho found that the dropout rate of students with emotional and behavioral disorders is double that of students with learning disabilities and mental retardation. Furthermore, they found that the graduation rates of these students is only half the rate of students with learning disabilities and mental retardation. An inescapable conclusion based on these data is that school district personnel across the nation are largely either unable or unwilling to properly implement educational programs for students with emotional and behavioral disorders. Teachers at the elementary and secondary levels who are committed to this area face an unusually difficult professional challenge, and they need a unique repertoire of knowledge and skills in order to carry out their responsibilities effectively.

The remainder of this chapter presents teachers with data-based considerations for the development of effective educational programs for students with emotional and behavioral disorders.

Critical Components of Curriculum in Transition Programming

Transition programming presents relevant content to students to help them develop the skills they need to live responsible and independent adult lives (Benz, Yovanoff, & Doren, 1997). The special educator, a multidisciplinary team, and the student together forge the goals and objectives of a program for individual students. Transition planning involves both long-range and short-range goals and objectives. The primary concern is the student's future integration into postsecondary environments.

Educational Components of Curriculum

Transition programming requires thoughtful planning and implementation of curriculum that is relevant, engaging, and useful to students. During these crucial school years, students with emotional and behavioral disorders have an opportunity to learn critical content they will need in order to live their adult lives. Concern for who students are, what and how they need to learn, and the search for appropriate curriculum and materials is at the core of transition programming.

Educational programming for students with emotional and behavioral disorders often leaves much to be desired. Knitzer, Steinberg, and Fleisch (1990) analyzed educational programs for students with emotional and behavioral disorders across the nation and found that these programs are largely dull and uninteresting and do not engage students' attention. They concluded, "Our observations confirm the haphazard nature of most curricula activities, sadly, even in programs notable for other strong components, such as a mental health presence or careful work with families" (p. 27). They found that control of behavior is the most commonly observable feature of classrooms and that there is little or no evidence of concern regarding relevant curriculum development or implementation. In order to accomplish the task of transition programming, Heal and Rusch (1995) provide data to support the development of students' academic skills and personal skills. They also provide evidence that students' family characteristics and links to agencies and community resources make a difference in positive adult outcomes.

Based on the data, teachers who focus directly on enhancing students' basic academic skills in a meaningful and relevant manner increase their students' chances of positive postsecondary outcomes. Thus, data support teachers' efforts to foster the development of students' skills in reading, writing, spelling, and mathematics. Furthermore, data support the focus on the development of study skills, such as listening, the ability to organize, comprehension, and problem-solving. They may focus very directly on fostering students' use of technology. An emphasis on developing academic and study skills increases the probability that students will be employed, will participate in the community, and will make successful adjustments as adults.

Community-Based Learning Components of Curriculum

In the process of teaching basic skills, teachers can use community-based learning, which anchors students in real-life experiences. For example, students can work with local businesses to understand the use of mathematics and computers. One community has a summer job-shadowing program for teachers. The teacher is paid a stipend in the summer to shadow an employee of a local business. This program gives the teacher an excellent idea of the skills expected in the workplace. Banks, stores, and other community organizations are often willing to donate materials and personnel time and to set up field trips and work programs, which can be critical to students in postsecondary settings.

More schools are participating in partnerships with businesses. Businesses may contribute both materials and employees' time to the school. For example, a school for students with significant behavioral disorders has a partnership with the local newspaper. The students, who write weekly articles for the newspaper, also visit the newspaper office weekly and learn how a newspaper operates. That newspaper also donates computer equipment to the school and participates in fund-raising activities with the school. Newspaper staff members participate in all special activities of the school: open house, Thanksgiving dinner, graduation, and so on.

Enhancing Students' Personal Living Skills

How can teachers enhance the personal skills of students with emotional and behavioral disorders? When teaching life skills, teachers can foster the development of their students' independence, their capacity to make choices that enhance their lives, and their ability to live balanced and responsible lives as adults. Educators can teach such functional skills as reading a newspaper with a focus on some specific outcome (e.g., knowing the latest social and political developments, analyzing the current weather pattern, reading want ads and supermarket ads to determine job issues and costs of food and housing, and learning about leisure activities in the community). While engaged in these life-skill-centered activities, students may be using basic reading, mathematics, spelling, and writing skills. Additionally, they are developing prosocial personal characteristics that may be important later in their lives. We recommend that after students finish working with the newspaper in the classroom, they take the newspaper home so the family has an opportunity to read it.

In transition programming, teachers cannot overemphasize the importance of students' daily living skills, and the teachers can creatively incorporate the development of these skills while teaching academic content and skills. While focusing on daily living skills, teachers can involve students in the community. For example, a teacher and students may become involved in a community project (such as building a house for Habitat for Humanity), may adopt a park, or may commit to the beautification of a particular area. The creativity behind such projects is limited only by the imagination of those involved. Teachers can confidently draw on the imagination of students, and together they can set out to accomplish the tasks they have undertaken. Reflecting on their accomplishments after each task is critical.

The importance of functional skills in transition programming must be acknowledged. There is no need for academic programming for students with emotional and behavioral disorders to be dull and uninteresting. A curriculum that incorporates the development of functional skills can offer students the opportunity to seek new information and to experiment with their own knowledge and skills. For example, a functional curriculum might focus on money management and organization for investment in stocks or mutual funds. Investments may be made by individuals, by class subgroups, or by the class as a whole. A money management project might be a critical link in the later positive use of money.

The development of students' leisure skills is another essential component of careful transition planning. Carson et al. (1995) included a leisure component in their analysis of successful adult adjustment and found that the number of young adults who met these criteria was surprisingly low. Their data indicate that more than 50% of high school graduates cannot be judged as making a successful adult adjustment. Teachers can develop leisure skills in their students by exposing them to various prosocial ways of spending time both indoors and outdoors. Teachers can foster the development of their students' natural talents in leisure activities by introducing them to ways of using these talents in their communities. For example, a student who has an interest in a sport can be encouraged to read about that sport and also to participate in developing that skill, to become acquainted with people who have excelled in the sport, and to follow the current news of that sport. Other students may have talent in the fine arts, which teachers can foster in a similar manner.

The community offers teachers an endless resource of meaningful experiences for students with emotional and behavioral disorders. Isolation characterizes many families of these students. Often they do not know their neighbors and seldom if ever participate in their communities. Involvement in the community offers students opportunities to make connections that might be crucial to their future participation in society. For example, a student with a particular interest in the welfare of animals may volunteer at a local animal shelter. This community involvement may pave the way for future involvement and even future employment. As a result of such an activity, students with emotional and behavioral disorders learn that they can be contributing members of society and can apply their knowledge and skills in meaningful ways. Again, the extent of community involvement is limited only by the imagination and persistence of teachers and students.

According to Sample (1998), best practices in transition programming incorporate vocational intervention, paid work experience, social skills curriculum, interagency collaboration, parent involvement, and individualized plans/planning. Other components critical to transition programming include communication skills, social skills, self-advocacy skills, awareness of personal needs and dignity, problem-solving skills, and conflict-resolution skills. Additionally, students with emotional and behavioral disorders have a particular need to develop their self-management skills, self-care skills, and self-awareness skills. While focusing on students' personal development, teachers can reinforce reading, writing, mathematic, and writing skills. Students can write letters to individuals and organizations to find out information of particular interest to them. They can read from sources that supply information of importance to them. They can calculate costs of supplies and services they might render or have rendered to them. The role of a curriculum that enhances students' personal skills is limited only by the imagination, energy, and resources of the teachers and students.

Self-Determination Skills

Finally, the development of self-determination skills is a critical part of effective transition programming (Schloss, Alper, & Jayne, 1993). Self-determination has been defined as "acting as the primary or causal agent in one's life and making choices and decisions regarding one's quality of life free from undue external influence or interference" (Wehmeyer, 1996, p. 246). Self-determination skills lead to an enhanced quality of life, increased student involvement in educational planning and in making decisions, and as options increase, there should be an increase in positive outcomes. Individuals with emotional and behavioral disorders exhibit self-determination skills when they act in accordance with their own preferences, interests, and abilities and are free from undue external influence or interference. They possess self-determination skills when they can self-regulate in order to analyze the skills to use in a situation and to examine the task at hand as well as their available repertoire of skills. These students can formulate, enact, and evaluate a plan of action with revisions when necessary. They exhibit self-determination skills when they can act on the beliefs that they have the capacity to perform behaviors needed in order to influence outcomes in their environment and that if they perform such behaviors, the anticipated outcomes result. Individuals who have developed their self-determination skills use a comprehensive and reasonably accurate knowledge of their own strengths and limitations in order to maximize positive outcomes.

Transition programs that successfully develop the academic and personal skills of students with emotional and behavioral disorders can make a critical difference in preparing these individuals to live either prosocial or antisocial adult lives. Transition planning is designed to motivate, inform, and prepare these students to live responsible lives and fully participate in a democratic society.

Common Questions of Educators of Students With Emotional and Behavioral Disorders

When Might Teachers Begin To Be Concerned About Students' Postsecondary Education?

Though focused documentation of transition planning begins in high school, teachers' concern about life skills and transition programming for students with emotional and behavioral disorders must begin in kindergarten and continue through grade school and high school. Once students begin to learn basic academic and social skills, they are paving the way toward successful postsecondary outcomes. Teachers, from kindergarten on, have an opportunity to teach students basic work skills, social skills, organizational skills, study skills, self-care skills, punctuality, and other life skills crucial to adult adjustment.

Does School Attendance Influence Positive Postsecondary School Outcomes for Students With Emotional and Behavioral Disorders?

A well-developed educational program can make a critical difference in the life of young adults with emotional and behavioral disorders. While in school these students have the opportunity to develop their personal and life skills as well as learn critical academic content and skills that data indicate influence positive adult outcomes (Carson et al., 1995; Heal & Rusch, 1995). Educational personnel who involve students' families and extended families have an opportunity to develop the networks that Heal and Rusch found to influence positive outcomes in students with disabilities in postsecondary settings.

What Causes Students With Emotional and Behavioral Disorders to Drop Out of School?

Kortering, Haring, and Klockars (1992) found that school-initiated interruptions, such as suspensions, influence the dropout rate of students with learning disabilities. Furthermore, they found that the extent of family intactness and the number of school transfers affect student dropouts. Farmer (1993) found that the extent of students' externalizing behaviors predicted the age at which students left school and increased the positive effects of such factors as students' academic ability and the aspirations of their parents. Students drop out of school for a host of academic and social reasons (Garnier, Stein, & Jacobs, 1997; Rumberger, 1987). Rumberger found that some students drop out because they believe that the school grounds are too dangerous, they did not get into desired programs, they could not get along with teachers or peers, and so on. Some students drop out because they fail courses and have a high absentee rate (Farmer, 1993). It is important for teachers to recognize that data indicate teachers can influence the dropout rate of students with emotional and behavioral disorders. By providing them with the best possible positive academic experience and a social program that addresses the development of their prosocial behaviors, teachers provide these students with the academic and behavioral programming they need.

What Can Teachers of Students With Emotional and Behavioral Disorders Do to Facilitate Their Students' Successful Transition to Adulthood?

This book is designed to provide teachers with a useful and practical resource to develop effective educational programs for students with emotional and behavioral disorders that will lead to their students' successful transition to adulthood. Using a relevant and meaningful curriculum, teachers can strive to develop the academic and social skills of students with emotional and behavioral disorders. They can teach their students to use learning strategies and study skills. Teachers can address diversity and provide a curriculum of hope. Teachers can strive to engage the students' attention, develop their higher-level thinking skills, and show them how to become involved in their families and communities. When teachers do these things they are preparing students for positive adult outcomes. We would also add that teachers must become excellent managers of their students' behaviors, thereby fulfilling their dual role in the crucial areas of curriculum and behavior. We have designed this book to focus primarily on critical curriculum issues. Walker, Colvin, and Ramsey (1995) and Johns and Carr (1995) present excellent resources for teachers on behavior management and on the development of effective behavior management programs.

Conclusions

Realistic expectations are at the core of effective transition planning. Students with emotional and behavioral disorders are often unrealistic and surprisingly out of touch with what the future might hold for them. Likewise, parents and guardians may themselves fail to imagine realistic future goals for their adolescent sons and daughters. Thus, school personnel may have the difficult role of discerning expectations that, on one hand, will not underestimate the potential of these adolescents, and, on the other hand, will not overestimate their potential. This requires much conversation, effort, planning, and at times expert communication skills on the part of school personnel. For example, how will parents who plan on sending their sons or daughters to medical school or law school be told that these may not be realistic options? Or, how will school personnel communicate with parents who want their sons or daughters to remain at home following high school, and who are unwilling to concern themselves with realistic issues about their children's future. In order to accomplish the intention of transition planning successfully, a team effort is required. Additionally, generous amounts of time, energy, and resources must be spent.

There is evidence to support the conclusion that transition programming might be best accomplished with concern for gender-specific outcomes (Benz et al. 1997; Blackorby & Wagner, 1996; Heal & Rusch, 1995; Levine & Edgar, 1995; Rojewski, 1996; Scuccimarra & Speece, 1990). For example, females are employed less often and at lower rates than males. Data indicate that marriage and pregnancy do not account for these differences (Benz et al., 1997). These data indicate that teachers may need to address their own perceptions of outcomes for girls. Do teachers treat girls differently than boys? Do teachers have similar expectations of males and females? Do teachers expect girls to fare differently than boys? What curriculum will best prepare girls to maximize their personal and worklife potential?

The outcomes data suggest rethinking critical aspects of curriculum for students with emotional and behavioral disorders. Alternative curricula during grade school and high school as well as alternative pathways toward graduation seem to be essential aspects of effective educational programming for these students. Creative programming that addresses options in content selection and an expansion of exiting criteria might enhance the potential of young adults with emotional and behavioral disorders. This book addresses what we believe to be critical components of effective programming as well as critical methods that teachers may use to ensure and enhance students' learning. For example, we believe that students need to learn in the natural environment as much as possible to increase their potential for the generalization of their knowledge and skills. We also believe that students must be taught strategies that will enable them to learn and maintain their knowledge and skills. Holding students to high but realistic expectations in the context of flexible and creative educational programming will enhance the possibility of positive adult outcomes for students with emotional and behavioral disorders.

Finally, effective educational programming that aims to maximize adult outcomes for young adults with emotional and behavioral disorders can be accomplished only by dynamic, informed, highly qualified, and creative professional personnel (Fink & Janssen, 1993; Wrobel, 1993). Teachers involved in the implementation of such programming must be aware of how crucial their role is in the future of these young adults. We believe that teachers must be committed to their professional tasks and uphold the Code of Ethics of the Council for Exceptional Children to the best of their ability. Furthermore, teachers must be supported by dynamic and creative inservice programming, which will involve not only teachers but also parents, community members, students, administrators, and others who work with these students. The development of ongoing inservice education programs will involve the investment of enormous amounts of time, money, and talent. However, we believe that society as a whole will benefit from the cost of assuring positive outcomes for adults with emotional and behavioral disorders.

Discussion Questions

1. How can you as a teacher convince a parent who dropped out of school that it is important that his or her child stay in school without offending the parent?
2. What steps can you take if you refer a student preparing for graduation to an agency and learn that the agency decides not to provide services to the student?
3. What steps can you take to assure that your classroom curriculum is meaningful to a student so that the student does not want to drop out of school?

References

Benz, M. R., Yovanoff, P,. & Doren, B. (1997). School-to-work components that predict postschool success for students with and without disabilities. *Exceptional Children, 63,* 151–165.

Blackorby, J., & Wagner, M. (1996). Longitudinal postschool outcomes of youth with disabilities: Findings from the national longitudinal transition study. *Exceptional Children, 62,* 399–413.

Carson, R. R., Sitlington, P. L., & Frank, A. R. (1995). Young adulthood for individuals with behavioral disorders: What does it hold? *Behavioral Disorders, 20,* 127–135.

Edgar, E. (1988). Employment as an outcome for mildly handicapped students: Current status and future directions. *Focus on Exceptional Children, 21,* 1–8.

Farmer, E. (1993). Externalizing behavior in the life course: The transition from school to work. *Journal of Emotional and Behavioral Disorders, 1,* 179–188.

Fink, A. H., & Janssen, K. N. (1993). Competencies for teaching students with emotional and behavioral disabilities. *Preventing School Failure, 37,* 11–15.

Frank, A., Sitlington, P., & Carson, R. (1991). Transition of adolescents with behavioral disorders—Is it successful? *Behavioral Disorders, 16,* 180–191.

Frank, A. R., Sitlington, P. L., & Carson, R. R. (1995). Young adults with behavioral disorders: A comparison with peers with mild disabilities. *Journal of Emotional and Behavioral Disorders, 3,* 156-164.

Gagne, R. (1994). A self-made man. In V. J. Bradley, J. W. Ashbaugh, and B. C. Blaney (Eds.), *Creating individual supports for people with developmental disabilities* (pp. 327–334). Baltimore: Paul H. Brookes.

Garnier, H. E., Stein, J. A., & Jacobs, J. K. (1997). The process of dropping out of high school: A 19-year perspective. *American Educational Research Journal, 34,* 395–419.

Hallahan, D. P., & Kauffman, J. M. (2000). *Exceptional learners: Introduction to special education* (8th ed.). Boston: Allyn and Bacon.

Heal, L. W., & Rusch, F. R. (1995). Predicting employment for students who leave special education high school programs. *Exceptional Children, 61,* 472–487.

Individuals with Disabilities Education Act, Public Law 101–476, 20, U.S.C. Chapter 33, Section 1414 et seq. (1990).

Individuals with Disabilities Education Act Amendments of 1997, Public Law 105–17, 20, U.S.C. Chapter 33, Section 1414 et seq. (1997).

Johns, B., & Carr, V. (1995). *Techniques for managing verbally and physically aggressive students.* Denver: Love.

Kennedy, M. (1996). Self-determination and trust: My experiences and thoughts. In D. J. Sands & M. L. Wehmeyer (Eds.), *Self-determination across the life-span: Independence and choice for people with disabilities* (pp. 35–47). Baltimore: Paul H. Brookes.

Knitzer, J., Steinberg, Z., & Fleisch, B. (1990). *At the schoolhouse door: An examination of programs and policies for children with behavioral and emotional problems.* New York: Bank Street Press.

Kortering, L., Haring, N., & Klockars, A. (1992). The identification of high-school dropouts identified as learning disabled: Evaluating the utility of a discriminant analysis function. *Exceptional Children, 58,* 422–435.

Levine, P., & Edgar, E. (1995). An analysis by gender of long-term postschool outcomes for youth with and without disabilities. *Exceptional Children, 61,* 282–300.

Maag, J. W., & Katsiyannis, A. (1998). Challenges facing successful transition for youths with E/BD. *Behavioral Disorders, 23,* 209–221.

Malmgren, K., Edgar, E., & Neel, R. S. (1998). Postschool status of youths with behavioral disorders. *Behavioral Disorders, 23,* 257–263.

Mattison, R. E., Spitznagel, E. L., & Felix, B. C. (1998). Enrollment predictors of the special education outcome for students with SED. *Behavioral Disorders, 23,* 243–256.

Neel, R., Meadows, N., Levine, P., & Edgar, E. (1988). What happens after special education: A statewide follow-up study of secondary students who have behavioral disorders. *Behavioral Disorders, 13,* 209–216.

Oswald, D. P., & Coutinho, M. J. (1996). Leaving school: The impact of state economic and demographic factors for students with serious emotional disturbance. *Journal of Emotional and Behavioral Disorders, 4,* 114–125.

Phelps, L. A., & Hanley-Maxwell, C. (1997). School-to-work transitions for youth with disabilities: A review of outcomes and practices. *Review of Educational Research, 67,* 197–226.

Rojewski, J. W. (1996). Educational and occupational aspirations of high school seniors with learning disabilities. *Exceptional Children, 62,* 463–476.

Rumberger, R. W. (1987). High school dropouts: A review of issues and evidence. *Review of Educational Research, 57,* 101–121.

Sample, P. L. (1998). Postschool outcomes for students with significant emotional disturbance following best-practice transition services. *Behavioral Disorders, 23,* 231–242.

Schloss, P. J., Alper, S., & Jayne, D. (1993). Self-determination for persons with disabilities: Choice, risk, and dignity. *Exceptional Children, 60,* 215–225.

Scuccimarra, D. J., & Speece, D. L. (1990). Employment outcomes and social integration of students with mild handicaps: The quality of life two years after high school. *Journal of Learning Disabilities, 23,* 213–219.

Sitlington, P., Frank, A., & Carson, R. (1993). Adult adjustment among graduates with mild disabilities. *Exceptional Children, 59,* 221–233.

Walker, M. M., Colvin, G., & Ramsey, E. (1995). *Antisocial behavior in school: Strategies and best practices.* Cincinnati: Brooks/Cole.

Wehmeyer, M. L. (1996). Self-determination as an educational outcome: Why is it important to children, youth, and adults with disabilities? In D. J. Sands & M. L. Wehmeyer (Eds.), *Self-determination across the life-span: Independence and choice for people with disabilities* (pp. 15–34). Baltimore: Paul H. Brookes.

Wehmeyer, M. L., & Schwartz, M. (1997). Self-determination and positive adult outcomes: A follow-up study of youth with mental retardation or learning disabilities. *Exceptional Children, 63,* 245–255.

Wrobel, G. (1993). Preventing school failure for teachers: Training for a lifelong career in E/BD. *Preventing School Failure, 37,* 16–20.

4

The Role of the IEP in the Education of Students With Emotional and Behavioral Disorders

Jeremy, a 15-year-old identified as having emotional and behavioral disorders, was having problems in his high school classes. He saw the special education teacher for three periods a day, but he spent the remainder of his day in general education classes, one of which was public speaking. That class so frustrated Jeremy that he cut it often. Concerned, Jeremy's mother went in to see the special education teacher. Jeremy's mother remembered that Jeremy's previous special education teacher had discussed his problems with verbal expression and had recommended that Jeremy not be integrated into the speech class. When Jeremy's mother asked the new special education teacher why Jeremy was mainstreamed in speech, the teacher responded that her schedule was so full that she did not have time to see Jeremy at that time. Jeremy's mother insisted that his IEP had recommended that he not be in a speech class. The special education teacher stated that she had not had time to review the IEPs of her new students but hoped to do so in a couple of weeks.

The Intent of the IEP

Unfortunately, we have known a few teachers like Jeremy's who placed the students' IEPs in a drawer and looked at them only when it was time to conduct the annual review. We have also known teachers who refuse to look at a new student's IEP for the first month or so because they do not want to have a bias or preconceived notion about a student. Both of these scenarios are unfortunate because the IEP should be the driving force in planning an effective educational program for the student. Wood (1992) calls the IEP a "road map for instruction" (p. 11).

The 1996 report from the Wingspread Conference on Accountability in Special Education called the IEP the "heart of the special education system" (National Association of State Directors of Special Education, p. 1). It is a safeguard for students and the students' families—it is the document that ensures that children receive specially designed instruction to meet their individual needs.

The Wingspread conference called the IEP both a process and a document. The process involves all of the individual planning steps taken by the team of individuals as they determine an appropriate educational program based on assessment, eligibility, and needs of the student. The document is the concrete confirmation of the decisions reached by the team. The IEP personalizes education by motivating the system to face the need for accommodations to assure that the student with individualized needs has an equal opportunity to education.

A number of revisions to the IEP process, designed to strengthen its role, were made in the Individuals with Disabilities Education Act of 1997 (IDEA 97) and its accompanying regulations. A teacher should not put the IEP in the drawer and forget it until it is time for the annual review; a new requirement assures that parents are updated on a regular basis (at the same time as report cards are issued) on the progress of the student toward that student's goals and objectives (or benchmarks).

Key Components of the IEP

Description of Present Levels of Performance

This statement of the child's present levels of educational performance must include how the child's disability affects the child's involvement and progress in the general curriculum. Section 300.347 of the regulations defines the general curriculum as the same curriculum as that for nondisabled children. What are the deficit areas of the student? What are the strengths of the student, upon which we can build success? Often, IEPs focus too heavily on deficits—what the student cannot do. This focus is discouraging to the student, the parent, and the teacher. Although it is important for us to outline the deficits so we know specifically what to do for the student, we must also keep strengths in mind so that the majority of each day is spent in providing successful experiences for the student. No child will want to come to school if most of every day is spent doing tasks that are too difficult. Every child should come to school and meet with success. IDEA 97 requires the IEP team to consider the strengths of the child and the concerns of the parents for enhancing the education of their child.

For the student with E/BD, the description of present levels of performance must include not only academic issues but also behavioral issues. For instance, the student with E/BD may engage in verbal aggression. The present level of performance must detail a description of the intensity, duration, and frequency of the verbal aggression. Consequently, a functional assessment of the behavior is a must in delineating the present levels of performance. In order to decrease verbal aggression, personnel must teach the student anger control and conflict resolution skills.

Goals and Objectives (or Benchmarks)

Goals and objectives should be based on present levels of performance: Where does the student need assistance based on the present levels of performance? IDEA 97 requires a statement of measurable annual goals, including benchmarks or short-term objectives, related to meeting the child's needs.

Appendix A to Section 300—"Notice of interpretation"—clarifies the difference between short-term instructional objectives and benchmarks. Short-term instructional objectives break down the skills described in the annual goal into discrete components. Benchmarks describe the amount of progress the child is expected to make within specified segments of the year. Benchmarks establish expected performance levels that allow for regular checks of progress that coincide with the reporting periods for informing parents of progress.

The appendix also points out that annual goals are not needed for each area of the general curriculum if the child's disability does not affect the ability to progress in that area. For the student who needs modifications or accommodations to be successful in a specific area of the general curriculum, the specific modifications or accommodations must be delineated on the student's IEP.

Specification of the Amount and Type of Special Education and Related Services

Where and how can the goals and objectives be met? The date by which the services will be convened should be part of this component.

The least restrictive environment must be addressed in this portion of the IEP. In determining the least restrictive environment, the IEP team should use the criteria delineated in *Sacramento City Unified School District Board of Education v. Rachel Holland* (1994).

1. Will the student derive educational benefit from the placement? Can the IEP goals be implemented in the placement chosen?
2. What are the noneducational benefits to the student? The examples used in this case were improved self-confidence and new friendships, and excitement about learning.
3. Is there detriment because the child is disruptive, distracting, or unruly, and would the child take up so much of the teacher's time that the other students would suffer from lack of attention?
4. What is the cost of the placement? Will the placement burden the District's funds or adversely affect services available to other children?

Section 300.347 (a)(4) and Sections 300.550–300.553 reaffirm the least restrictive environment standards, which require an explanation of the extent to which the child will not participate with nondisabled children in the general education class and in extracurricular and nonacademic activities; and that each child with a disability be educated with nondisabled children "to the maximum extent appropriate" (Sec. 300.550 [(b)(1)]). The questions and answers section in Appendix A provides further clarification: Services and educational placements must be individually determined in light of the child's unique needs to reasonably promote the child's educational success. Of critical importance is the statement in the appendix that a student need not fail in the general education classroom before another placement can be considered.

In considering the statement of special education and related services, the IEP team must determine the supplementary aids and services to be provided as well as the program modifications or supports for school personnel that will be provided for the child to advance appropriately toward attaining the annual goals, including involvement and progress in the general curriculum.

Evaluation Procedures and Schedules

How often will the goals and objectives be reviewed? These procedures and schedules should be outlined at the time of the IEP. IDEA 97 mandates that the progress of the student toward the goals and objectives of the IEP must be reported to the parent at the same time as report cards are issued for all students.

Transition Services

According to IDEA 97, transition services must be included in all IEPs when the student reaches the age of 14. Beginning at that age, and updated annually, there must be a statement of the transition service needs of the child under the applicable components of the child's IEP that focus on the child's course of study (such as participation in advanced placement courses or a vocational education program). Beginning at the age of 16 (or younger, if determined appropriate by the IEP team), there must be a statement of needed transition services for the child, including, when appropriate, a statement of interagency responsibilities or any needed linkages.

Transition services are defined in Section 300.29 as a coordinated set of activities for a student that is:

1. Designed within an outcome-oriented process that promotes movement from school to postschool activities, including postsecondary education, vocational training, integrated employment (including supported employment), continuing and adult education, adult services, independent living, or community participation.
2. Based on individual students' needs and considers the student's preferences and interests.
3. Includes instruction, related services, community experiences, and the development of employment and other postschool adult living objectives, and if appropriate, the acquisition of daily living skills and a functional vocational evaluation.

Beginning at least one year before the child reaches the age of majority under the state law, a statement that the child has been informed of his or her rights must be provided.

According to Bateman (1996), transition services are a coordinated set of activities that promote movement from school to postschool activities. The IEP meeting must include a representative of the public agency providing and supervising the transition activities. The student must also be involved.

Consideration of the Evaluation Results

The results of the initial or most recent evaluation of the child should be considered. This requirement is designed to assure that programming for the student is based on diagnostic information. The heart of special education is the diagnostic-prescriptive approach—the element that Dr. Sam Kirk cited as what was special about special education. This approach is best summarized by Kirk and Chalfant (1984):

1. Assess a child's special physical, intellectual, social, emotional, and educational needs—a comprehensive evaluation. Kirk believed that it was critical to learn as much as possible about a child's abilities and disabilities in all developmental areas.

2.   Determine the focus of the instruction through the development of the goals and objectives on the IEP.
3.   Decide how instruction should be delivered through the use of task analysis and specialized instructional techniques.
4.   Measure the child's progress after having received special education.

The diagnostic-prescriptive approach is critical for students with emotional and behavioral disorders. If we are unable to meet these children's individual needs, they become frustrated and consequently increase behavioral problems.

Strategies to Address Behavioral Interference of Learning

In the case of a child whose behavior impedes his or her learning or that of others, the IEP team shall consider, when appropriate, strategies, including positive behavioral interventions and supports, to address that behavior. A common theme throughout IDEA 97 is the use of positive behavioral interventions. We know from a long history of research that a positive focus is the most effective means of changing student behavior. Lewis and Sugai (1999) state that even though peer attention is a powerful motivator for students, teacher attention is also a useful positive reinforcer. A reinforcer is any action or event that follows a behavior and is associated with increases in future rates of that behavior. If we want to decrease inappropriate behavior, we must positively reinforce appropriate behavior. Critical to the development of a behavioral intervention plan are the positive behavioral interventions to be used.

For any student with behavioral concerns, a behavioral intervention plan based on a functional assessment is mandated.

Individual Language Needs

The IEP team must consider the student's language needs. For children with limited English proficiency, their language needs as they relate to the IEP must be considered. The extent to which a child who has a disability and limited English proficiency receives English instruction or instruction in the child's native language, the extent to which the child will participate in the general curriculum, and the extent to which the child needs English language tutoring must be determined by the member of the IEP team. School districts are required to provide students who have limited English proficiency with alternative language services that enable them to acquire English proficiency.

Visually Impaired Students

In the case of a child who is blind or visually impaired, instruction in Braille and the use of Braille must be provided unless the IEP team determines otherwise (designated criteria for that determination are given). The IEP team must make individual determinations for each child who is visually impaired based on relevant evaluation data. The IEP team's determination of whether instruction in Braille is appropriate cannot be based on factors such as the availability of alternative reading media (e.g., large print texts, recorded materials, and computers with speech input).

Individual Communication Needs

The IEP team must consider the communication needs of the child. In the case of a hearing-impaired student, the IEP team must consider the additional special factors relating to the child's language or communication needs. The range of communication and related needs of hearing-impaired students must be appropriately addressed in evaluation discussions and placement decisions.

Assistive Technology Devices and Services

The IEP team shall consider whether the child requires assistive technology devices and services. Section 300.308 adds a provision that clarifies that a public agency must permit a child to have access to a school-purchased assistive technology device at home or in another setting if necessary to ensure a free appropriate public education.

Statement of Necessary Individual Accommodations

There must be a statement of any individual accommodations in the administration of state or districtwide assessments of student achievement that are needed for the child to participate in such assessment.

According to Section 300.138 of the IDEA regulations, each state must demonstrate that children with disabilities are included in general state and districtwide assessment programs, with appropriate accommodations and modifications if necessary. States must also develop guidelines for the participation of children with disabilities in alternative assessments for those children who cannot participate in those state and districtwide assessment programs.

Section 300.347 clarifies the IEP team's responsibility to make individual modifications in the administration of state or districtwide assessments of student achievement. If the IEP team determines that the child will not participate in the assessment (or part of such an assessment), the team must provide a statement of: "(A) Why that assessment is not appropriate for the child; and (B) How the child will be assessed." In summary, the IEP is the document that delineates meaningful benefit for the student.

Document Portability

We believe that the IEP should be written so that if a student moves anywhere in the country, the new teacher could pick up the document and be able to plan an effective educational program for the student. In one district, students were required to have an assignment notebook to assist in developing organizational skills. The special education teacher believed that because all of the students in her class used an assignment notebook, there was no reason to put it on the IEP. However, if the student were to move to another district in which assignment notebooks were not used, the new teacher would not know that it was appropriate for the student.

Who Constitutes the IEP Team

IDEA 97 and its accompanying regulations clarify the mandated participants in the IEP Team.

The Parents of a Child With a Disability

Each local education agency or state education agency shall ensure that the parents of each child with a disability are members of any group that makes decisions on the educational placement of their child. Section 300.345 of the IDEA 97 regulations outlines the steps that school personnel must take to ensure the parents' opportunity to participate, which include: notifying parents of the meeting early enough to ensure that they will have an opportunity to attend, scheduling the meeting at a mutually agreed on time and place, and giving proper notice that delineates the purpose, time, and location of the meeting. It further states that if neither parent is able to attend, school personnel shall use other methods to ensure participation such as individual or conference phone calls. The section does specify whether an IEP can be held without a parent present. In fact, an IEP meeting can be held without a parent if school personnel are unable to convince the parents that they should attend. The burden of proof is on school personnel, and detailed records to obtain the parent's participation must be kept.

At Least One General Education Teacher of Such Child (if the child is, or may be, participating in the general education environment)

The general education teacher, as a member of the IEP team, shall, to the extent appropriate, participate in the development of the child's IEP, including the determination of appropriate positive behavioral interventions and strategies and the determination of supplementary aids and services, program modifications, and support for school personnel.

Appendix A of the regulations (p. 12477) notes that the general education teacher may not be required to participate in all decisions made as part of the meeting or be present throughout the entire meeting. An example is given: The general education teacher would have to participate in the discussions on how to modify the general curriculum, but the teacher might not have to participate in discussions regarding physical therapy needs of the child if the teacher is not responsible.

The appendix to the regulations also states that the IEP team need not include more than one general education teacher of the child, *unless* the participation of more than one general educator would be beneficial to the child's success; then it would be appropriate for more than one to attend. The commentary states that there should be discussion with the parents before the IEP meeting to determine which general educators should attend which parts of the IEP meeting.

At Least One Special Education Teacher (or, where appropriate, at least one special education provider of such child)

This requirement can be met by either the child's special education teacher or, as appropriate, another special education provider such as a speech-language pathologist, physical or occupational therapist, or others, if the related service consists of specially designed instruction and is considered special education under the appropriate state's standards. It is the duty of the school district to ensure that all individuals who are necessary to meet the child's unique needs develop the IEP. The special education teacher or provider is supposed to be the person who is, or will be, responsible for implementing the IEP.

A Representative of the Local Education Agency (who is qualified to provide or supervise the provision of specially designed instruction, is knowledgeable about the general curriculum, and is knowledgeable about the availability of resources of the local school district)

The public school can designate another IEP team member as the public agency representative provided that the individual is not serving as the special educator or the general education teacher.

An Individual Who Can Interpret the Instructional Implications of Evaluation Results (who may be a member of the team described in the roles of other individuals)

Public schools find it helpful to have a member or members of the eligibility team as part of the IEP team for initial and subsequent meetings to develop a child's IEP. It is critical that there be a strong linkage between the evaluation and the determination of goals and objectives for the student.

At the Discretion of the Parent or the Agency, Other Individuals Who Have Knowledge or Special Expertise Regarding the Child (including related services personnel as appropriate)

Parents are assisted at their child's IEP meetings if another person can accompany them. Some parents report that they are too nervous to listen and take notes at the same time, so they bring a friend or advocate to take notes for them. Other parents bring a friend for emotional support.

The Child With a Disability, Where Appropriate

Teachers and parents together should determine whether it is appropriate for the child to attend all or part of the IEP meeting. When transition services are being considered, the student must be invited to attend so that the student has a voice in planning for the transition from school to post-school activities. If the student does not attend the IEP meeting, the public agency shall take other steps to ensure that the student's preferences and interests are considered.

Roadblocks to Effective Use of the IEP

What keeps members of the educational staff from being able to effectively use and implement IEPs?

Lack of Training and Knowledge

An IEP that is poorly designed and crafted cannot be used effectively. Teachers may need ongoing training in creating appropriate and effective IEPs. Training must include how to clearly delineate each student's present level of educational performance, how to determine the student's educational needs based on the disability, and how to write goals and objectives that are measurable and reasonably calculated to confer educational benefit. Training must also include how to determine whether a student is able to participate in statewide and local assessments and, if so, what specific accommodations are needed for that assessment and for educational programming throughout the year. A thorough understanding of how to meet all of the requirements of the IEP process is a must for all IEP participants.

There may be times when parents are much better versed in specific methodologies than the educators are. Educators must stay current on methods of instruction through reading and staff development.

CHAPTER 4

Lack of Support in the Implementation of the IEP

When the special educator attempts to implement the IEP, others in the school may prevent the teacher from doing so. For example, the IEP states that a student identified as E/BD (who is in a self-contained E/BD classroom) is to be mainstreamed into music class. The music teacher decides that he does not want the student in his class. Another example might involve specific assistive technology that is written into the IEP, and the school district has budget cuts and will not purchase the technology.

Large Caseloads

Large caseloads sometimes do not give the teacher adequate time to plan and teach. The special education teacher may see students throughout the entire day and not have any planning period. In that case it is very difficult for the teacher to have the time to provide consultation to the classroom teachers who have the student in the general education setting. Because the teacher does not have a break within the school day, the paperwork has to be done on the teacher's own time. This leads to burnout of special educators.

Inadequate or Inaccurate Assessment Information

An individual test does not mean an evaluation; nor does an assessment by a single individual. Because the diagnostic-prescriptive model is a key component in the delivery of special education services, all evaluations must be multidisciplinary and must be thorough to determine the deficits, strengths, and interests of the student. An evaluation must determine whether a processing deficit is present, at what rate the student learns, and social and emotional factors that may be impacting the child's educational performance.

Pressure Against Individual Plans

Teachers are sometimes pressured by school district officials to base the IEP on what is available in the district or to ignore IEPs. We have heard numerous stories from teachers who were told that their school district was going to become a "full-inclusion" district, and therefore all students would be in the general classroom all day. The teacher would serve as a consultant to the general education teachers. These districts totally ignored the content of the IEP and ignored the mandated individualization for each child.

Teachers are often pressured to use a standard, computer-generated format for IEPs. Although the computer is an excellent tool for completing paperwork, blanket goals and objectives for all students in the special class are not acceptable.

Nevertheless, we have seen situations in which the same goals and objectives were used for all students served by a specific team. Remember, the "I" in IEP stands for "Individual."

Pressure From Classroom Teachers To Provide Tutoring Services Rather Than Specially Designed Instruction

We have seen this more in secondary programs where a student is mainstreamed in a high school general education class. The classroom teacher refuses to make accommodations and refuses to accept suggestions for making accommodations from the specialist. Instead, the classroom teacher wants the specialist to tutor the student using the same book and keep the student up with the general classroom. The student, however, needs accommodations such as the ability to tape-record the material and to listen to the material multiple times. The student also needs to learn a specific strategy for learning the content and a specific strategy for taking notes during a lecture.

Pressure From Many Sources To Act Unilaterally Rather Than in Accordance With the IEP

For example: A principal wants a teacher to provide more services for more students, which means it is necessary to decrease the amount of time a particular student receives. Another common example is seen when the student is failing a general education class, and the general education teacher wants the student out of the regular class but doesn't want to have a new IEP and wants the special education teacher to add more time without convening a new IEP meeting. The IEP may delineate that the student needs 60 minutes weekly of social work services, but the teacher is told that the social worker is available only one day a week in the school and the student will receive only 30 minutes weekly.

Failure To Recognize Parents as Active Participants in the IEP

The parents of the student with E/BD bring critical information to the table in writing an effective IEP: the student's strengths and weaknesses, the student's likes and dislikes, the student's attitude toward school, and the student's goals after school. School personnel should do whatever is possible to establish the IEP at a mutually agreeable time, set aside enough time for the meeting so the parent does not feel rushed, and make the parent(s) feel comfortable at the IEP meeting.

The Top 10 Common Problems in IEPs

After many years of observing and viewing a variety of IEPs for E/BD students across the country, we have compiled a list of 10 common problems associated with IEPs.

1. Failure to separate eligibility from placement.

    Because a student meets eligibility criteria for E/BD, it cannot automatically be assumed that the student will be placed in a class for students with E/BD. The student's needs could be met in a general education classroom with support services from a behavior management specialist. The process is twofold. The first part is the determination of eligibility for special education. In this process, the team must determine whether the child has a disability and whether that disability has an adverse effect on educational performance. The second part of the process occurs after eligibility is established. At this time, participants must determine the needs of the child based on the evaluation and current levels of performance. Placement decisions are then based on where the child's needs can be most appropriately met according to the least restrictive environment.

2. Missing critical information.

    An example: The student has failed the vision or hearing screening; the parents have divorced within the last three months; the student has been absent 50% of the time. Such information is important in gaining an appropriate picture of where the student is and what the needs of that student are.

3. Failure to provide accurate descriptions of the current levels of educational performance.

    For example: "Johnny has poor attendance." "Billy is physically aggressive." "Mary reads at a third-grade level." One could ask the following questions: "What is poor attendance?" "What is physical aggression, and how often does it occur?" "Does third-grade level mean word recognition or passage comprehension?"

4. Failure to clearly identify the special education services and the necessary related services.

    One of the authors was recently reviewing an IEP of a student who had moved into a district. On one page, the IEP said the student was integrated into some general education classes but did not say how many, and the IEP did not delineate how much time during the day the student was in special education. Another common occurrence is that a related service may be listed but the amount of time that the student receives the related services is not listed.

5. Goals on the IEP not based on deficits described in the present levels of performance and not based on the adverse effects on educational performance.

As an example, the present levels of performance have identified that the student easily loses his temper and throws books on the floor and knocks over desks twice a day on average. However, when one reviews the student's goals and objectives, there is no goal present to learn anger management skills. Instead, the goals and objectives are related only to the improvement of reading and math skills. Another example is when a student has a significant learning disability in the area of visual memory, and there is no goal to address that deficit area.

6. Failure to provide enough information in the objectives, including not having an accurate baseline and having unrealistic expectations.

A student may exhibit difficulty in time on task, and a goal is developed to increase time on task. Yet there is no information on how much time the child currently can stay on task—a baseline has to be established. Or, there may be a baseline that shows that the child is able to stay on a paper-and-pencil task in math for two minutes, and the objective specifies that the student will be able to stay on task for 30 minutes. To expect the student to progress from attention to task for 2 minutes to attention to task for 30 minutes may certainly be unrealistic.

7. Failure to identify reasons for rejection of placement.

In some IEPs, placement in a general education class is rejected because—it is stated—it is "not appropriate." An explanation should be given. In addition, consideration should be given to how it could be made appropriate for the student.

8. IEPs that do not reflect the amount of time spent in special education and general education and what is happening with the student.

For example: The IEP may state that the student is receiving 50 minutes of resource services daily from the E/BD teacher; however, an investigation of the child's day shows that he or she is receiving those services only every other day. It is also common for an IEP to state that a student is in E/BD instructional class all day, when in fact that student is integrated into music, art, PE, and a speech class. The IEP should reflect what is actually happening with the student.

9. Failure to identify other needs and disabilities that the student may have.

> An example: A student might have an identified learning disability as well as emotional and behavioral disorders. However, there is no mention in the IEP that the student has an auditory-processing deficit that is exhibited when the student is expected to follow an auditory directive from the teacher. The student needs to have a visual cue as well as a verbal direction. One student who had a very slow processing time would take at least one minute to process a request and then perform the task requested. If teachers did not know of this disability or did not address it on the IEP, they might not understand why the student was not doing what was requested of him.

10. Integration into general education classes not driven by the IEP but by a level system.

> The decision about integrating a student into general education classes must be made by the IEP team, not by a level system.

Making the Most of the IEP

> An IEP cannot be used effectively if it is not crafted carefully. How can the IEP team do that?

Evaluation

> The IEP should be based on appropriate assessment information including testing, observation of a student's educational performance, any processing deficit, learning style, and a functional analysis of behavior. It is expected that an evaluation of each student is completed every three years. Additionally, the special education teacher is continually engaged in ongoing assessment through observations, standardized achievement tests, and, for students with E/BD, an ongoing functional analysis of behavior.
>
> The three-year evaluation is conducted by a multidisciplinary team including at least one teacher or other specialist with knowledge in the area of the suspected disability. Additionally, for students suspected of having a learning disability, the IDEA regulations state:
>
>> Each public agency shall include on the multidisciplinary evaluation team: (a)(1) The child's regular teacher, or (2) If the child does not have a regular teacher, a regular classroom teacher qualified to teach a child of his or her age, or (3) For a child of less than school age, an individual qualified by the State educational agency to teach a child

of his or her age; and (b) At least one person qualified to conduct individual diagnostic examinations of children, such as a school psychologist, speech-language pathologist, or remedial reading teacher. (Federal Register, 34 CFR 300.540)

No longer can only one person perform the evaluation and declare that a student is eligible for special education; for the protection of the student it is a team effort.

It is critical for students with E/BD that behavioral observations and evaluations and a functional assessment of behavior are conducted. A functional assessment is defined as a process of identifying personal and environmental events that contribute to the occurrence of target behaviors and assist in organizing the information to select appropriate interventions for the student. The purpose of a functional assessment is threefold: (a) to determine the variables that may be associated with the problem behavior; (b) to identify the function of the problem behavior; and (c) to examine the consequences of the behavior that may be contributing to its maintenance. It is a proactive and positive approach to reduce inappropriate behavior and increase appropriate skill development and certainly increases the likelihood of a positive outcome following intervention efforts.

A simple way to remember how to do a functional assessment is to relate the process to the mnemonic ABC:

A: Antecedents—what comes before the behavior
B: Behavior—operationally defined
C: Consequences—what comes after the behavior

Once the information is gathered, the evaluator should attempt to determine the purpose that the misbehavior serves. All behavior serves one of these functions:

Attention-seeking: The child performs the challenging behavior in order to secure or maintain someone's attention.
Escape: The child performs the challenging behavior when he or she does not want to perform a particular task.
Tangible: The child exhibits a challenging behavior in order to obtain or keep an object.
Sensory: The child performs a challenging behavior because of a need for stimulation.

The special educator can then plan an intervention based on this critical information, which provides for the child's needs in a socially appropriate way and for a brief, consistent consequence for the misbehavior.

Bateman (1996) offers very helpful suggestions to assure an appropriate evaluation. She maintains that it is important to individualize the evaluation and assess the child in all of the areas related to the suspected disability. One standard battery or standard procedure administered to all children is, in her words: "unprofessional and unacceptable, even though too common" (p. 5). She also warns:

> Don't rely on any formula or quantitative guideline to determine eligibility. The more elaborate the formula, the sillier it will appear to a judge. The law requires professional judgment be relied on, and sole reliance on any quantitative guideline is prohibited. (p. 6)

Figure 4.1 demonstrates how, beginning with the evaluation process, the educational system should determine the need for special education and related services:

What Deficits Interfere With Learning?

After the evaluation is completed and the levels of performance assessed, deficits for which goals and objectives will need to be written must be identified. An example: Through evaluation and a statement of the present levels of performance, a student has been identified as having difficulty with attention to task. The current performance level is defined as: Attention to task is currently 2 minutes on an independent second-grade level activity. The student is able to

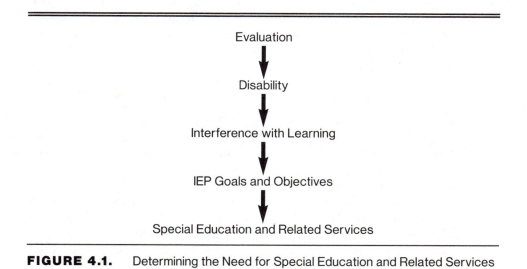

FIGURE 4.1.   Determining the Need for Special Education and Related Services

do second-grade work. This is a definite deficit that interferes with learning in a second-grade classroom. Based on the knowledge that there is a deficit, a goal and an objective can be written to address it.

For students identified as E/BD, it is critical that specific behavioral problems are described along with their frequency and duration. For instance, the statement "Johnny is physically aggressive" is not enough. What is the teacher's definition of physical aggression? Is it hitting other students in the classroom or on the playground? Is it throwing books? Is it throwing furniture? Definitions of physical aggression vary and it is important to be as specific as possible. It is equally important to note how often physical aggression occurs. Once a month? Once a week? Five times a day?

Writing Appropriate, Meaningful, and Effective Goals and Objectives

Students must gain meaningful benefit from an IEP. Clearly written goals and objectives can provide us with the information needed to show that benefit. Imagine a student who engages in verbal aggression 10 times a day each time he is given an assignment in the classroom, although the work is at an appropriate level for the student. The verbal aggression is defined as swearing very loudly so that all students in the classroom can hear. That is the present level of performance. The goal: To decrease verbal aggression in the classroom. The objective might be: Given an assignment at the appropriate third-grade level, Johnny will start the assignment, refraining from becoming verbally aggressive (swearing) so that there are no more than 5 such occurrences during any day. As the student progresses, benefit is seen because the number of incidents involving verbal aggression has decreased from 10 to 5. Needless to say, the teacher should be implementing a behavioral intervention plan to gain this progress.

Determining Appropriate Accommodations and Modifications for the Student

Section 504 of the Rehabilitation Act of 1973 states that reasonable accommodations must be made for students. Such accommodations are adaptations or adjustments in the classroom that will assist the student in learning skills. The National Information Center for Children and Youth with Disabilities (1996) outlines some sample accommodations. For note-taking, accommodations may include: use of a tape recorder in the class, use of another student's notes, a note-taker, a study guide provided by the teacher, use of a computer or typewriter. Test-taking accommodations may include: extended time on the test, taking the test in a quiet area, having someone read the test to the student, having the student take the test orally. Additional accommodations may include: preferential seating, textbooks-on-tape, extended timelines, and so on.

Accommodations do not modify the same curriculum content. Modifications, however, do change curriculum content. A modification might be to change the number of spelling words a student is required to learn or to utilize a high-interest, low-vocabulary book.

When considering reasonable accommodations, it is important that the student and teachers who will be implementing the accommodations be involved in those decisions. I once attended a staff meeting that concerned a student who had an auditory memory deficit and required repetition of what was said, and he needed to visually see the material to learn it. Most participants wanted to allow the student to use a tape recorder for lecture classes. The student did not want to use a tape recorder because he didn't like to listen to the tape after class. He wanted to learn how to take notes. His desire was an example of information from the IEP driving curriculum and a good example of student self-advocacy. In the same meeting, all teachers were present and all but one had stated they were willing to provide the student with "word banks." One teacher sat quietly throughout the discussion and finally asked: "What is a word bank?" If only one or two of the student's general education teachers attend the meeting, accommodations are recommended, and often, the other teachers are not made aware of these. An effective communication system must be established so that teachers know what accommodations have been recommended. Teachers are often reluctant to make accommodations because they do not know how to do so or do not have the time to make the accommodations. As the IEP team develops those accommodations, it is important that teachers be provided the opportunity to receive training in how to make accommodations.

The IEP team must also be cognizant of which accommodations are reasonable and which are not. We have found that unless teachers are involved in the decision-making process, the team might not be able to evaluate an accommodation in terms of what is reasonable in the classroom setting.

Planning an Effective Behavioral Intervention Plan to Meet the Needs of the Student

A behavioral intervention plan should be based on a functional assessment of the student's behavior, and should be designed to meet the goals and objectives of the student. If the goal for the student is to decrease verbal aggression (defined as swearing at the teacher when given a direction that the student does not want to do), the behavioral intervention plan should be designed to assist the student in reaching that goal. At the same time, the goals and objectives and the behavioral intervention plan should also drive a portion of the student's curriculum. The teacher must teach the student alternative ways to deal with anger other than verbal aggression. (The teaching of social skills will be discussed later.)

Point Systems

One of the major flaws in classes for children with E/BD is the lack of individualization in point systems and level systems. Although these techniques may be key components in operating an effective E/BD classroom, they are often not individualized and not based on the needs identified on the IEP. How will point systems and level systems be implemented and adjusted to the individual needs of the child? Point systems are effective only if they are paired with positive verbal reinforcement. Often teachers become mechanical engineers so busy recording points and charting that they don't make those greatly needed positive comments to the students. The behaviors targeted for the student's point sheet should be based on both the classroom rules and behaviors identified on the student's IEP.

Time intervals should be based on the level of the student. We have seen teachers establish point systems for first graders that provide points once an hour, which is a long time for a young student to wait for feedback. Five or 10 minutes may be a more appropriate interval for young students; 20 or 30 minutes may be appropriate for older students, depending on the student's developmental and social maturity level. I was working with a special education teacher of junior high school students with multiple needs, who I observed were at a social level of about 5 years. They needed frequent positive reinforcement. I worked with the teacher to establish a point system based on 5-minute intervals.

If skill deficits are part of the point system, the teacher must provide instruction in those deficit areas. A skill deficit refers to a behavior that the student has not yet learned. A performance deficit is a behavior that is currently exhibited by the student, but not to satisfactory criteria. If the teacher is uncertain if the student has a skill deficit or a performance deficit, he or she should assume it is a skill deficit and teach the skill. Scheuermann and Webber (1996) encourage social skills assessments and observational recordings to determine whether the student has a skill deficit or a performance deficit.

Finally, point systems are based on the premise that beyond positive verbal feedback, the student will receive some other type of positive reinforcement based on the number of points received (such as a tangible item purchased in a "store," free time, movie, and so on). Those reinforcers must be based on the interests and level of the student. The IEP is an excellent vehicle for learning what motivates the student; the parent knows what the student does and does not like and how the student likes to spend his or her free time. Motivators for the student should be identified on the IEP.

Level Systems

The pitfalls of level systems have been studied by Scheuermann and Webber (1996). They define level systems as consisting of "target academic and social behaviors arranged in a sequential hierarchy of 'levels,' ranging from the most basic skills at the lowest level to the most complex skills at the highest level" (p. 21). There are several problems with level systems. Teachers who plan to implement such systems must be sure that procedural safeguards are followed and the individualized needs of the student are addressed. Level systems should not determine access to general education classes. The law is clear; IEPs determine integration into general education classes—not level systems. Educational placement and access to nondisabled peers should not be used as level-system privileges.

Another problem with level systems is that all students are expected to attain the same behaviors at the same mastery schedule. For instance, the teacher may identify work completion or attention to task as a behavior that must be exhibited to progress in the level system; yet one student has a different skill level and may not be able to attend to a task as long as another student. Although it is appropriate to have some behaviors or expectations on the level system based on the rules of the classroom, it is also important that individual target behaviors be identified through the IEP process. The criteria for progressing through the level system should also be addressed individually. According to Scheuermann and Webber (1996), it is not appropriate to have a policy that has all students begin the level system at the lowest level or the middle level or highest level. The decision for the appropriate level for the student should be made by the IEP team.

Additionally, privileges should not be arranged hierarchically, with those most desired available at only the highest levels. If reinforcers are not individualized, school personnel must carefully investigate whether the reinforcers are in fact such for individual students.

Consequences for inappropriate behavior should also be addressed within the context of the IEP. Will the consequence for inappropriate behavior be a drop of level? Scheuermann and Webber (1996) recommend that it should not be. They recommend that consequences for inappropriate behaviors be independent of the level system. In any case, that decision should be made by the IEP team.

As the IEP team determines the individual effectiveness of a level system for a student, the team must determine whether the student is making satisfactory progress through the level system. For example, if the team has determined previously that the student should enter the level system at level 1 and a year later sees that the student has never moved from level 1, the group must reevaluate whether this system is effective for the student. Are the behavioral expectations appropriate for the student? Has the student been taught the skills to meet the behavioral expectations? What are the reinforcers that the student earns within the level system? Scheuermann and Webber (1996) outline possible reasons for lack of student progress within a level system: The student does not have the necessary prerequisite skills for the expected behaviors identified as targets on the level system; the student does not know how to perform those target behaviors; mastery criteria may not be reasonable and attainable; mastery criteria are not sufficient to ensure that the student really learns the target behaviors; reinforcers are not effective; and consequences for inappropriate behaviors are more appealing than consequences for engaging in the appropriate target behaviors.

Scheuermann and Webber (1996) stress the importance of targeting self-management skills in the level system. It is important to incorporate such skills as self-monitoring, self-evaluation, self-reinforcement, or a combination of the three into the level system. Self-management skills are necessary for generalization of behavior gains and certainly necessary for success in less restrictive environments. Students with E/BD typically do not exhibit such skills; therefore, they should be an integral part of the curriculum for E/BD students.

As teachers evaluate a level system, they should answer the following questions:

- Is integration into general education classes determined by the IEP rather than the level system?
- Is the entry level in the system determined by the IEP committee?
- Is placement on the level system based on current valid assessment?
- Are skill deficits considered when planning the student's level system? Are those skills then taught as part of the curriculum?
- Does each student have individual target behaviors based on the IEP in addition to those designated for the whole group?
- Are reinforcers individualized?
- Are advancement criteria appropriate for each student and based on the student's developmental level?
- Is each student's progress on the level system monitored frequently?
- Are self-management skills incorporated into the level system? (Chapter 10 of this book is devoted to the teaching of self-management skills.)
- Do behaviors that are addressed in the level system maintain over time and generalize to other environments?

Contracting

Contracting may also be an effective behavior management technique to be incorporated into the IEP. We recommend contracting as most appropriate for students in fifth grade and above. The length of time of the contract is dependent, as a point system is, on the age and maturity level of the student. The general rule of thumb is to start with a short-term contract to assure success for the student. When negotiating a contract with a student, the teacher should zero in on one behavior. At one school, I advised that a contract be developed for a student. When I followed up with the school and asked how the contract was progressing, staff members responded that it wasn't working at all. The student's behavior had deteriorated. When I inquired about the details of the contract that had been developed, I was told a list of 12 behaviors had been made that the student was expected to exhibit. I then asked what reward the student would receive for following the contract. The staff stated: "Nothing, she is just supposed to do these things and these are the consequences she will get if she doesn't follow these 12 expectations." Needless to say, this was contracting gone amuck.

A reward for following the behavior expected on the contract should be appropriate for the student. That reward does not have to be a material item, and if it is, it should not be an expensive one. We have found that attention from an adult is a powerful motivator for some students. One student likes to spend time with an adult at the end of every day if she has refrained from verbal aggression and can also earn a soft drink from the teacher if she wears her glasses every day. Consequences for not following the contract should be natural and logical. Johns, Carr, and Hoots (1995) provide a list of natural and logical consequences for inappropriate behavior. The purpose of the contract is to gain ownership from the student to work on the behavior; therefore, it is important for the student, parent, and teacher to sign it. It is also important to provide the student with a daily review of the contract and to post it where the student can see it.

The use of restrictive behavioral intervention must be addressed on the student's IEP. Teachers may not act unilaterally to determine that a restrictive intervention is appropriate for a student. Procedures that deny access to education for a portion of the day (such as time-out, in-school suspensions) or procedures that are intrusive in nature, such as the use of physical intervention or a helmet for head-banging, must be specified on the student's IEP. In a videotape, Johns and Carr (1994) outline the legal issues surrounding the use of safe physical intervention. That tape stresses that any such use must be addressed and specified on the student's IEP.

Transition Planning

Students who are above the age of 14 must be involved in their own IEPs to determine an appropriate plan for them to achieve their life goals after the completion of school. Transition planning includes discussing and planning for such areas as the student's employment, postsecondary education, independent living, eligibility for various adult services, community participation, and vocational evaluation. According to Agran (1997), federal law acknowledges that for too long students have had no say in their education and their input, which was long denied, is now valued. The traditionally passive role of the student in educational decision-making is no longer acceptable. Activities must be based on the student's needs, preferences, and interests.

Transition planning provides an excellent opportunity for a student to individually reflect about plans for the future, what the student wants to do, and what types of training or experience the student needs in order to prepare and how the school can help in meeting the student's future goals. Discussion of the student's transition plan will drive the curriculum for the student.

Agran (1997) stresses teaching a strategy to students to prepare them for the transition planning process. That strategy, called IPLAN, includes:

I: Inventory your strengths, weaknesses, goals, and choices for learning
P: Provide your inventory information
L: Listen and respond
A: Ask questions
N: Name your goals

What Assessments Will Be Conducted to Determine Student Progress?

Does the district have a districtwide assessment or is there a state-required assessment? Will the student participate in that assessment or will the student be provided with alternate assessment? If the student does participate in the assessment, what accommodations will need to be implemented? There is much discussion about whether identified special education students should participate in local and statewide assessments. While this discussion continues, it is important to remember that deciding if a student should or should not be included in those assessments should be made by the IEP team and should be delineated on the IEP. If the student does not participate in the state or local assessment, the IEP team must be able to justify why the student cannot participate. If the student can participate but needs accommodations, such as extended timelines or a modified test site or clarification of directions, those must be delineated in the IEP.

In What Least Restrictive Environment Can Specially Designed Instruction Be Provided?

After goals and objectives have been carefully crafted, the next question is how can those goals and objectives be met? In what setting? Can behaviors be controlled and changed in a general education class? In a resource class? In an instructional program? Or in a specialized setting? Are behavior problems of such a serious nature that the safety of other students is at stake? Can factors in the environment be changed? The school district has to have available a full continuum of alternative placements, including general education classrooms with supplementary aids and services, resource services, special classes, and special schools. When making the placement decisions, consideration must be given to any possible effect on the child or on the quality of the services that he or she needs. Most important, the placement must be based on the individual needs of the child and must be reviewed annually. Vaughn, Bos, and Schumm (1997) point to mainstreaming as (although not required by law) one way to achieve placement in the least restrictive environment. They believe that the essential element of mainstreaming is shared responsibility on the part of all educators in the school toward students with disabilities. According to them, "Mainstreaming includes accommodations designed to facilitate the participation of students with disabilities in all aspects of public education including transportation, instruction, extracurricular activities, and access to facilities" (p. 29). Even if a student is placed full-time in a special classroom or in a special school, the extent of opportunities to participate with nondisabled peers must be addressed in the IEP.

Placement options and questions that need to be asked in determining whether those placement options are appropriate are as follows.

General Education Classroom

Is the student able to function in the general education classroom all or part of the day with or without modifications? Can the student spend the day in the classroom if a behavioral intervention consultant or the E/BD teacher provides assistance to the classroom teacher?

General Education Classroom With Supplementary Aids and Services

Are there any aids or services that could be provided within the classroom to meet the student's needs? What are those aids and services? What does the classroom teacher need in order to meet the child's needs? If modifications are needed, what are they?

Resource Services

The student receives assistance for less than the majority of the day from a resource teacher. Does the student need reduced distractions and more individualized instruction?

Instructional Program

The student spends the majority of the day in a special class. Will the student participate in any general education classes and, if so, what will those be? How will coordination occur between special education and general education teachers?

Instructional Program in a Specialized Setting

What is the justification for placement outside the student's home school setting or general education building? Will there be opportunities for the student to interact with nondisabled peers?

Residential Program

Is placement being made for educational reasons? Placement is determined after goals and objectives have been established. Where can those goals and objectives best be met?

Promoting Parent-Educator Partnerships Through the IEP: Tips for the Educator

Parents are a required and integral part of the IEP process. The IDEA reauthorization emphasizes that concept, stressing that school district personnel must assure that parents are on an "equal footing." After all, they live with the child and know more about the child's needs and interests than the educator does. It is therefore critical that the parent be a partner in the IEP process. However, we, as educators, often establish roadblocks that prevent parents from being full participants in the process. The following are some helpful hints to assure that the parent feels comfortable in the IEP.

- Hold meetings at a time that is mutually agreeable to all participants.
- Avoid assembly-line IEPs. When teachers schedule eight IEP meetings in the same day and establish a tight time schedule, parents feel rushed and don't feel they can ask the questions they might have.
- Offer coffee or tea at meetings.
- Offer the parent the seat next to the person chairing the meeting. Individuals will look at the person who is chairing the meeting, so parents will also gain from that eye contact.
- Introduce everyone at the meeting and explain their roles.
- Let parents tape-record the meeting if they wish to do so.
- Explain the purpose of the meeting.
- Avoid having the IEP form completed before the meeting. We have seen teachers come into meetings with parents and present the completed form. This is inappropriate. The development of the IEP should be a group process with parent input.
- Avoid educational jargon.
- Accentuate the child's strengths—review those first. Then discuss deficit areas. No parent (especially those of E/BD students) wants to come to a meeting to hear only negative statements about his or her child. Often, parents are also struggling with the child's behavior and don't need to be reminded of the difficulties numerous times.
- Ask for the parents' input throughout the meeting: "Do you also see this behavior at home?" "What does your child like to do in his free time?"

- If the parent makes statements you don't agree with or find offensive, comment first on those statements you agree with and then discuss the points you do not agree with.
- Have parents participate in writing goals for their child. They usually have in mind particular behaviors or skills that they would like to see their child achieve.
- Most important, see things from the parents' perspective. Remember that the parents live with the child and have their own issues they must deal with.

In summary, the IEP should be the cornerstone of the child's special education program and thus should provide the framework for appropriate curriculum planning for the student.

Discussion Questions

1. How can you voice a dissenting opinion during an IEP meeting?
2. How do you approach a parent during an IEP meeting when it is clear that the parent has unreasonable expectations or is negative about the child?
3. What types of medical information are critical to consider during an IEP?

References

Agran, M. (1997). *Student directed learning: Teaching self-determination skills.* Pacific Grove, CA: Brooks/Cole.

Bateman, B. (1996). *Better IEPs: How to develop legally correct and educationally useful programs.* Longmont, CO: Sopris West.

Federal Register, March 12, 1999 (Volume 64, Number 48). 34 CFR Parts 300 and 303.

Johns, B., Guetzloe, E., Yell, M., Scheuermann, B., Webber, J., Carr, V., & Smith, C. (1996). *Best practices for managing adolescents with emotional/behavioral disorders within the school environment.* Reston, VA: Council for Children with Behavioral Disorders.

Johns, B., & Carr, V. (1994). *Safe physical intervention: The Garrison Model for dealing with physical aggression.* Video. Garrison School, 936 West Michigan, Jacksonville, IL 62650.

Johns, B., Carr, V., & Hoots, C. (1995). *Reduction of school violence: Alternatives to suspension.* Horsham, PA: LRP.

Kirk, S., & Chalfant, J. C. (1984). *Academic and developmental learning disabilities.* Denver: Love.

Kovac, M. (1996). *A student's guide to the IEP.* Washington, DC: National Information Center for Children and Youth with Disabilities.

Lewis, T., & Sugai, G. (1999). Effective behavior support: A systems approach to proactive schoolwide management. *Focus on Exceptional Children, 31*(6), 1–24.

Maloney, M., & Pitasky, V. (1995). *The Special Educator 1995 desk book.* Horsham, PA: LRP.

National Association of State Directors of Special Education. (1996). *Enhancing individual student accountability through the IEP: Report of the Wingspread Conference on accountability in special education.* Alexandria, VA: National Association of State Directors of Special Education.

Sacramento City Unified Sch. Dist. Bd. of Educ. v. Rachel H., 20 IDELR 812 (9th Cir. 1994).

Scheuermann, B., & Webber, J. (1996). Level systems: Problems and solutions. *Beyond Behavior, 7*(2), 12–17.

Vaughn, S., Bos, C., & Schumm, J. (1997). *Teaching mainstreamed, diverse, and at-risk students in the general education classroom.* Boston: Allyn and Bacon.

Wood, J. (1992). *Adapting instruction for mainstreamed and at-risk students.* New York: Merrill.

20 U.S.C. 1400 et seq. *Amendments to the Individuals With Disabilities Education Act.*

PART THREE

Focus on
the Curriculum

5

A Meaningful and Relevant Curriculum

Carlus, a high school freshman, is in a class for students with behavioral and developmental disorders. He has difficulty reading; at best he reads at a fourth-grade level. He says he will leave school when he is 16—only a couple of months away.

Justin is a fifth grader who was recently referred and placed in a BD classroom. When the teacher attempts to give Justin a worksheet to complete, Justin responds, "Why do I have to learn that?"

hese typical statements, made by many students throughout the county, should cause all teachers to reflect on the relevance and meaning of what they are teaching students like Carlus and Justin.

Salend (1994) believes that successful techniques for motivating students are those that personalize instruction with respect to students' skills, interests, experiences, and career goals. How can we achieve "personalized meaningful instruction"? Frymier (1985) offers a good definition of *meaningfulness:* "the extent to which that which is perceived 'makes sense' or is seen as significant or potentially useful to the student" (p. 13). He believes that students must be able to see personal relevance or potential usefulness for the information.

Strength-Based Curriculum

According to Gallagher (1997), students with E/BD need to hear that they are competent individuals. Therefore, they need to see that they have strengths. She recommends that teachers provide students with a checklist that identifies their interests and special skills. She provides this example:

I am really good at doing _____ at school.

I am really good at doing _____ at home.

I am really good at doing _____ in my neighborhood.

If I were to have a chance to choose one thing I would like to learn in school, I would choose _____.

What motivates me the most to do well in school is _____
_____

The instructional equipment I like to use the most is _____
_____

When I work hard, I want the teacher to _____.

I can do written assignments if I can do them _____.

When I am not in school, I would like to learn about _____.

I have a special interest in _____ and would like to _____.

I know how to _____. (pp. 7–8).

The Individuals with Disabilities Education Act stressed the importance of identifying deficits of students in order to plan an appropriate educational program for those with disabilities. Deficits were identified and goals were written to address those deficits. Although this is a critical component of specialized instruction, it is equally important to determine the strengths of the child and to plan a curriculum that focuses on those strengths. The most recent reauthorization—Public Law 105-17—now addresses the importance of accentuating the strengths of the child.

If we wish to keep students' interest and motivate them to stay in school, we must accentuate those strengths. When we look at the professions that individuals choose, we find that those choices are based on what the individual likes to do and does well. For instance, nurses do not choose that profession unless they are interested in working with people who are ill and unless they have strengths in that area. Why should we expect students to want to do work that deals only with deficits? If we want to motivate students to come to school, we must focus our curriculum on their strengths.

Osher (1996) discusses the longstanding success in the mental health movement of the strength-based approach. Two such approaches have been the Re-ED model and Kaleidoscope. In the 1960s Nicholas Hobbs developed the Re-ED model as an alternative to hospitalization. It focused on interventions that developed competence and enabled self-fulfillment. Chicago's Kaleidoscope also developed an unconditional, strengths-based, consumer-driven, wraparound program in the 1970s to return children from out-of-state placements (p. 27). Osher reported on a meeting held among five major federal agencies, families, service providers, and youth on the Social and Emotional Disorders National Agenda. Those present identified effective practices for enabling children and youth to succeed at home, at school, and in the community. A clear consensus was that effective schools and programs "focus on strengths, recognize progress, and reward effort" (p. 28).

A common problem in our high schools is the assumption that all students should go to college; many schools, in fact, devalue students who do not go to college. We must recognize that a trade school may be what is needed for students who have talent working with their hands. We must work with students to determine their most appropriate career path based on their strengths.

Interest-Based Curriculum

A teacher was struggling to motivate one of her students to read. The student, who was in high school, could read only at a third-grade level and appeared to have given up. During the IEP process, I asked the parents what the student liked to do. The parents responded that all the student did was sit in front of the TV and watch Showtime (a movie channel). I suggested that the teacher might want to improve the student's reading skills using the *Showtime Guide*. The teacher did exactly that. She used the *Showtime Guide* to come up with questions. The student had to read the guide in order to respond. She built vocabulary lists around the words in the guide. Some high school students who share this student's discouragement with reading might be motivated by a reading program built around the state's driver education manual.

Gallagher (1979), who stresses the importance of heightening students' interest in reading materials, notes that a teacher can observe if a student's performance changes when the material is altered. Such alterations might include enclosing the items on worksheets in colorful outlines or replacing words such as *apples, ball, wagons,* and so on, with words such as *10-speed bike, jeans, motorcycles,* and *skateboards.* One teacher substituted the names of students in the class for the fictitious names used in books she read to her students.

Although we do not recommend that teachers use many worksheets, we do suggest that students can be motivated by amusing activity sheets interspersed with worksheets. Teachers might also slip in sheets that tell students they can pick a game, use the computer, or draw for five minutes. Preferably, these sheets should be based on activities that the student likes to do.

Rademacher, Cowart, Sparks, and Chism(1997) devised a quality assignment-planning worksheet that can be used by teachers to create assignments for diverse learners. The worksheet, part of a comprehensive instructional routine for creating interesting classroom assignments, was designed to guide the teacher's thinking through a series of four steps. The steps in using the quality assignment planning worksheet are:

P: Plan the purpose of the assignment
L: Link assignment to student needs and interests
A: Arrange clear student directions
N: Note evaluation date and results. (p. 14)

For the "L" section of planning, teachers ask the following questions:

How can the assignment be made relevant for students?
How can personal choices for variation and challenge be incorporated?
What are pitfalls to successful completion of work?
What are solutions to these pitfalls?

The acronym HALO can prompt teachers' thinking on how choices within the assignment will address the needs of

H: High achievers
A: Average achievers
L: Low achievers
O: Other students, such as limited English proficiency students and special education students.

Although this planning tool was designed to be used in general education class-rooms, it is most appropriate for classes of E/BD students in which achievement levels of students will vary.

To accompany the planning worksheet, an assignment idea chart was also created. The top part of the Assignment Idea Chart contains verbs from Bloom's Taxonomy of Thinking; the bottom half is an assignment that matches the verb. The purpose of the chart is to help teachers design assignments that differ from the frequently used worksheet format.

Function-Based Curriculum

Shea and Bauer (1987) describe two types of curriculum used in schools that do not meet the needs of our students with emotional and behavioral disorders. One such curriculum is based on the developmental-cognitive approach—an approach based on students moving through various developmental levels; success at each level is required for movement to the next level. Shea and Bauer believe that this type of curriculum approaches instruction in a manner that often leads some students to say, "This is baby stuff." Others may ask, "Why do I have to learn that?"

The second approach—the remedial-behavioral approach—is based not on a specific order of skills a student should learn, but on a specific set of skills to improve the child's ability to interact effectively within a given environment. Shea and Bauer believe that this approach does not solve the problem of the need for generalization to other environments and may block discovery of other key concepts in teaching.

Finally, Shea and Bauer (1987) discuss a functional curriculum in which goals and objectives for instruction are based on an environmental assessment. This curriculum motivates the individual because teaching is based on the natural environment of the student. Shea and Bauer believe that in order to plan an appropriate functional curriculum, the teacher should ask: Why should the skill be taught? Is the skill necessary to prepare students to function in the most appropriate environment for that student? Could students function if they did not learn the skill?

Quinn and Rutherford (1997) define the functional curriculum as "one that allows the program to meet a student's cognitive, vocational, social, and behavioral needs" (p. 22). This curriculum focuses on developing skills that are job-related and geared to daily living as well as being socially relevant. Henley, Ramsey, and Algozzine (1996) believe that a functional curriculum should include life skills that are taught both in the classroom and in the community. Academic skills are taught in a practical manner. Math can be taught by having students pay bills, balance a checkbook, and prepare a budget. Reading skills would be reinforced by having students use a cookbook, assemble appliances from directions, or repair items in the home by consulting a manual. As these authors state: "Everyone must ultimately function in a community setting regardless of the level of schooling pursued or accomplished. This means that life skills preparation is important for all students at all levels of schooling" (pp. 247–248).

Students can learn important social skills and job preparation skills through community service. In addition, community service teaches students the value of giving to others. A student who did community service at a facility for students with severe and profound disabilities discovered he wanted to do this sort of work after he finished his schooling. He later got a job in such a facility.

One of the purposes of education as outlined in the new IDEA is to prepare students for independent living. If we are to reach that goal, we must teach students the skills they need to live on their own and to meet their basic needs.

Age-Appropriate Curriculum

Students with E/BD are aware that they have academic deficits that arise either as a result of learning problems or learning disabilities or as a result of missing instruction because of behavioral problems they exhibited in the classroom. They are also aware of the level of a particular book—even if the reading level is coded. Students with E/BD want to "save face" with their peers and are very sensitive to working in a book that may be at a lower level than the one their peers are reading. Obviously, it is not appropriate to give a seventh grader a first-grade reading book, even if that student can only read books at that level. Such a practice is demeaning to the student and lets other students in the class know that the student is not able to read as well as most others in the class.

In their work with young children, McCormick and Feeney (1995) used the example of a 3-year-old female who was functioning near the 18-month level. They reported that providing even such a young child with materials and toys at that level of functioning would both contribute to a negative self-concept and stigmatize the child in the eyes of her peers. They believe that the child should have the same materials as her peers. The materials could be modified if necessary. For older students, the teacher has the option either to modify the materials or to utilize high-interest, low-vocabulary books that are more appropriate for the student.

Lynch and Beare (1990) studied the quality of IEP objectives and their relevance to the instruction of students with mental retardation and behavioral disorders. The subjects in the study were 48 elementary and secondary students with mild behavioral and intellectual disabilities who were placed in self-contained or resource rooms in eight school districts in the northwestern part of Minnesota. Twenty-five of the students were in programs for those with emotional and behavioral disorders; 23 were in programs for students with mental retardation. The analysis rated IEP objectives for the presence or absence of 10 components:

age-appropriate material, relation to demands of general education, transition, relevance, interaction, teaching across settings and materials, teaching in natural settings, generalization, specificity, and parent involvement. Age-appropriate objectives were defined as being within one grade level of chronological age.

Classroom observations were conducted, following the examination of the IEPs, in order to describe the relationship between what was written in the IEP and what was observed. It was found that the IEP objectives reflected the category of disability; that is, for students identified as E/BD the objectives primarily focused primarily on behavioral management. The IEP objectives were judged adequate on all categories for appropriate practice. It was found that within the age-appropriate and functionality categories, there was an average of 62%.

However, it was found that even though an individual student's IEP objectives reflected functionality, generalization, and age-appropriateness, the student did not necessarily engage in activities that reflected the indicators. Observations showed that the students' activities were not age-appropriate. Lynch and Beare speculated that this may have been the result of lowered expectations for the ability of the students to be successful in chronological age-equivalent curriculum. (Throughout this book, we stress the importance of high-expectations for students and a challenging curriculum.)

Based on their study, Lynch and Beare (1990) stress the importance of learning to view education as consisting of more than adjustment to the general education curriculum. Minimally, the curriculum should include prevocational, vocational, and social skills instruction that is functional to the student in environments outside the general education classroom. Teachers have opportunities to be very creative in teaching skills by using more appropriate age-level materials. For example, math skills for a seventh grader may be better taught using ads in the newspaper, the point system in the classroom, or material that is of great interest to the student.

We have observed teachers giving junior high and high school students worksheets that the students perceive as "babyish." With the availability of high-interest, low-vocabulary materials and materials based on students' life skills, there is no need to give inferior materials to students. Such materials fail to motivate students and demean them. As Curwin (1994) states: "When school tasks are too easy, students perceive them as condescending, babyish, and not worth doing" (p. 28). He notes that there is very little value in achieving something that is too easy because there is no pride in accomplishing it. Children need to be challenged, yet not overwhelmed. That balance is a delicate one to achieve.

Likewise, there is a fine balance between materials and activities that are not babyish and those that meet the social and emotional needs of the students. For example, some secondary students may be chronologically 16, but socially and emotionally much younger. As we work with them, we should not give them babyish materials, although we may want to utilize activities that are typically used with younger students. We have found that students may have missed some activities when they were younger and still need to have them as part of their experiences. An example: A teacher of junior high school students liked to read them children's stories, such as *Charlotte's Web*. The students would sit spellbound throughout storytelling time. One of the girls (a street-smart young lady) asked if she could hold the book up as the teacher read it. Another example: A junior high school teacher of students with emotional and behavioral disorders sponsored an optional brown-bag lunch once a week. The students would bring their lunch and the teacher would read a story. Although this activity was optional, she found that all of her students participated every week and even some of the general education students asked to participate and did so. Teachers have found that some junior high and high school students like puppet shows.

If we are to reach students with E/BD, we must work to motivate them to stay in school. Personalization of instruction through the mechanisms described in this chapter is an important key to that motivation.

Discussion Questions

1. How can we best determine the strengths of our students?
2. When it appears that all of the interests of a student are centered on activities that are of an illegal nature, how can we channel the student's energies toward other interests?
3. How do we balance the need for age-appropriate materials with "fun" activities that students may have missed when they were younger?

References

Curwin, R. (1994). Helping students rediscover hope. *Journal of Emotional and Behavioral Problems, 3*(1), 27–30.

Frymier, J. (1985). Motivation to learn. *Kappan, 9,* 13–14.

Gallagher, P. (1997). Promoting dignity: Taking the destructive D's out of behavior disorders. *Focus on Exceptional Children, 29*(9), 1–19.

Gallagher, P. (1979). *Teaching students with behavior disorders.* Denver: Love.

Henley, M., Ramsey, R., & Algozzine, R. (1996). *Teaching students with mild disabilities.* Boston: Allyn and Bacon.

Lynch, E., & Beare, P. (1990). The quality of IEP objectives and their relevance to instruction for students with mental retardation and behavioral disorders. *Remedial and Special Education, 11*(2), 48–55.

McCormick, L., & Feeney, S. (1995). Modifying and expanding activities for children with disabilities. *Young Children, 50*(4), 10–17.

Osher, D. (1996). Strength-based foundations of hope. *Reaching today's Youth: The Community Circle of Caring Journal, 1*(1), 26–29.

Quinn, M., & Rutherford, R. (1997) Alternative programs for students with social, emotional, or behavioral problems. In L. Bullock & R. Gable (Eds.), *The Second CCBD Mini-Library Series: Successful interventions for the 21st century.* Reston, VA: Council for Exceptional Children.

Rademacher, J., Cowart, M., Sparks, J., & Chism, V. (1997). Planning high-quality assignments with diverse learners. *Preventing School Failure, 42*(1), 12–18.

Salend, S. (1994). *Effective mainstreaming: Creating inclusive classrooms.* Upper Saddle River, NJ: Merrill.

Shea, T., & Bauer, A. (1987). *Teaching children and youth with behavior disorders.* Englewood, NJ: Prentice-Hall.

6

The Central Role of Teaching Social Skills

Blaine was participating in a pizza party for students who had perfect attendance for the month. When he wanted another piece of pizza, he snapped his fingers at one of the teacher assistants. The assistant, who was very upset, later learned that at the dinner table Blaine's father snapped his fingers to get what he wanted from Blaine's mother. Obviously, finger-snapping for food was inappropriate and offensive behavior at school, but it was a behavior that Blaine had learned at home.

We can no longer assume that all children come to school knowing how to behave and how to respond appropriately in varying social situations. Some children believe that the only way to express anger is to hit someone or to yell until they get attention. Albert, a 15-year-old student who was involved in a gang did not know how to wait his turn to speak and continually strove, like a 3- or 4-year-old, to get the teacher's attention. He became very upset if someone else in his instructional E/BD class received attention. Tyler, a 16-year-old, is in a regular high school but is scorned by other students because he continually acts like a Power Ranger. Jenny, a 10-year-old receiving resource services from the special education teacher in the building, speaks very quietly and cannot assert herself to make her needs known. All of these students need to be taught appropriate social skills.

Mathur and Rutherford (1996) state that adequate social development can be considered the foundation of personal and social adjustment in life. Deficits in social skills are linked to poor social adjustment, mental health problems, delinquency, and low self-concept. According to Deshler, Ellis, and Lenz (1996): "Social skills knowledge is just as important as content knowledge" (p. 371). They believe that poor social skills in school are related to the following factors: (1) limited opportunities to learn; (2) negative academic and social self-concept; and (3) social isolation.

According to Shores and Jack (1996), children and youth are identified as having behavioral disorders based on their excesses and their deficits of social behavior. They respond to available social stimuli in unpredictable ways.

The teaching of social skills should be an integral part of any program for E/BD students. We have observed E/BD teachers who work on developing students' skills in reading, math, and writing, but fail to spend time in the direct teaching of social skills. But when we ask people in business and industry what skills they want workers to have, they consistently answer: "We want them to be able to get along with other people." Business and industry leaders can teach students job-specific skills but need workers who have appropriate social skills. If we are to prepare our students for the world of work, we must provide direct instruction in social skills.

Mathur and Rutherford (1996) define social skills as socially acceptable patterns of behaviors that allow students to gain social reinforcement and acceptance and avoid aversive social situations. "A socially skilled person is capable of managing his or her social environment by understanding and responding to social situations effectively" (p. 21). They believe that the purpose of training in social skills should not be restricted to teaching a specific social skill in one context but to promoting overall social functioning that includes a wide repertoire of social skills that produce socially acceptable responses in various social situations. Further, they define social competence "as a composite or multitude of generalized social skills that contribute to a person's overall social functioning, whereas social skills refer to situationally specific patterns of behaviors that are identifiable and definable. The ultimate purpose of teaching specific social skills is to promote the overall functioning or social competence of the individual. . . . Social skills are the basic ingredients of social competence" (p. 22).

Warger and Rutherford (1993) make the following distinctions between social skills and social competence. Social skills are specific, identifiable, discrete, learned behaviors that result in positive social consequences in social situations. Social skills are viewed as part of the broader construct known as social competence. "Social competence is an observer-based judgment about a person's social functioning, whereas social skills are specific behaviors that form the basis for socially competent behavior" (p. 21). Gresham (1998) believes that the degree to which children learn to establish, develop, and maintain satisfactory interpersonal relationships with their peers and adults is the essence of social competence.

Social skills programming has many facets. As teachers plan the teaching of social skills to students, they must ask these questions (outlined by Mathur and Rutherford [1996]).

What are the social skills deficits?

What are the reasons for the deficits? Does the student have adequate knowledge of the skill?

Does the student have enough opportunity to use the target skills? (p. 23)

Are reinforcement contingencies effectively arranged to promote the response? (p. 23)

They suggest that "targeting the peer group rather than the student for social skills training, and altering the classroom environment to facilitate positive peer networks and to discourage negative peer influences are examples of strategies that need to be examined in future social skills research" (p. 23).

In summarizing, Mathur and Rutherford (1996) state that the success of social skills training depends on several factors including:

1. Social validity of target skills.
2. A sound conceptual basis for social skill deficits.
3. Precision and comprehensiveness in assessment procedures.
4. Clarity in description of social skills interventions.
5. Attention to contextual factors.
6. Systematic programming for generalization. (p. 26)

Walker, Colvin, and Ramsey (1995) believe that the two major indications of the success or failure of any social skills training effort are:

1. Whether the student targeted acquires and demonstrates unlearned social skills or uses already acquired skills in a more competent manner, and

2. Whether the process of acquiring the skill leads to improved social effectiveness and acceptance by key social agents in the student's world (p. 235).

Quinn, Kavale, Mathur, Rutherford, and Forness (1999) conducted a meta-analysis of 35 studies investigating the effects of social skill interventions for students with emotional and behavioral disorders. The results showed that the use of universal social skill interventions—those that are given to whole groups of students with emotional and behavioral disorders—has produced less than substantial changes in behavior. These researchers determined that group interventions are not as effective; rather what students with E/BD need is an increase in specially designed individualized instruction. They also argue that the cost of not teaching social skills is extremely high.

Gresham (1998) summarizes social skills training research that shows a weak effect, particularly for students with emotional and behavioral disorders. However, he believes that the poor outcomes can be attributed in part to these factors in the research: use of socially invalid and insensitive outcome measures; failure to match social skills interventions to specific social skills deficits; and failure to program for functional generalization. He advises that social skills training not be utilized as a stand-alone intervention but as an integral part of the curriculum.

In this chapter we will discuss the critical components of social skills training, utilizing a multifaceted approach. Those components include:

1. Direct instruction.
2. The teachable moment.
3. The teacher as a role model for appropriate social skills.
4. Recognition of appropriate social skills throughout the day.
5. Special group projects.
6. Conflict resolution.
7. Teaching self-management, including social skills strategies and anger management.

This chapter will also discuss the selection of social skills materials for the classroom.

Direct Instruction of Social Skills

Rutherford, Quinn, and Mathur (1996) point to research that validates the effectiveness of social skills training approaches in promoting specific social skills of students with E/BD. In direct instruction of social skills, we must:

1. Select the target student(s).
2. Determine what type of prosocial skills are desired. Such prosocial behaviors might include: dealing with anger appropriately, accepting consequences of

behavior, listening, accepting compliments, responding to failure, cooperating with peers, and so on.

3. Determine what types of inappropriate behaviors the student currently displays.
4. Determine if the student can't or won't demonstrate the prosocial skills.
5. Establish a group or groups for teaching social skills.

After assessing through observation, behavior-rating scales, and functional assessment, the teacher must determine if the student has a skill deficit. According to Bullock and Fitzimmons-Lovett (1997), if there is a skill deficit, direct instruction is essential. Teachers should examine commercially available materials to teach the skill. We stress the importance of modifying and adapting materials so that they are relevant to the students' backgrounds and so that the materials meet the needs of the students. Bullock and Fitzimmons-Lovett believe that there is no one ideal social skills curriculum. When teaching, it is important to incorporate the components of effective instruction:

1. Teach the skill by breaking it into small steps.
2. Demonstrate and model the skill.
3. Have students practice the skill using role-playing. Role-playing provides students with practice of the targeted social skills. According to Rutherford, Quinn, and Mathur (1996), role-playing provides the student with a safe environment for practicing the steps and the strategies necessary to develop target social skills. They suggest that the teacher present a variety of role-playing situations in order to allow the student to use the same strategies in different social situations.
4. Provide feedback and reinforcement for practice.
5. Systematically provide a program for generalization of social skills. We know that students often are not able to generalize the social skills that we are teaching them to other settings. Rutherford, Quinn, and Mathur (1996) discuss the use of opportunity teaching for promoting generalization of social skills in natural settings such as hallways, cafeterias, other classrooms, and so on. The technique calls for cueing or prompting students who have missed an opportunity to use the social skill in the other environment. Students are provided with corrective feedback when they apply the social skills incorrectly and are praised for appropriate demonstration of the skills.

ASSET is a commercial program designed to develop social skills of adolescents with special needs who demonstrate difficulties in social functioning. The program, which has also been used in regular classrooms, emphasizes the following eight fundamental skills: giving positive feedback, giving negative feedback, accepting negative feedback, resisting peer pressure, being able to negotiate, solving personal problems, following directions, and conducting conversations.

Each skill is then divided into components that are sequenced for instruction. ASSET employs a nine-step process to teach social skills to secondary students by using commercial materials. The nine steps are:

1. Review previously learned skills and evaluate and integrate homework.
2. Explain the skill that is the focus of the current lesson.
3. Explain the reason the skill needs to be learned.
4. Provide examples of situations in which the skill can be used.
5. Examine the skills that are needed. A skills sheet that lists component skills is provided to the students.
6. Use videotapes for modeling.
7. Provide opportunities for verbal rehearsal. Students practice saying the skill components and play games and engage in activities that teach them the skills.
8. Provide the opportunity for students to role-play, performing the subskills and overall skills.
9. Provide homework so that the students can practice the subskills and skills outside of the classroom.

The Teachable Moment

Often when a behavioral problem occurs, the teacher will provide a consequence for the student and then will forget the incident. Unfortunately, the teacher has missed the "teachable moment"—the opportunity to take a negative situation and turn it into a learning experience. We cannot assume that the student knows the appropriate response to the situation. It is possible that the student needs to be taught. The teacher has a perfect opportunity to teach the child how to respond appropriately, so that the student does not get in trouble again. An example: Mumbling, so no one else can hear, Jimmy addresses Billy by an inappropriate name. Billy gets mad and hits Jimmy. Billy gets into trouble because no one heard Jimmy. Billy receives an appropriate consequence, but the teacher should also use this event to teach Billy what he could do if this situation occurs again. The teacher should consider that Billy may have a "short fuse" that comes from a family in which violence may be a frequent occurrence. Billy's father may have taught him that when someone irritates you, hit. Billy did what he knew how to do. More appropriate options must be explored with Billy.

Once the student is calm, the teacher can help the student assess and process the event by asking: What happened? What did you do? What can you do the next time it happens? In the example, the teacher would ask Billy, "What happened?" Billy would have immediately said: "Jimmy called me a name." (Students typically will focus on what someone else did.) The teacher would then ask: "What did you do?" Then Billy would reluctantly state that he hit Jimmy. The teacher would then ask: "What could you do the next time that Jimmy calls you a name?" Billy might first state that he could hit Jimmy again. The teacher would then ask the student if that was an appropriate response. Billy would say, "No." The teacher could then say, "What else could you have done?" Billy would respond: "I could ignore him." The teacher would reinforce the student positively and then might ask the student if there was anything else the student could do. Billy might say that he could tell the teacher. The teacher would reinforce the student again. The teacher would then leave the student with a positive word, expressing confidence that the student can handle the situation appropriately if another incident would occur. The teacher should also reinforce the student for speaking calmly.

The Teacher as a Role Model for Appropriate Social Skills

It is important for teachers to remember that they are role models for their students. How teachers treat students, how teachers deal with anger, frustrating situations, or a crisis sets the tone for the classroom. We firmly believe that we must treat children with respect if we wish to gain respect. When teachers reprimand students in front of others, point their fingers in students' faces, or yell at them, they send messages to students that they do not respect them. No adult wants to be treated in such a negative manner; we should remember not to treat students negatively.

Recognizing Appropriate Social Skills

We know that positive feedback for appropriate behavior is critical. As Walker, Colvin, and Ramsey (1995) state: "As with the acquisition of academic skills it is important to look for spontaneous displays of expected behavior and to provide behavior-descriptive praise for them" (p. 134). Johns and Carr (1995) concur: "Teachers should never miss an opportunity to honestly accent the positive. In our opinion, at least 70% of the comments teachers give students each day should be positive" (p. 25).

An example: Aubrey has a whole repertoire of inappropriate behavior, and the bus ride to school with 14 other students is very difficult for him. One day there was a major problem with three students on the bus, which the bus driver came in to report. Almost immediately, all staff members assumed that Aubrey was one of the three. However, Aubrey was not involved at all. As a matter of fact, he had stayed in his seat and ignored the trouble. He even apologized to the bus driver for the trouble. When the principal learned how Aubrey had handled the situation, she went to the classroom and asked to see Aubrey privately. Aubrey immediately thought he was in trouble. However, the principal proceeded to tell him that she had heard about the trouble and was very proud of the mature way that Aubrey had handled the situation. Aubrey was very proud of himself.

Special Group Projects

Walker, Colvin, and Ramsey (1995) believe that all students in a classroom should be exposed to a core set of skills from which all of them can benefit. A group project is an appropriate method of exposing an entire class or school to these skills. Group projects might include:

Pom-Pom Day. The goal is to teach students how to give and receive compliments. Warm fuzzy pom-poms, which are to be worn around the neck, are given to students and staff members. The task for each participant is to give and to collect pieces of yarn from the pom-pom. To do this, participants must give a compliment to another participant.

Giving thanks during the month of November. The goal is to teach students to say, "Thanks" when someone does something nice for them. Students throughout the school are given thank you cards. A bulletin board or large poster for each class is placed in a central location. Students write thank you notes to those within the school and classroom who do something nice for them. The thank you notes are placed on the bulletin board. The object is to see which class can have its bulletin board filled first.

Reflecting on the things for which we are thankful. The goal is to teach students to reflect on the positive things in their lives. Students and staff are asked to make a poster depicting 50 things they are thankful for. The posters are displayed in the hall.

Holiday gifts. The goal is for students to reflect on their strengths. Students and staff members use construction paper and ribbon to create "packages" that can be displayed in the hall. Gift tags identify the participant's package. On the package, participants describe their talents and strengths.

New Year's Resolution. The goal of this project is to set and attain a goal for the month. Each student and staff member is given a sheet of paper on which the participant writes down a goal to accomplish during the month of January. The sheets are posted for all to see. Prizes are given to participants who meets their January goals.

Start each day with a smile. The goal of this project is to stress the importance of a smile. For a month, as students enter the building, they are greeted by staff who observes if the students are smiling. When a smile is seen, a smiley face coupon is given to the student. At lunch, a drawing is held for a smiley face cookie. At the end of the month, all coupons are entered into a drawing for a giant cookie.

Teachers will find these projects most effective when the whole school or the whole classroom participates.

Conflict Resolution

According to Johnson and Johnson (1995), violence prevention programs alone are not sufficient. They must be supplemented by programs in conflict resolution, a key component in any effective curriculum for students with emotional and behavioral disorders. Johns and Keenan (1997) believe that if we can teach students to abandon violence and resolve conflicts in other ways those students will not only have more positive relationships with peers and peace of mind, they will want to use the techniques increasingly in their everyday life.

Conflict resolution teaches negotiation skills and higher level thinking. Life is full of situations individuals must negotiate. Through conflict resolution, students learn how to negotiate. Conflict resolution is also more effective than suspensions and detentions in shaping appropriate behaviors. Rather than removing students from a situation and allowing them to escape the problem, conflict resolution teaches students to face the problem and resolve the conflict peacefully.

The process we use has been adapted from the work of Fred Schrumpf (1991):

A. Bring the two parties who have the conflict together.
B. Have the parties sit facing each other with the mediator at the head of the table.
C. The mediator opens the session, introducing himself or herself as the mediator; and each disputant introduces himself or herself. The mediator then provides the ground rules, which are:

   1. The mediator is neutral and does not take sides.
   2. The session is confidential; no one in the room discusses the proceedings with anyone.
   3. Each party is to respect the other party by listening and by not interrupting when the other is speaking.
   4. It is important for both parties to cooperate in order to resolve the dispute.

The mediator should obtain a commitment from the parties to follow the ground rules.

D. The mediator then begins the process of gathering information.

   1. Each disputant is asked to tell his or her side of the story. "Will you each tell me what happened?"
   2. The mediator listens, summarizes, clarifies, repeats statements, rephrases to check accuracy, sums up the statements of the disputants.
   3. The mediator then repeats the process asking for additional information. "Is there anything you want to add?"
   4. The mediator then restates both sides of the situation.
   5. The mediator then focuses on common interests, asking such questions as: What do you want? If you were in the other person's shoes, how would you feel? If you could ask the other person to do one thing, what would it be?
   6. After gaining insight into the students' interests, state what the interests are.

7. The mediator then asks the disputants to come up with possible solutions that might satisfy both parties.
8. The mediator then asks the disputants to evaluate options and choose solutions.
9. The mediator then writes the agreement and closes by asking each participant to sign it.

Teaching Social Skills Through Self-Management Strategies

Our goal should be to teach students how to manage their own behavior. Self-management is discussed in greater depth in Chapter 10 but it is important to discuss some social skills strategies that students can be taught to use in solving interpersonal problems. According to Vaughn, Bos, and Schumm (1997), the goal is "to teach students to identify their problems, goals, and a wide range of alternative strategies for effectively solving their problems" (p. 85). They believe that four components are critical in problem-solving: problem identification, generation of alternative solutions, identification and evaluation of the consequences of the alternative solutions, and solution implementation.

Vaughn, Bos, and Schumm (1997) discuss two strategies that were developed by Vaughn to teach students a method to solve problems. The first strategy, known by the acronym FAST, suggests students to consider problems, identify alternatives, and evaluate the consequences. The steps of FAST are:

F: Freeze and Think. Students must identify the problem and view it from their own perspective as well as from the perspective of the other student(s) involved.

A: Alternatives. Students generate alternative solutions and learn how to categorize the solutions generated.

S: Solution Evaluation. Students select several of the options and evaluate the consequences of the alternatives.

T: Try It. Students practice and implement the solution, evaluating its effectiveness. If it is not effective, the student goes back to step two (Alternatives).

SLAM, another strategy developed by Vaughn and compatible with FAST, aims to teach students to accept and respond in an appropriate manner to negative feedback from others.

S: Stop. Students stop what they are doing and take a breath when they receive negative feedback.

L: Look. When a student receives negative feedback, the student should stop all activity and look at the person who gave the negative feedback.

A: Ask. The student should ask questions to clarify the meaning of what the other person has said.

M: Make. The student makes an appropriate response to the other person.

PEACE is an effective strategy developed by Lantieri and Patti (1996) for teaching students how to handle a conflict:

P: Practice calming down. Take deep breaths and tune into your feelings.

E: Express your point of view. Be strong without being mean.

A: Agree to work it out. Listen well. Acknowledge the other person's feelings.

C: Choose a solution that works for everyone. Brainstorm lots of possibilities first.

E: Encourage others to be nonviolent. See conflict as a problem to be solved, not a contest to be won. (p. 44)

Another strategy (taken from *Anger Management for Youth: Stemming Aggression and Violence* by Eggert [1994]), which will also be discussed in the chapter on self-management, is known as COPING. It aims to teach students to use self-talk phrases to cope with anger:

C: Calm down: Say, "calm down" or "stop."

O: Overcome the negative; opt for control: Say, "Overcome. Easy does it. I am in control."

P: Prepare; problem-solve; plan: Say, "think, problem-solve, remember your plan."

I: Identify; invite alternatives rather than using insults: Say, "Imagine success. Don't use insults."

N: Name the angry feelings and negotiate: Say, "I'm angry, I need to think about negotiation."

G: Go; get on with the plan; give praise to self and others: Say, "Way to go!! Good job!" (p. 114).

During the process of teaching these strategies to students, teachers will find that role-playing each step is critical because it helps students become aware of their own inappropriate behaviors. Deshler, Ellis, and Lenz (1996) give these guidelines for effective role-playing:

a. Establish clear objectives.

b. Identify roles to be played and specify how each player should act.

c. Establish what participants should think about and observe during role-playing.

d. Remember that participation in role-playing is more effective than observation.

e. Role-playing should be at least partially scripted. (p. 398)

Deshler, Ellis, and Lenz (1996) recommend three self-monitoring activities that can be included in the process of teaching social skills to students. The first is interviewing. As a form of modeling this technique, the teacher asks students if they are aware of their own behavior, if they know why their behavior is a problem, if they have ideas as to why they engage in the behavior, if they desire to change their behavior, and what alternatives could be used to change the behavior. Interviews can be used to monitor the students' progress and help them participate in devising and then monitoring the chosen intervention process.

Keeping a journal is another self-monitoring technique. The students keep notes on their social interactions and the progress of interventions. By keeping a journal, students can reflect on their own behavior. Common options include having students make notes whenever they perform a newly learned skill, at certain times or once or twice during the day.

Keeping a record of one's own behavior is the third self-monitoring technique. The students can use a tally sheet to keep track of the incidents involving a particular behavior. A tally sheet can be attached to the desktop or to a notebook cover.

Rosenthal-Malek (1997) stresses the importance of using metacognitive strategies to teach students social skills. She teaches children as young as 3 years of age how to interact cooperatively by using a self-interrogation strategy. Such strategies consist of a series of questions that the student employs during a problem-solving situation. For instance, to help the child to interact appropriately in a free-play situation, the student is taught six general self-interrogation questions:

1. Stop and think!
2. What (or who) do I want to play with?
3. What will happen if_____?
4. How do I feel (happy, sad, angry)?
5. How does my friend feel (happy, sad, angry)?
6. What (or who) else could I play with? (p. 30)

In the area of self-management, anger management and control are essential. Walker, Colvin, and Ramsey (1995) believe that it is important to teach students to recognize when they are angry and the emotional psychological arousal that accompanies anger; to identify the situations and events that seem to trigger intense anger; to recognize the unpleasant consequences that can result from intense expressions of anger; and to learn appropriate methods of expressing anger and dissatisfaction.

Goldstein and Glick (1987) have developed a very important program for adolescents. Aggression Replacement Training consists of three coordinated interventions. The first, Structured Learning, is a set of procedures designed to enhance prosocial skills levels. Modeling, role-playing, performance feedback, and transfer-training are used. The second, Anger Control Training, teaches antisocial behavior inhibition. Moral Education, the third intervention, is centered around dilemma discussion groups.

Skillstreaming, another excellent structured learning approach, was developed for early childhood students, elementary students, and adolescents. Goldstein, Sprafkins, Gershaw, and Klein (1980) define this structured learning approach for the adolescent as "a psychoeducational intervention designed specifically to enhance the prosocial, interpersonal, stress management, and planning skills of the aggressive, withdrawn, immature, and 'normal' but developmentally lagging adolescent" (p. 11).

Selecting Social Skills Curriculum

Sugai (1995) offers this checklist to be used in determining whether a published social skills curriculum should be utilized.

1. Is a behavioral or cognitive-behavioral approach to teaching social skills emphasized?
2. Are prerequisite teaching skills for using the curriculum indicated?
3. Are the chronological ages and developmental levels of the students who would benefit from the curriculum indicated?
4. Are adaptations and accommodations for individualizing instruction provided?
5. Has the curriculum been field-tested? (p. 3)

Discussion Questions

1. What activities can be used for whole school social skills?
2. How would you go about planning social skills activities for a whole school?
3. If you were asked to mentor a teacher of students with emotional and behavioral disorders and that teacher said he or she did not have time to teach social skills during the day, what would be your response?

References

Bullock, L., & Fitzimmons-Lovett, A. (1997). Meeting the needs of children and youth with challenging behaviors. *Reaching Today's Youth: The Community Circle of Caring Journal, 1*(3), 54–61.

Deshler, D., Ellis, E., & Lenz, B. K. (1996). *Teaching adolescents with learning disabilities: Strategies and methods.* Denver: Love.

Eggert, L. (1994). *Anger management for youth: Stemming aggression and violence.* Bloomington, IN: National Educational Service.

Goldstein, A., & Glick, B. (1987). *Aggression replacement training.* Champaign, IL: Research Press.

Goldstein, A., Sprafkin, R., Gershaw, N. J., & Klein, P. (1980). *Skillstreaming the adolescent.* Champaign, IL: Research Press.

Gresham, F. (1998). Social skills training: Should we raze, remodel, or rebuild? *Behavioral Disorders, 24*(1), 19–25.

Hazel, J. S., Schumaker, J. B., Sherman, J. A., & Sheldon-Wildgen, J. (1981). *ASSET: A social skills program for adolescents.* Champaign, IL: Research Press.

Johns, B., & Carr, V. (1995). *Techniques for managing verbally and physically aggressive students.* Denver: Love.

Johns, B., & Keenan, J. (1997). *Techniques for managing a safe school.* Denver: Love.

Johnson, D., & Johnson, R. (1995). *Reducing school violence through conflict resolution.* Alexandria, VA: Association for Supervision and Curriculum Development.

Lantieri, L., & Patti, J. (1996). Waging peace in our schools. *Reaching Today's Youth, 1*(1), 43–47.

Mathur, S., & Rutherford, R. (1996). Is social skills training effective for students with emotional or behavioral disorders? Research issues and needs. *Behavioral Disorders, 22*(1), 21–27.

Quinn, M. M., Kavale, K. A., Mathur, S. R., Rutherford, R. B., & Forness, S. R. (1999). A meta-analysis of social skill interventions for students with emotional or behavioral disorders. *Journal of Special Education, 7*(1), 54–64.

Rosenthal-Malek, A. (1997). Stop and think: Using metacognitive strategies to teach students social skills. *Teaching Exceptional Children, 29*(3), 29–31.

Rutherford, R., Quinn, M., & Mathur, S. (1996). *Effective strategies for teaching appropriate behaviors to children with emotional/behavioral disorders.* Reston, VA: Council for Children with Behavioral Disorders. Mini-Library Series on Emotional/Behavioral Disorders.

Schrumpf, F. (1991). *Peer mediation.* Champaign, IL: Research Press.

Shores, R., & Jack, S. (1996). Special issue on research needs and issues in education for students with emotional and behavioral disorders. *Behavioral Disorders, 22*(1), 5–7.

Sugai, G. (1995). Selecting and designing social skills instructional materials. An unpublished handout presented at the International Conference on Behavioral Disorders Preconference Workshop, Dallas, TX, October 7, 1995.

Vaughn, S., Bos, C., & Schumm, J. S. (1997). *Teaching mainstreamed, diverse, and at-risk students in the general education classroom.* Boston: Allyn and Bacon.

Walker, H., Colvin, G., & Ramsey, E. (1995). *Antisocial behavior in school: Strategies and best practices.* Pacific Grove, CA: Brooks/Cole.

Warger, C., & Rutherford, R. (1993). Co-teaching to improve social skills. *Preventing School Failure, 37*(4), 21–27.

7

Multicultural Education for Students With Emotional and Behavioral Disorders

During a module on cultural diversity for teachers who were working toward attaining their credentials for teaching students with E/BD, several of the students made comments like, "This is really a waste of our short time together." "We don't need this; it isn't required for my teaching license." "We don't have a culturally diverse family living within a hundred miles of my school."

Note: Portions of this chapter have been adapted from Comprehensive Programming for Middle and Secondary School-Aged Youth: Strategies and Procedures for Academic and Non-Academic Instruction, by Eleanor Guetzloe. In L. M. Bullock and R. A. Gable (Eds.) *Addressing the Social, Academic, and Behavioral Needs of Students with Challenging Behavior in Inclusive and Alternative Settings.* Copyright 2001 by the Council for Children with Behavioral Disorders, Reston, Virginia. Adapted with permission.

*O*ur nation and our world continue to become more diverse with each passing day. Trends in school populations suggest that an ever-increasing percentage of minority children are attending our nation's schools. In fact, by the middle of the 21st century, Caucasian Americans will have become a numerical minority (Burns, Fenstermacher, Godfrey, & McCormick, 1998). Demographers have predicted that by the year 2056, more than 50% of the population of the United States will be people of color (Howey & Zimpher, 1991). Further, there is a documented overrepresentation of students from certain minority groups in special education, particularly African American and Hispanic students (CCBD Multicultural Concerns Task Force, in press; Culatta & Tompkins, 1999; Polloway & Smith, 1992). For example, African Americans represent only 12% of the school population, but 28% of the total enrollment in special education (Culatta & Tompkins, 1999). This overrepresentation is particularly noticeable in special education for students with emotional and behavioral disorders.

Even if there are no students with ethnic, cultural, or linguistic differences in a particular classroom, school, or community, there is still a critical need for fostering a sense of understanding, acceptance, and celebration of human differences in all our children—those with E/BD as well as those without. Multicultural education should be a major focus of the curriculum in all of our schools.

What Is Multicultural Education?

In answering this question, we must address both what multicultural education is and what it is not. Multicultural education has been defined by Friend and Bursuck (1999) as "approaches to education that reflect the diversity of society" (p. 490). It is much more than a curriculum or a subject focused on learning about diverse cultures. It is not just social studies, but is rather a thread or theme running through the entire curriculum (Tiedt & Tiedt, 1995). Multicultural education requires the creation of a classroom in which the cultures of all students—and their families—are acknowledged and valued.

For purposes of this discussion, multicultural education includes such programs as the acquisition of English as a second language (ESL), bilingual education, antibias curricula, and all other specialized instruction that addresses cultural diversity. The major focus will be on variables that are alterable within the school and normally addressed by the classroom teacher.

Multicultural education is not just an activity for the last 30 minutes of school on Friday (Dettmer, Thurston, & Dyck, 1993). The principles of multicultural education should be infused throughout the curriculum, throughout the school day, and throughout the entire school year. Multicultural concepts should pervade all subject areas—reading, writing, language arts, mathematics, science, social studies, art, music, physical education, vocational education, and all other areas of study.

Even a subject like weather that seems far removed from culture can lead to a valuable multicultural experience. When I was teaching a fifth-grade class many years ago, I was not satisfied with the sequence of the curricula, particularly in social studies and science, which were primarily "textbook dependent." I rearranged the sequence in which the various topics would be presented according to what might be of greater interest at certain times of the school year. For example, we were in Florida and it was logical to study weather during hurricane season in the early weeks of each fall term. We addressed many issues related to the effects of weather conditions and climate on all people (e.g., food, shelter, clothing, transportation, vocations, and celebrations). The multicultural focus of this first unit set the tone for the entire school year.

Many of my students were children of members of the armed forces. Some of them (and their parents) had been born in other countries, and some were biracial. As the parents became aware of our multicultural focus, they volunteered to bring in photographs, clothing, arts and crafts objects, musical instruments, and other artifacts from other countries. They also made presentations to the class about their experiences in other countries around the world; their presentations included songs, dances, and activities that greatly enhanced our curriculum. Many of the parents spoke several languages, and the students were able to learn a few simple words and phrases in a variety of languages (e.g., "Hello." "How are you?" "Farewell." "Please." "Thank you." "My name is . . . ." "What is your name?"). We used one section of a large bulletin board for our ongoing study: the topic of the day, the language of the week, and pictures with the caption "Where is this place?" We maintained a calendar that showed holidays and festivals of many cultures. We studied art, music and musical instruments, dances, games, athletic events, food, clothing, jewelry and adornment, hairstyles, homes, transportation, money, commerce, stories, legends, holidays, religions, history, heroes, and customs of not only the ethnic groups represented in the school but also many other cultures in our nation and around the world. We did this all year and related our explorations of culture to every possible topic.

Multicultural education was still a new concept, and I did not understand that I was carrying out its mission. This project was simply an exciting and enjoyable way to encourage the students to look at the ways in which other human beings live and work.

Multicultural Education: The Origins and the Mandates

Multicultural education in the United States grew out of the civil rights movement of the 1960s, which called for the reform of curriculum to reflect the histories, cultures, and views of minority groups. Among the early responses to the call were (a) recognition of ethnic holidays and (b) the addition of special courses, usually in the area of social studies, to the high school curriculum.

According to Baca and Cervantes (1989), the mandates of multiculturalism in education are to: (a) increase knowledge about cultural diversity, (b) foster positive attitudes toward cultural pluralism, and (c) provide learning environments in which students from every culture can develop to their fullest potential. Banks (1991) suggested that multicultural education has four major dimensions:

1. Integration into content—infusing ethnic and cultural content into various subject areas in a natural and logical way.
2. Construction of knowledge—having students learn how perspectives, frames of reference, implicit cultural assumptions, and biases affect the ways in which knowledge is constructed.
3. A pedagogy of equity—facilitating the achievement of students from diverse cultures through the use of different teaching and learning styles (making the learning experience available as equally as possible to all students).
4. An empowering school culture—examining the school culture for bias and prejudice, developing strategies to alleviate these problems, and providing opportunities that enhance self-esteem for all students.

Major Issues Related to Multicultural Programs for Students With Disabilities

In the special education literature, recommendations for multicultural programs for students with disabilities generally fall into one of several categories: (a) teacher attitudes, values, knowledge, and skills; (b) the referral, assessment, and identification process; (c) instructional strategies; and (d) behavior management and therapeutic interventions. Each of these components will be briefly discussed below.

Teacher Attitudes Toward Other Cultures

To be effective and comfortable with multicultural education, teachers need to assess their personal beliefs and attitudes toward cultures other than their own and work to change any thinking that could interfere with their understanding and appreciation of diverse cultural groups. Vaughn, Bos, and Schumm (1997) suggested that teachers who are preparing for involvement in multicultural education should take time to learn about their own cultures and how culture influences beliefs and actions. They should also read books that survey the histories of cultural groups in the North American continent. Dettmer, Thurston, and Dyck (1993) designed a self-assessment list, which should be helpful to such teachers. The following statements, adapted from those included in the checklist, are indicators of an individual's interest in becoming more culturally aware, sensitive, and competent:

- I read literature to increase my understanding and sensitivity about the strengths, hopes, and concerns of people from other cultures.
- I speak out against prejudicial, stereotypical thinking and speech at every opportunity.
- I include contributions of culturally diverse individuals and groups as an integral part of the school curriculum.
- I select and obtain bias-free multicultural materials to use in my classroom.
- I invite families and members of the community from various cultural backgrounds to be classroom speakers, visiting experts, interpreters, or instructional assistants.
- I display photographs and other materials in my classroom that show culturally diverse people working and socializing together.

Acquiring a new worldview about diversity will take practice for many teachers, whether they are in general or special education. To become culturally competent, teachers will probably have to engage in considerable study of countries, languages, and cultures other than their own. The good news is that there is an abundance of literature and other materials available that can help to bring the world (and all its cultures) to the classroom. Advances in technology, including the availability of the internet, have made the consideration, evaluation, and selection of suitable instructional resources much easier—far beyond what schools were able to provide in the past.

Basic Suggestions for Teachers: How to Get Started

Many teachers will not have the luxury of participating in self-assessment and training (either preservice or inservice) in multicultural education. There are, however, a number of things that can be done to ensure a positive classroom environment for students from diverse cultures, particularly those who also have E/BD.

- Learn about the cultures of your students. Study their histories and ask questions of their family members and other authorities. Study literature on the various cultures represented in the class or school.
- Create a classroom climate in which all students feel physically and psychologically safe.
- Treat all students with respect and insist that your students treat each other (and you) with the same respect.
- Help all students to foster pride in their cultural backgrounds.

- Develop lessons in diversity based upon the students' backgrounds, neighborhoods, and life experiences.
- Use effective, research-based teaching methods and techniques when teaching about diversity.
- Develop the classroom management and discipline plans to fit the cultural beliefs and expectations of the students (e.g., communicating with or without eye contact, standing close or far away, touching or not touching, speaking privately or in public).

What Special Educators Need To Know About Multicultural Education

Several authorities have made specific suggestions of the knowledge and skills needed by teachers in multicultural education programs. Hafner and Green (1992) identified five clusters of skills teachers need to be effective in teaching culturally diverse students:

1. Proficiency in helping students whose first language is not English to acquire skills in the English language.
2. Understanding the students' native languages and developing teaching strategies in those languages.
3. Adjusting the curriculum to meet the needs of culturally diverse students.
4. Encouraging student interaction in the classroom.
5. Collaborating with students' parents and the community.

Multicultural Competencies for Teachers of Students With E/BD

The Behavioral Institute for Children and Adolescents (1994) conducted a study of the knowledge and skills related to cultural and linguistic diversity that should be possessed by teachers of students with E/BD. Participants in the study have rated the following as critical areas of knowledge (things the teacher should understand):

- Variations in beliefs, traditions, and cultural values.
- Major theories regarding the relationship of diversity to E/BD, including social-cultural influences on behavior.
- Effects of cultural and linguistic diversity on assessment.
- Personal culture and beliefs and influence on perceptions.
- Community and cultural norms and expectations.

According to this study, teachers of students with E/BD should also exhibit the following observable skills related to diversity:

- The ability to support ethnic and cultural differences in students.
- The ability to create a supportive climate that values diversity.

■ The ability to work with students, parents, and professionals of diverse cultural and ethnic backgrounds (including the abilities to adapt teaching style and techniques to learning styles and to adapt interaction style to fit local customs).

Assessment of Students With Behavior Problems and Cultural Differences

The issue of culturally appropriate assessment is probably most relevant for certain populations (i.e., African American and Asian American students) who are often overrepresented and underrepresented, respectively, in educational programs for students with E/BD (Cartledge, Kea, & Ida, 2000; Ishii-Jordan & Peterson, 1994; Singh, Ellis, Oswald, Wechsler, & Curtis, 1997). Federal law provides for nonbiased assessment, but the primary attention in assessment is usually directed at language needs rather than cultural differences. Especially when culturally and linguistically diverse students are being referred for suspected emotional problems, their cultural traditions and values must be carefully considered (Nuttall, Sanchez, Osorio, Nuttall, R. N., & Varvogli, 1996). Many behaviors seen by teachers as different, annoying, or frightening may actually be cultural in origin—and not symptoms of emotional problems. Daniel Valdez-Agrait, a school psychologist, shared the following example (cited in "Understanding the 'why,'" 1999).

> A child of Puerto Rican background was referred for acting out behaviors. The child was described as irritable and said to report having psychotic hallucinations and visions in which he prayed with deceased Indians.
>
> Valdez-Agrait set up an interview with the child and the family in their home—"It is very important to visit the home to note any cultural signs." As it turned out, Valdez-Agrait, who has expertise in Puerto Rican folk culture and religious traditions, immediately noticed that a piece of bread had been tacked to the front door and an altar placed in the hallway. He interviewed the child and family, only to confirm what he had suspected—the child's mother was involved in what her culture calls entierro—praying to wandering souls to help them rest in peace. "The important thing to remember is that in Puerto Rico, entierro is considered normal and a sign of spirituality." (p. 6)

In the absence of other significant symptoms (which, according to Valdez-Agrait, is always an important consideration), the intervention recommended in this case was to accept the child's report (of talking to dead Indians) as real and to encourage the mother to select prayer times during normal waking hours.

A Model for Multicultural Assessment

A comprehensive model for multicultural assessment of students with emotional and behavioral disorders has been developed by Nuttall et al. (1996). The authors suggested that the socioemotional assessment of culturally and linguistically different children requires specific data about language development patterns, family migration history, culture-specific child-rearing practices, family and individual degrees of acculturation, and the educational history of both student and family, in addition to standard information about the nature, degree, frequency, and duration of the behavior(s) in question.

Cultural issues should be considered during every step of the assessment process: referral; selection of examiner; interviews with family, child, and teachers; observations; selection and use of assessment tools; and the interpretation of results.

Reducing Bias in Assessment

The Minnesota Department of Children, Families, and Learning (1998) developed a document entitled *Reducing Bias in Special Education Assessment for American Indian and African American Students,* which contains information on the following:

- Different types of diversity and their impact on special education.
- Tools for gathering information about diversity factors.
- Suggested adaptations to assessment procedures to account for diversity.
- A framework for documenting the assessment team's consideration of diversity issues and its ruling out of exclusionary factors when determining eligibility.
- A framework for assessment procedures that can be expanded to address the needs of other diverse student populations.

These guidelines include background information about American Indian and African American cultural traits, characteristics, and communication styles, which should be helpful to teachers in working with both students and families.

Consideration of Culture and Learning Styles

Several authorities have compiled information gleaned from research about cultural preferences and learning styles, which should be considered, along with the classroom setting, during the special education referral and assessment process.

Franklin (1992) summarized 23 years of research regarding common cultural values of African Americans that affect their learning and interaction styles. For example, although white infants were frequently given manipulable objects to explore, African American infants were held by their families most of the time (which resulted in their being more person-oriented than object-oriented). Speech between African American mothers and children was in a call-and-response pattern, and children were encouraged to be assertive and to develop their own response style along with other creative abilities. Further, African American students were found to need—and aggressively seek—teacher attention, acceptance, nurturance, encouragement, and reassurance. If positive attention is not given, they may become frustrated, angry, and disruptive (all of which could be interpreted as symptoms of emotional problems).

Vasquez (1998) described several distinctive learning traits of Hispanic students that can be distinguished from traits of students from the mainstream society. For example, Hispanic youngsters prefer cooperation with other students, especially in goal-setting activities, rather than competition with peers and working in isolation. They strive for the honor of the family and for the pride the family will have in them, so simple statements such as "Good work. You should be proud of yourself!" may not be effective reinforcers. A positive statement congruent with their cultural beliefs might be, "I will send your very best work home to your parents."

Nel (1993) discussed several of the most important value conflicts between Native American students and the mainstream school culture. For example, generosity, sharing, and cooperation, expected of Native American youngsters in their home and community (rather than competition), may be viewed by a teacher as lack of motivation. Praising individual students in public (rather than the entire group) would be embarrassing to them. It is an instinctual reaction for a Native American student to help a friend (who may not know the answers to a test). The concept of life as an unhurried natural progression contributes to students' being late to class or failing to turn in assignments on time. To prepare for these differences in perceptions, Nel suggested the establishment of a cultural orientation for both students and parents as well as inservice training for faculty in cultural knowledge and sensitivity.

Guild (1994) summarized research on the learning styles of several cultural groups that may have implications for both instruction and classroom management. She noted that Mexican Americans regard family and personal relationships as very important, are likely to seek personal relationships with teachers, and are more comfortable with broad concepts than with component facts and specifics. African American students, who favor vocal interaction, loyalty in personal relationships, and physical activity generally respond well to discussion, active projects, and collaborative work. Native American students tend to have reflective thinking patterns and generally develop acute visual discrimination and skills in the use of imagery. In contrast, white Americans value independence, objectivity, and accuracy, which translate into learning styles that focus on competition rather than collaboration and on analytical rather than global thinking. Guild concluded that using such information in positive and sensitive ways will help educators value and promote diversity in all aspects of the school.

Providing an Appropriate Educational Program

Several mandates of current federal law have particular implications for planning an appropriate curriculum for students with both E/BD and cultural differences. First, the language and communication needs of the student and family must be considered in the planning and implementation of a student's individualized education program. Students who normally speak a language other than English may need bilingual special education services—using the students' native language (along with English) as the means of delivering special instruction that meets the students' individual needs. Second, any student with a disability must also be guaranteed access to the general curriculum, which means that the lessons in which the student is engaged will reflect the topics, knowledge, and skills that are studied by a student of the same age without a disability. For a fifth-grade student, for example, the curriculum must be the same curriculum (with specialized instruction, adaptations, and modifications) as that presented to a fifth grader without a disability. A primary concern for a student with E/BD from a diverse background, therefore, is to address the academic, cognitive, and emotional needs related to E/BD, as well as those related to diversity, within the parameters of the regular curriculum.

Addressing Cultural Factors in Instructional Planning

Most educators believe that students are more motivated and perform at higher levels when instructional methods and techniques are suited to the student's individual learning characteristics, which include the effects of culture. It is important to note, however, that all students from the same cultural background will not have the same learning preferences. The individualized education program of a student with a disability must be based upon his or her individual needs and strengths, and each child's needs are different. Necessary modifications in, and adaptations to, the curriculum should be determined and specified by the IEP team, as provided in federal law.

The following general areas are considered most amenable to curriculum accommodations and modification (Munson, 1987):

- Instructional level
- Content
- Instructional materials
- Format of directions and assignments
- Instructional strategies
- Mode of teacher input
- Mode of student response
- Individual instruction
- Test administration
- Grading policies

Specific Suggestions for Bilingual Programs

In a bilingual program, academic tool subjects are taught in both English and the student's native language. Pierangelo (1995) suggested the following guidelines (which are appropriate for all students) for evaluating, selecting, and adapting materials for exceptional bilingual children:

1. Assess the specific language abilities of each student.
2. Include appropriate cultural experiences (acceptable in the child's culture) in selected materials.
3. Ensure that material progresses at an appropriate rate for the students.
4. Adapt only materials that require modifications.
5. Follow a consistent format for evaluating materials and documenting their success.

Making Adaptations

Pierangelo (1995) also listed the following suggestions for making the adaptations necessary for effective bilingual education, which would, again, be appropriate for any student:

1. Adjusting supplemental material.
2. Audiotaping or videotaping directions.
3. ProvidIng for alternative responses.
4. Rewriting brief sections of instructional materials to lower the reading level.
5. Outlining the material for a student before he or she reads a selection.
6. Reducing the number of pages or items on a page that the student is expected to complete.
7. Using a simpler task rather than a more complex one.
8. Breaking long tasks into shorter subtasks.
9. Developing simple study guides.
10. Providing additional practice to ensure mastery.

Teachers should also use illustrations (both examples and nonexamples) and manipulable objects that are relevant to and socially acceptable in the student's culture.

Modifying Instruction

Choate (1997) suggested the following guidelines for planning and modifying instruction to meet the needs of students with language or cultural differences:

- Incorporating students' multicultural contributions into lessons.
- Building concrete and vicarious experiences prior to each lesson.
- Using pictures and other visual cues to explain, illustrate, and translate concepts.

- Giving students a written script of oral directions and lessons.
- Furnishing positive corrective feedback on vocabulary and grammar.
- Using a whole-language approach to explain syntactical differences and to bridge gaps among students' oral language, reading, and writing.

Components of an Appropriate Educational Program for Students with E/BD

In addition to access to the general education curriculum, an appropriate program for any student with E/BD should include the following, which must often be modified to meet the individual needs of students with cultural or linguistic differences: (a) academic tool subjects (e.g., reading, writing, listening, and mathematics); (b) instruction in social skills; and (c) therapeutic interventions, including behavioral change, counseling, and affective education, as well as outlets for creativity (e.g., creative writing, art, music, drama, and dance) (Guetzloe, 1996). These are, of course, in addition to (not instead of) the provision of access to the general education curriculum, as previously mentioned.

Meeting Special Education Needs First

In the IEP for a student with a disability, individual needs and strengths should be considered as the basis for planning an appropriate education program. For culturally and linguistically diverse students with disabilities, the necessary special instruction and related services, as included in the IEP, must be given primary consideration. It is important to use teaching strategies and procedures that address the strengths and needs of individual students, including those presented by ethnic, linguistic, and cultural differences.

Curriculum and instructional strategies for students with E/BD are the major focus of this entire text. Specific suggestions for addressing linguistic and cultural differences are discussed in the following sections, but it is by no means an inclusive listing of appropriate strategies.

Combining Best Practices

As suggested by Di, Stewart, and Lisner (1998), the most effective instructional practices for students with E/BD and those for students with cultural differences can be combined very easily. These authors recommend the use of direct instruction, cooperative learning, learning strategy instruction, and instruction in social skills as appropriate for students with cultural differences.

Using Practices That Are Effective Across Cultural Groups

For approximately 15 years, the National Center to Improve the Tools of Education (NCITE) has conducted research on the features of instructional design that accommodate the needs of students who do not achieve success in school (including those from diverse cultures). Six major features of instruction common to practices suitable for students across ethnic groups are as follows (Burke, Coulter, & Grossen, 1998; Dixon, Carnine, & Kameenui, 1996):

- Big ideas (organizing instruction around fundamental concepts with a range of examples rather than insignificant details).
- Primed background knowledge (instruction in prerequisite skills).
- Conspicuous strategies (identifying and teaching distinct learning strategies as well as when and where to use them).
- Mediated scaffolding (personal guidance, assistance, and support from the teacher, followed by transition to less teacher direction).
- Judicious review (well-planned review, sufficient for learning to occur, distributed over time, varied for generalizability, and cumulative).
- Strategic integration (connecting new knowledge with information the student already understands).

Including Students in Planning

Nieto (1992) suggested including culturally and linguistically diverse students in the development of lessons and instructional methods. Children can and will identify what they like and dislike and what they feel comfortable doing. By including their recommendations, a teacher begins the process of acknowledging and accepting diverse opinions and attitudes.

Focusing on Group Activities

Active and inclusive learning, apparently preferred by several cultural groups, can be facilitated by focusing on group activities, peer or cross-age tutoring, and community-based activities.

Using Games as Teaching Aids

As discussed by Salend (1994), the use of games in teaching academics is particularly motivating for students with disabilities. Multicultural games, such as Mancala (from Africa) and Sungka (from the Philippines), have been suggested for teaching both academics and social skills (de la Cruz, Cage, & Liam, 2000). Games that provide concrete experiences and are also enjoyable are particularly useful before teaching abstract concepts.

Selecting Suitable Materials and Resources

As mentioned previously, there are many resources related to appropriate content and instructional strategies for use in the multicultural education of students with E/BD. The teacher will be able to read the literature on cultural diversity; select materials that are suitable for the ages, academic levels, and cultures of the students for whom they are intended; and evaluate the outcomes, as previously suggested. One of my favorite resources is *Teaching Tolerance,* a publication of the Southern Poverty Law Center, a nonprofit legal and educational foundation. Published twice a year, this journal is available at no cost to educators. The publication contains descriptions of successful programs, thematic instructional units, folk literature, art, music, games, computer networks and software programs, videotapes, and many helpful suggestions for multicultural education of students of all ages. A recent issue included descriptions of an antibias club in a suburban high school (Collins, 2000), a sidewalk library in Brooklyn, New York (Walker, 2000), and an interactive multimedia curriculum that combines "two distinct 'ways of knowing'—Native American tradition and high-tech innovation" (King, 2000, p. 10). (For further information, teachers can contact Teaching Tolerance, 400 Washington Avenue, Montgomery, AL 36104.)

Considering Diversity in Providing Therapeutic Interventions

A positive school and classroom environment, including positive behavioral interventions and positive behavior support, is absolutely essential to the success of any educational program for students with E/BD. The only modifications required for students with cultural or linguistic diversity would be those related to communicating acceptance of—and respect for—all students and their families. Some of the components that should be considered in developing culturally appropriate interventions are briefly discussed below. (Provisions related to working with families are also discussed in Chapter 15.)

A Welcoming School Climate

Welcome signs in every language spoken by students and their families can be posted at the entrance to the school. There should also be a classroom, lounge, or other place for families to gather. Add a selection of journals, magazines, videos, and decorations that illustrate the acceptance and celebration of diversity in the school.

Ancillary personnel and other individuals (staff or volunteers) who speak the languages represented in the school should be available to act as interpreters, classroom instructional assistants, lay counselors, speakers, tutors, and participants in festivals or other special programs. These individuals will need to be knowledgeable about school policies and procedures as well as informed about the languages and cultures of the students and their families.

Differences in Nonverbal Communication Styles

Teachers must be aware of the effects of their styles of interacting and their influence on the behavior of the students and their families. Garcia (1982) discussed differences in nonverbal communication that may affect behavior management in a classroom that includes students from diverse cultural backgrounds.

In Latino cultures, women who sit on tables in public places are viewed as crude. Women teachers who sit on tables in their classrooms may therefore convey a message of crudeness, which could be embarrassing to the students. Native American students may not respond with direct eye contact when teachers speak, because they have been taught that looking directly into the eyes of an elder—or a person in an authoritative position—is disrespectful. Haptics (touch), in terms of how teachers touch (or avoid touching) their students, may be interpreted very differently by individuals from different cultures. Garcia (1982) suggested that all of these nonverbal modes of communication can convey ethnic and cultural biases of which the teacher is not even aware.

Family Involvement in Establishing the Classroom Management System

Parents and families should be encouraged to become actively involved in the development of the classroom plan for behavior management. Collaborative relationships should also be established with colleagues who are knowledgeable about other cultures and who may offer information about the effects of cultural diversity on students' behaviors. It is particularly important to understand the families' perceptions regarding classroom rules, expectations, rewards, and aversive consequences (if any are to be used). If the students' families do not understand the components of the classroom management system, or if any of the components are not positively perceived in their respective cultures, someone with competence in the parents' culture should be present when the system is explained to parents. (For other information about working with families, see Chapter 15.)

Student Involvement in Establishing Positive Interventions

Students can also help in the establishment of positive interventions and behavior support by defining their values, concerns, and attitudes. These definitions can be used as a foundation for the development of classroom rules and expectations.

Selection of Culturally Appropriate Consequences

Teachers often use specific objects or activities as reinforcers in the classroom management system. The choice of reinforcers—for both desirability and cultural acceptability—must be made carefully.

Culturally Appropriate Counseling and Other Mental Health Services

A number of authorities have discussed the need for counselors, therapists, and other mental health providers to include culture as an essential aspect of the counseling process (Camino & Spurlock, 1994; Lee, 1996; Nuttall et al., 1996; Sue & Sue, 1990). Individuals who provide related services (e.g., consulting teachers, counselors, and school psychologists) must also employ techniques that are congruent with the values, beliefs, and perceptions of families of culturally diverse students with disabilities (Daugherty & Stanhope, 1998; Garcia, 1982; Nuttall et al., 1996; Sue & Sue, 1990).

Instruction in Social Skills

Social skills instruction is an important component of the educational program for students with E/BD. In selecting skills to be targeted for instruction, teachers should consider not only the students' developmental levels (including language abilities) but also their sociocultural environment and the degree to which the specific social skills will be valued and reinforced by others in the home and neighborhood (Cartledge & Milburn, 1995; Rivera & Rogers-Adkinson, 1997).

Teaching Social Responsibility

Social responsibility has been defined by Berman (1990) as an interest and concern for the well-being of others and the environment. Social responsibility can be taught throughout the curriculum by examining real-world issues related to the topic under consideration (e.g., the impact of mathematics and statistics on the political process) (Berman, 1990; Salend, 1994).

Social responsibility curricula also afford opportunities for students to participate in community service activities that benefit others. (Further discussion of community service for students with E/BD will be found in Chapter 8.)

Using Therapeutic Group Approaches

Camino and Spurlock (1994) recommended group approaches for counseling or teaching social skills that may be particularly suitable for those whose cultures (a) emphasize cooperation and (b) value the group over the individual (e.g., Native American). They also suggested teachers read African folk stories when working with African American youngsters. Specific audiotapes were recommended (e.g., *African American Folktales,* as read by Brock Peters and Diana Sands) as particularly useful for young children. A folk story with a "message" from any culture could be used as the basis for a group discussion of values or social skills.

Outlets for Creativity

The program for students with E/BD should include activities (such as art, crafts, music, dance, drama, and creative writing) that provide outlets for creative abilities and talents (Guetzloe, 1989). All of our world's cultures have made significant and unique contributions to the creative arts, which are often a source of great joy and pride. These activities are not only enjoyable but also therapeutic, which make them valuable in a multicultural program for students with E/BD.

Discussion Questions

1. How can a teacher assure that curriculum materials are bias-free?
2. Think about a classroom observation you have done. Did you observe any discussion of the contributions of culturally diverse individuals and groups?
3. How do you deal with a parent who is upset that her child is in the same class as a child with a different cultural background?

References

Baca, L. M., & Cervantes, H. T. (1989). *The bilingual special interface.* Columbus, OH: Merrill.

Banks, J. A. (1991). The dimensions of multicultural education. *Multicultural Leader, 1,* 4.

Behavioral Institute for Children and Adolescents. (1994). *E/BD teacher competencies.* Arden Hills, MN.

Berman, S. (1990). Educating for social responsibility. *Educational Leadership, 48*(3), 75–80.

Burke, M. D., Coulter, G., & Grossen, B. (1998). Instructional design and videodisk technology. In R. E. Schmid & W. Evans (Eds.), *Curriculum and instruction practices for students with emotional and behavioral disorders* (pp. 27–35). Reston, VA: The Council for Children with Behavioral Disorders.

Burns, C. W., Fenstermacher, K. M., Godfrey, T. Y., & McCormick, M. E (1998). Multicultural education: Current status and future directions. In D. Daugherty & V. Stanhope (Eds.), *Pathways to tolerance: Student diversity.* (pp. 25–29). Bethesda, MD: National Association of School Psychologists.

Camino, I. A., & Spurlock, J. (1994). *Culturally diverse children and adolescents.* New York: Guilford.

Cartledge, G., Kea, C. D., & Ida, D. J. (2000). Anticipating differences—celebrating strengths. *Teaching Exceptional Children, 32*(3), 30-37.

Cartledge, G., & Milburn, J. F. (Eds.). (1995). *Teaching social skills to children and youth.* Boston: Allyn and Bacon.

CCBD Multicultural Concerns Task Force (in press). *Working with culturally diverse children, youth, and their families: Best practices in assessment, instruction, and personnel preparation.* Reston, VA: Council for Children with Behavioral Disorders.

Choate, J. S. (1997). Special needs of special populations. In J. S. Choate, *Successful inclusive teaching* (pp. 18–35). Boston: Allyn and Bacon.

Collins, K. (2000, Spring). No place for bigotry. *Teaching Tolerance,* pp. 26–27.

Culatta, R. A., & Tompkins, J. R. (1999). *Fundamentals of special education: What every teacher needs to know.* Upper Saddle River, NJ: Merrill.

Daugherty, D., & Stanhope, V. (Eds.) (1998). *Pathways to tolerance: Student diversity.* Bethesda, MD: National Association of School Psychologists.

de la Cruz, R. E., Cage, C. E., & Liam, M. J. (2000, January-February). Let's play mancala and sungka: Learning math and social skills through ancient multicultural games. *Teaching Exceptional Children, 32*(3), 38–42.

Dettmer, P., Thurston, L. P., & Dyck, N. (1993). *Consultation, collaboration, and team-work for students with special needs.* Boston: Allyn and Bacon.

Di, X., Stewart, S., & Lisner, M. (1998). Multicultural education and students with emotional/behavioral disorders. In R. E. Schmid & W. Evans (Eds.), *Curriculum and instruction practices for students with emotional and behavioral disorders* (pp. 3–12). Reston, VA: Council for Children with Behavioral Disorders.

Dixon, R., Carnine, D. W., & Kameenui, E. J. (1996). *Instructional tools for students with learning difficulties.* Reston, VA: Council for Exceptional Children.

Franklin, M. E. (1992). Culturally sensitive instructional practices for African-American learners with disabilities. *Exceptional Children, 59*(2), 115–122.

Friend, M., & Bursuck, W. D. (1999). *Including students with special needs: A practical guide for classroom teachers.* Boston: Allyn and Bacon.

Garcia, R. L. (1982). *Teaching in a pluralistic society.* New York: Harper & Row.

Gollnick, D. M., & Chinn, P. C. (1983) *Multicultural education in a pluralistic society.* St. Louis, MO: Mosby.

Guetzloe, E. (1996, April). Components of an effective program for students with emotional and behavioral disorders. Paper presented at the Annual International Convention of the Council for Exceptional Children, Salt Lake City, UT.

Guetzloe, E. C. (1989). *Youth suicide: What the educator should know.* Reston, VA: Council for Exceptional Children.

Guild, P. (1994). The culture/learning style connection. *Educational Leadership, 51*(8), 16–21.

Hafner, A. L., & Green, J. S. (1992). *Multicultural education and diversity: Providing information to teachers.* San Antonio, TX: Southwest Regional Laboratory (ERIC Document Reproduction Service No. ED 342 762).

Howey, K. R., & Zimpher, N. L. (1991). Restructuring the education of teachers: Descriptions and discussions. Reston, VA: Association of Teacher Educators.

Ishii-Jordan, S., & Peterson, R. L. (1994). *Multicultural issues in the education of students with behavioral disorders.* Cambridge, MA: Brookline.

King, C. (2000, Spring). From cradleboard to motherboard. *Teaching Tolerance,* 10–13.

Lee, W. M. L. (1996). New directions in multicultural counseling. *Counseling and Human Development, 29*(2), 1–11.

Minnesota Department of Children, Families, and Learning. (1998). *Reducing bias in special education assessment for American Indian and African American students.* St. Paul, MN.

Munson, S. M. (1987). Regular education teacher modifications for mainstreamed mildly handicapped students. *Journal of Special Education, 20*(4), 489–502.

Nel, J. (1993). Preventing school failure: The Native American child. *Preventing School Failure, 37*(3), 19–24.

Nieto, S. (1992). *Affirming diversity: The sociopolitical context of multicultural education.* White Plains, NY: Longman.

Nuttall, E. V., Sanchez, W., Osorio, L. B., Nuttall, R. N., & Varvogli, L. (1996). In M. J. Breen & C. R. Fiedler (Eds.), *Behavioral approach to assessment of youth with emotional/behavioral disorders: A handbook for school-based practitioners* (pp. 451–501). Austin, TX: Pro-ed.

Pierangelo, R. (1995). *The special education teacher's book of lists.* West Nyack, NY: Center for Applied Research in Education.

Polloway, F. A., & Smith, J. E. (1992). *Instruction for students with language disabilities.* Columbus, OH: Merrill.

Rivera, B. D., & Rogers-Adkinson, D. (1997). Culturally sensitive interventions: Social skills training with children and parents from culturally and linguistically diverse backgrounds. *Intervention in School and Clinic, 33*(2), 75–80.

Salend, S. J. (1994). *Effective mainstreaming: Creating inclusive classrooms* (2nd ed.). New York: Macmillan.

Singh, N. N., Ellis, C. R., Oswald, D. P., Wechsler, H. A., & Curtis, W. J. (1997). Value and address diversity. *Journal of Emotional and Behavioral Disorders, 5*(1), 24–35.

Sue, D. W., & Sue, D. (1990). *Counseling the culturally different: Theory and practice* (2nd. ed.). New York: John Wiley.

Tiedt, P. L., & Tiedt, I. M. (1995). *Multicultural teaching: A handbook of activities, information, and resources* (4th ed.). Boston: Allyn & Bacon.

Valdez-Agrait, D. (1999). Understanding the "why" of behaviors in children from different cultures. *Research Connections in Special Education, 4,* 6.

Vasquez, J. A. (1998). Distinctive traits of Hispanic students. *Prevention Researcher, 5*(1), 1–6.

Vaughn, S., Bos, C. S., & Schumm, J. S. (1997). *Teaching mainstreamed, diverse, and at-risk students in the general education classroom.* Needham Heights, MA: Allyn & Bacon.

Walker, T. (2000, Spring). Street smart. *Teaching Tolerance,* 22–25.

8

A Curriculum of Hope: Focusing on Helping Others

By the time Steven was 10 years of age, he and his brothers had witnessed his father tie his mother to a railroad track and leave her to be run over by a train. When his father left the area, Steven and his brothers untied her and took her home. Steven's father went to prison for a short period of time, but after he was released, his wife allowed him to return to the home. Steven and his siblings continued to witness a high degree of violence. When Steven came to school, he always had a very sad look on his face; he had indeed lost hope for a calm, safe future.

Note: Portions of this chapter have been adapted from "Developing a Sense of the Possible," by Alan M. Blankstein and Eleanor Guetzloe. In *Reaching Today's Youth, 4*(4), 2–5. Copyright 2000 by National Education Service. Adapted with permission.

first became interested in the effects of hope while studying the effects of hopelessness for a book about youth suicide. I agonized over a consuming need for accuracy. A book with inaccurate information about teaching reading might result in a delay in a child's learning to read, but inaccuracies about the treatment of a suicidal child could result in a death.

Hopelessness is among the most important factors associated with suicidal behavior in young people. According to Frederick (1985), suicidal youngsters suffer from haplessness (encountering problems that are not of their own doing), helplessness (having no control over the outcomes), and hopelessness (thinking that things will never get any better—and that suicide is the only answer). Several other researchers documented a significant relationship between hopelessness and suicide (Beck, Steer, Kovacs, & Garrison, 1985; Dyer & Kreitman, 1984; Kazdin, French, Unis, Esveldt-Dawson, & Sherick, 1983).

In attempting to formulate positive suggestions for prevention, I listed all the risk factors known to be associated with youth suicide and addressed each with an if-then approach, which seemed logical (if simplistic). For example, if a student suffers from unrealistic expectations or overprogramming, then goal-setting, self-evaluation, and self-monitoring would be valuable individual study topics. If social isolation is a problem, then training in assertiveness, communication, and social skills would be advisable. Problems of stress could be addressed by teaching self-control, coping skills, problem-solving, time management, and relaxation exercises (Guetzloe, 1989, p. 175).

I had trouble, however, addressing hope. Hope is known to be a factor in resilience, the study of which was at the time a relatively new and very exciting field of research, but well-designed studies on the nature, origins, or development of a sense of hope were not to be found. I decided to promulgate my own suggestions, attempting, at the very least, to do no harm.

What Is Hope?

Hope is defined in the *American Heritage College Dictionary* (1993) as both a noun and a verb: "to wish for something with expectation of its fulfillment; to have confidence, trust [noted as an archaic definition]; to look forward to with confidence or expectation; to expect and desire; a trust or reason for hope," (p. 654). The word optimism does not appear as a synonym. The definition of optimism, however, includes the following reference to hope: "a tendency to expect the best possible outcome or dwell on the most hopeful aspects of a situation" (p. 958).

What Research Tells Us About Hope

In comparison to the enormous body of literature about problems associated with the lack or loss of it, there is a relative paucity of research on hope itself. According to Martin Seligman (1991, 1995), hope is an optimistic explanatory style, the tendency or ability to explain misfortune in temporary and specific terms. Jonas Salk has referred to hope as "psychological immunization" (cited in Seligman, 1995, p. 5). Snyder (1994) suggested that hope has two components: the will or energy to reach one's goals (willpower) and the ability to generate routes to achieving them (waypower).

The Importance of Hope

Authorities have been suggesting for many years that a positive mind-set is powerful medicine in the battle against serious disease, and there is now a growing body of statistical evidence that supports this assumption. Researchers at Mayo Clinic in Rochester, Minnesota, recently completed a follow-up survey on patients who had been classified 30 years earlier as optimists or pessimists ("Look at the Bright Side," 2000). The researchers compared the patients' expected and actual survival rates and found that the optimistic group's survival rate was significantly better than expected. They also found a 19% increase in risk of death among the pessimistic group.

Seligman (1991), basing his thoughts on studies of both animals and humans, offered several reasons for the apparent link between explanatory style and the immune system. First, preventing feelings of helplessness apparently helps to keep immune systems in working condition. Second, optimists are more likely to take action that prevents illness—to stick to health regimens and seek medical advice when illness strikes. Third, optimists are more likely to avoid bad events (and bad events often lead to illness) such as reckless accidents and violent acts. Finally, optimists tend to have more social supports—deep friendships and love—that are important for physical health. Based on such findings, the Mayo Clinic researchers suggested that certain clinical interventions might make patients more optimistic and thus improve their responses to medical treatment.

Where Optimism Comes From

According to Seligman (1995), parents and teachers have considerable responsibility for the development of both optimism and pessimism. He strongly suggested that pessimism can originate from (a) genetics; (b) parental pessimism;

(d) pessimistic criticism from parents, teachers, or coaches; and (e) experiences of helplessness (rather than mastery).

> As parents and teachers, you should remain alert to the likelihood that many experiences of success for a child will lead to optimism. You should go out of your way to help a child follow up one success with another and another. The right coaching from you will support and maintain a child's optimism, and the right crucial experiences will set that optimism in concrete. (Seligman, 1995, p. 88)

Seligman further explained the "right crucial experiences" with a story about what he termed "the Hoving effect" (pp. 108–109). Thomas Hoving, curator of the Metropolitan Museum of Art in New York, was, at the time of the story, a 19-year-old sophomore at Princeton University—self-described as "flunking out, anxious, low of self-esteem, and unsure of judgment" (cited in Seligman, 1995, p. 109). One successful experience in a sculpture seminar (he was only one of eight students who described a "sculpture" honestly and accurately) changed his attitudes about himself—and his life.

Seligman is convinced that one single, crucial, transforming event can markedly alter pessimism or optimism by changing a young person's theories about who he or she is and what he or she is worth. The lesson of Hoving's story is obvious: Such an event could occur on any day, at any time, in the home or school.

How Children Learn Hope

How do children learn hope? How do they learn other things? Effective instructional strategies and techniques can be applied to learning hope—as they are to reading, writing, mathematics, social studies, science, and any other subject in the curriculum. Such effective strategies include (a) success-oriented instruction (e.g., positive, realistic expectations, goals, and objectives) for both individual students and the group; (b) effective instructional techniques (e.g., direct instruction, errorless training, positive materials, positive models, cooperative learning, and constructive evaluation); (c) changing the social roles of students in the home, school, and community (from problems to participants, producers, and providers); (d) addressing students' problems through special topics and activities; and (e) providing integrated experiences based on helping others (Guetzloe, 1989, 1997).

Specific experiences that foster and enhance hope:

- Being nurtured and protected by primary caregivers.
- Learning to anticipate and achieve wants and desires.

- Modeling the optimistic behavior of significant others.
- Being exposed to media and materials about hope and optimism and to individuals who portray these behaviors.
- Being rewarded for optimistic statements, attempting new or difficult tasks, and persevering.
- Being exposed to the community in a positive way: meeting community leaders, engaging in altruistic experiences that enhance dignity and promote self-esteem, and receiving positive recognition for their involvement.

Practical Strategies for Teaching Hope

As noted, hope can be taught in the same ways that we teach anything else in the home, school, and community. The instructional methods must be both humane and effective and should include (a) establishment of attainable goals, direct instruction, errorless training, and constructive evaluation; (b) modeling optimistic behavior; (c) being exposed to media and materials about hope; and (d) being reinforced for trying, persevering, and making optimistic statements. Specific strategies include (Guetzloe, 1997):

- Ensuring physical and psychological safety. It is absolutely essential that students feel safe in school—from intruders, from the faculty and staff, and from one another. They must not be subjected to harsh punishment, ridicule, or humiliation. School must be a place they want to be.
- Providing appropriate faculty and staff. Teachers of hope should be knowledgeable, skilled, charismatic, courageous, confident, trustworthy, and optimistic. They must exhibit a strong sense of community and a high regard for society and its laws. They must also maintain every ounce of dignity of which they are capable and have a sense of humor.
- "Setting children up" for success. Often, when teachers begin to plan for a special event, they simply announce that it is going to happen. A "setup" for practicing hope would begin with a discussion about the possibility of the event and what fun it would be if the class could do it.

Eventually, a student will ask, "Can we do this? Can we go?" Rather than just saying, "Yes," the answer can be, "We don't know yet, but we hope so." Teachers would, of course, ensure (in advance) that the event will be approved, guaranteeing an opportunity before even beginning the discussion, but that fact would be kept a secret. Students are then involved in the planning and implementation of the activity—and the hope.

- Using a "language of hope." Teachers should use words of hope more often in the classroom. Stories selected for reading aloud to students can include such messages as (a) hope, (b) striving to meet goals, and (c) attempting difficult tasks (e.g., *The Little Engine That Could*). Songs (or instrumental background music, after students have learned the words and themes) can focus on hope and other positive messages (e.g., "High Hopes," "Always," or "A Cockeyed Optimist").

- Modifying explanatory styles. Seligman (1991, 1995) developed specific techniques for teaching optimism to young people. His program for fostering and practicing optimistic explanatory styles, intended for use by parents, could easily be included in the school curriculum for both children and adolescents.
- Reinforced modeling. Role playing in the classroom, involving students, teachers, instructional assistants, and trained volunteers, can be used to teach the language of hope, problem-solving approaches, and other related social skills.
- Providing positive models in the classroom. Teachers and other instructional staff must also exhibit a sense of hope. Other positive and appropriate models can be invited to school to share their experiences. It is particularly important to select models from the same cultural backgrounds as the students with whom they will speak (people who have "been there"). If individuals are not available, videos, excerpts from television programs, filmstrips, records, and pictures that portray hope can be substituted.
- Using positive materials. Instructional materials should be selected that show human beings and society in a favorable light. Special assignments can challenge students to find stories with happy endings and poems, songs, and jokes that are not only positive and funny but also suitable for sharing at school. Games that address specific issues related to hope (e.g., courage, self-control, self-expression, and anger management) are commercially available and suitable for classroom use. Such materials, of course, should be carefully screened by the teacher before use in the classroom.
- Including special topics in the curriculum. Units, modules, and activities that address specific issues of interest or concern to individual students or the entire group can be integrated into existing course or content areas. Examples include assertiveness training; juvenile law; grooming and dress; outlets for creativity—art, music, writing, dance, and drama; prescriptive physical education (e.g., weight loss, weight gain, or body-building programs); life sports—golf, tennis, handball, running; and use of leisure time (Guetzloe, 1989).
- Mentoring by positive and responsible individuals. The advantages of mentoring to foster and enhance hope in young people has been well established in the literature. We must issue a caveat, however, that the mentors must be responsible individuals who will (a) take the obligation

seriously, (b) be present at the appointed times, and (c) agree to serve as a mentor for an extended period—often for more than a year.

- Providing integrated and meaningful experiences. Experiences that help to foster hope include helping others, meeting community leaders and other important individuals, participating in positive events in the school and community, and receiving favorable publicity in the media. Children (and adults) need to know what they might be able to accomplish in order to establish appropriate goals for themselves—high but attainable expectations. They need real experiences that show them what might be possible.

What Students With E/BD Need in the Curriculum

Students with E/BD need every educational experience available to students without disabilities—and much more. They need academics, social skills, computer skills, thinking skills, life skills, physical education, moral education, recreation, vocational education, career and job exploration, job placement, and follow-up assistance well into their adult lives. They may have missed so many experiences that usually occur naturally in families and communities long before children come to school. They may have not eaten in restaurants, learned to swim, or gone camping with their families. They may not have been welcomed in neighborhood recreational facilities, community organizations, or even churches. Even if they have been exposed to positive learning situations—in the home, neighborhood, school, and community—their behavior and its effect have interfered with learning the lessons offered.

The curriculum for students with E/BD must be more effective, therapeutic, and more motivating than that for students without disabilities. Further, the entire program should provide for meeting every student's individual (and sometimes very basic) needs. In that respect, the curriculum is also therapeutic, ameliorating the problems that have contributed to the student's being identified as having E/BD.

Instruction in Basic Skills

As noted by Curwin (1993), for students with poor academic achievement, the classroom is a breeding ground for feelings of inadequacy and worthlessness. It is essential that students master the basic academic skills of reading, writing, speaking, and mathematics, so they can be successful in the real world as well as in the school environment. These tool subjects can be incorporated into instructional units or out-of-school experiences.

Integrated, Thematic Instruction

One of the most positive, meaningful, and effective strategies for keeping all members of a group engaged in a learning experience is the integrated thematic unit in which all skill and content areas are related to a certain topic or theme. The use of units in the regular school program is very common in the areas of science, social studies, and health. It is not a new idea in special education. Ingram (1935) suggested the use of instructional units as an appropriate strategy for "slow learners." Meyen (1981) wrote an entire text (the first edition of which was published in 1972) on the development and use of instructional units in both regular and special education. More recently, Wigginton (1985) and Ensminger and Dangel (1992) described the components of the Foxfire approach, including the planning and implementation of integrated units of study, as an example of best practice in special education.

Opportunities for Socialization

Social skills, which students with E/BD often lack, are not learned in a study carrel. These students, to a greater extent than others, need to learn to communicate and work with one another in a natural environment—a group setting—under adequate supervision.

Appropriate Instructional Materials

Materials should be relevant to the students' lives and understandable because they relate to what the youngsters see in newspapers, on television, in their neighborhoods, and in the community (e.g., newspapers, current magazines, "bites" of videos or movies, and pictures of real people and places). Whenever possible, classroom lectures and discussions should be enhanced with concrete, manipulable materials (e.g., the real thing or a working model). We must not resort to "infantile" materials for teaching basic skills, but rather select materials with content that is appropriate for the chronological ages of the students. Positive materials should be selected that show human beings and society in a favorable light. Students can be challenged to find stories with happy endings and poems, jokes, or songs that are both funny and suitable for sharing at school.

- ■ Students with E/BD need instruction in social skills every day—all day. Appropriate skills can be selected from the many good commercial materials and the techniques of reinforced modeling can be used to teach any skill. Many published materials include suggestions for teaching such skills as anger control, moral reasoning, assertiveness, and aggression replacement.

■ Materials should be used that encourage student interaction (under supervision). Students need to learn to talk to one another and adults—appropriately, without put-downs, arguments, or fights. Plays (even Shakespeare) and "after school special" television shows are useful for this purpose.

■ As mentioned above, students with E/BD are in dire need of positive and effective models—both in and outside of the school. In the classroom, appropriate models can be provided not only by real people but also by videos, excerpts from television, filmstrips, records, pictures, and books (listed in descending order of probable effectiveness).

According to Katz (1997), learning about others who have overcome similar adversities can help to instill a sense of hope in young people. In Katz, I discuss a project in San Diego—the Learning Development Services Resilience Project—(p. 170) that offers such opportunities to children, families, and young adults. Participants who have overcome adverse conditions in their early years are videotaped as they answer four questions:

1. What have you learned?
2. As you look back, what are some of the strengths that you feel you had, or that you developed, that helped you through the tough times?
3. Were there any turning-point experiences that you can remember that led to change for the better?
4. Based on what you have learned, what would you tell others who are going through what you went through?

The participants are allowed to talk for as long as they like. The tapes are then made available to families and young people who have faced similar adversities but who have lost hope that their situations can change. "These tapes show them that things can change; they can hear and see it from those who have overcome similar challenges" (Katz, 1997, p. 80).

Implementing a "Preventive Curriculum"

In addition to the subjects required in the general curriculum, students with E/BD should be offered components or modules on a variety of topics related to specific cognitive, physical, or emotional concerns. These topics can be easily integrated into coursework (even in the regular classroom) and can be considered a "preventive curriculum" for students who do not exhibit emotional problems. Such offerings include:

■ Basic skills (for those who need developmental or remedial work).
■ Learning strategies (organizational skills, mnemonics, study skills, self-questioning, and error monitoring).

- Stress reduction (including time management, organizational skills, and relaxation training), coping skills, problem-solving, decision-making, self-control, and assertiveness training.
- Prescriptive physical education (weight gain, weight loss, bodybuilding, and exercise).
- Individual "life" sports (tennis, racquetball, handball, golf, swimming, and running).
- Expressions of creativity (art, music, dance, drama, and creative writing).
- Health problems (nutrition, hygiene, orthodontics, acne, substance abuse, and sex education).
- Grooming and dress (clothing selection, color analysis, and cosmetics).
- Communication skills.
- Juvenile law.
- Marriage, family life, and child care (and related legal issues).
- Use of leisure time (hobbies, community service, and recreational reading) (Guetzloe, 1989).

Incorporating Positive and Effective Consequences

Current federal law requires that behavioral intervention plans for students with disabilities include positive behavioral interventions and supports. In programs for students with E/BD, we should always emphasize natural, logical, and positive consequences. Natural consequences are neither contrived nor delivered by the teacher or another adult. They result instead from defying (or following) a law of science (e.g., the consequence of touching a hot stove, leaning back too far in a chair, driving too fast, holding both prongs of an electric plug while plugging it into a socket, or sticking a tongue on a frozen railroad track, all of which are aversive) or a "law" of human nature (smiling at someone and eliciting a smile in return, which is positive). Logical consequences—both positive and aversive—are related to the behavior in question and therefore easily understood (e.g., having no homework because classwork was finished or cleaning the wall on which obscenities were written). At the early stages of teaching a behavior management system, it may be necessary to use concrete rewards (e.g., "funny money" or tokens related to the activity or unit of study; be sure when working with secondary students in particular that the tokens cannot be counterfeited).

When implementing token systems, it is necessary to select desirable backup reinforcers—items or activities for which the points or tokens can be traded. A menu of available reinforcers should be posted in the classroom, with new items added often, so that satiation does not occur. Elementary students may prefer primary reinforcers, small trinkets, printed certificates, or "happygrams" to take home to the family. The most desirable backup reinforcers for secondary students are usually related to "work avoidance" (e.g., earning time for extra physical activity, listening to music, running errands within the school, or being excused from homework). Specific items that seem to appeal to adolescents are travel-sized shampoos and lotions, used clothing, photographs (of teachers or class-mates), or other things that can be gifts for parents and significant others. Backup reinforcers may be highly individualized (something that appeals to one student may not appeal to another); a variety of items or activities should be available.

Service Learning as Curriculum

The concept of youth service as curriculum is not new. Recommendations for including service as part of the school experience appeared from time to time in educational reports and reform proposals throughout the twentieth century (Conrad & Hedin, 1991). For example, Kilpatrick (1918) argued for the adoption of a "project method," in which learning would take place outside the school and involve efforts to meet community needs. Since the passage of the National and Community Service Act in 1990 (which provided funding for service programs in schools and colleges and support for a full-time postsecondary service corps), there has been a dramatic increase in the number of such programs (Kielsmeier, 2000). A follow-up study on service programs, conducted by the U.S. Department of Education in 1999, found that 64% of all public schools and 83% of public high schools now offer some form of community service for their students (Skinner & Chapman, 1999).

There is no question about the positive outcomes of service programs. Conrad and Hedin (1991) reported on program evaluations previously conducted and concluded that community service (a) fosters social, personal, and academic development and (b) can be a worthwhile, useful, and enjoyable experience. As Conrad and Hedlin stated, "The case for community service as a legitimate educational practice receives provisional support from quantitative, quasi-experimental studies and even more consistent affirmation from the reports and testimony of participants and practitioners" (p. 749).

Billig (2000) provided a summary of findings from research conducted on public school programs, grades K-12, during the period from 1990 to 1999. She organized the findings into the broad areas in which service learning has an impact: (a) personal and social development, (b) civic responsibility, (c) academic learning, (d) career exploration and aspiration, (e) schools, and (f) communities. Positive results were cited in every area, although the author cited limitations of the research. She urged the readers to review the original studies for further information. Billig also discussed a variety of mediating factors (e.g., the intensity or duration of a project) that affect the outcomes. She made a number of suggestions for achieving stronger results.

Woerhle (1993) suggested helping activities for specific age groups, from preschool to 12th grade, that were carried out by a school and found to be both developmentally appropriate and successful. The following items are part of the list:

- For 3- to 5-year-olds: Feeding birds; making decorations for nursing homes and soup kitchens; and helping 6th graders wrap Christmas gifts for needy children.
- For grades 1 and 2: Delivering holiday decorations to residents of nursing homes; reflecting (in a group) on the question "Was I a good friend today?"
- For grades 3 and 4: Continuing with and expanding on school and local activities.
- For grades 5 to 8: Participating in recycling projects, environmental cleanups, and tree plantings.
- For grades 9 and 10: Creating a one-term course on "Poverty, Homelessness, and Community Service" that concluded with a trip to New York City, during which students prepared, shared, and delivered meals to homeless individuals and shelters.
- For grades 11 and 12: Serving in day-care centers, tutoring centers, and nursing homes; participating in Habitat for Humanity in southern Appalachia; and shopping for the elderly.

There are issues related to service programs. Despite the positive outcomes, community service programs are not without controversy. Authorities continue to argue about issues (some trivial) such as defining service programs, including a hyphen in the term (i.e., service-learning), fitting the goals and objectives into an assessment rubric, giving course credit for the experiences, and proving that the experiences will prepare students for high-stakes tests. This is an unfortunate shift in thinking—from a focus on what is helpful to the students, community, nation, and world to an obsession with accountability.

Do Students With E/BD Participate in Service Learning?

Although sufficient empirical data are not available to substantiate the involvement of students with E/BD in the regular education service programs, access to the general curriculum is now mandated for any student with a disability. If the general curriculum includes service learning activities for students without disabilities, as has been reported in the extant literature, these experiences must be made available for the student with E/BD.

A number of researchers and practitioners have discussed the inclusion of service learning in the curriculum for students with E/BD, most often in special settings or as part of a small-group experience, in or out of school. Panico (1998), a manager of a public school for troubled adolescents, reported a successful intervention with Melvin, a young person who had previously resisted all efforts to engage him in an interpersonal relationship. During a Saturday morning work session with Habitat for Humanity, for which Panico was a volunteer, the two "connected" (over a broken electric switch and an old plumbing system) and Melvin became interested in the work of the volunteer group. This incident led to the school's forming an alliance with Habitat; the program is still evolving.

Lantieri (1999), who helped to found the Resolving Conflict Creatively Programs (RCCP) in 1985, discussed the need for more focused intervention for young people who "fall through the cracks" (p. 84). A new RCCP program, which is now in place in Anchorage, Atlanta, New York City, and Vista (California), is delivered by two trained adults in weekly group sessions over a 30-week period. The groups consist of students known to be at risk along with others who are known to be positive leaders, and the sessions focus on team building and conflict resolution. Each group also develops a social action project that will benefit the community. The projects of the groups included fixing dinner for a family in need, making Easter baskets for a center for individuals with retardation, creating a peace quilt, collecting and delivering books and art materials for a children's hospital, planting shrubs around a school, broadcasting peace messages each morning on a school loudspeaker, and collecting food for the needy and delivering it to the food collection warehouse (an event that was featured on a local television news program). More than 150 young people have participated in these projects, and the evaluations (by an independent evaluator) showed substantial growth in the participants in terms of skills (e.g., conflict resolution, listening, and anger management), positive attitudes toward school, and self-esteem. In Lantieri's words, these youngsters have become "hooked on altruism" (p. 87).

Students at the Cloverdale Learning Centre, an alternative public school in Surrey, British Columbia, washed windows of town buildings, picked up litter, prepared meals for a soup kitchen, washed cars, and participated in other projects to improve their community. At the same time, they raised money for charity, learned about volunteerism, gained self-esteem, and improved the image of the school, according to their principal. The proceeds of their campaign, "Habits of the Heart," will go to the Canadian Association for the Mentally Handicapped ("Cloverdale students," 2000).

These are not unusual stories. Students with E/BD—and those at risk of being so identified—do participate every day in programs like these across the country. They are involved in service activities, and they are successful in these programs.

Does Service Learning Really Teach Hope?

Coming full circle—back to the topic of hope and the curriculum for students with E/BD—we find that a number of researchers and practitioners specifically

An Integrated Experience by Eleanor Guetzloe

Several years ago, I served as principal investigator and director of a federally funded interagency project in a local school district. Our primary target population consisted of students of middle school age who were identified as having emotional and behavioral disorders and whose families were poor.

As we began our planning, the project staff and advisory council held several large meetings in the community, to which all families of children with E/BD were invited. We simply asked them what they needed—for their children and for themselves. They responded that their children needed after-school and weekend recreation and other activities—a place to play where they were safe and accepted. This became the primary focus of our grant program.

The school placements of the students were not "inclusive," but were primarily special classes, day treatment centers, and residential programs, so we planned and implemented inclusive recreational and service activities for the hours after school and on weekends. The criteria for selecting activities were that they were (a) "normalizing" experiences, (b) "socially acceptable" to the students with E/BD and their nonhandicapped peers, (c) reasonable in cost, and (d) could be expected to continue when the project funding ceased.

The first activity in which the students participated was Coastal Cleanup, a national activity that takes place along the entire coastline of the United States in the early fall of each year. A local environmental group invited us to help with this effort and assigned us the intercoastal shoreline of a local island that is also the community beach. Before the big day, the students discussed environmental concerns in their classes and studied the forms (furnished by the environmental group) to be used in recording the number, type, and weight of the items they might find in the shallow water and on the shore.

The cleanup was on a hot Saturday morning. Several teachers, parents, mental health professionals, and project council members attended to help with the work and to furnish transportation (without compensation). I bought food and drink for everybody (for which I was never repaid, which is a policy story too long to discuss here), procured baseball caps for everyone, and brought along emergency supplies (water, extra shoes, old shirts, and a first aid kit).

The students with E/BD (including a few who were allowed to leave a psychiatric hospital for this occasion) endured sun, heat, insects, sandspurs, and each other all day. Standing in the sun, they listened quietly to a lengthy lecture (on procedures to be followed) by a junior college professor. They picked up, categorized, and hauled away an enormous amount of trash;

▶

competed cheerfully over which group could bring in the largest single piece of debris; and occasionally came back to the car for soft drinks and conversation. After a very hot morning, we found a shady spot on the beach side of the island, had lunch, cooled off in the gulf, packed up, and went home.

That's the whole story. It was a great day. There were no incidents of inappropriate behavior. Everyone—including parents, teachers, and council members—had a good time. When the students were having lunch, one could have mistaken the group for a Sunday School class. They sat together at picnic tables without adults, conversed, ate a great deal, and looked decidedly undisturbed.

This incident was not isolated. We found that any activity that was an "ordinary" experience, away from the classroom, and aimed at helping others was a winner.

In another project, middle school students were to read aloud to very young elementary school children with physical disabilities. Several of the middle school boys, some of whom had never read an entire book, practiced reading their selections during "group," and then rode with the school psychologist (who took driving safety lessons so she would be allowed to furnish their transportation) to the elementary school. The youngsters with E/BD "adopted" the younger group, helped them during play period at school, and took them to see Santa in a local mall during holiday season. The photographs of their work with the younger children brought tears to the eyes of some of the council members.

One amusing and significant episode in this activity was recorded by the school psychologist (the same person who also taught reading during group and served as bus driver). One of the older youngsters admitted that he could not read, but wanted to participate. The psychologist accompanied him to the school library and helped him select a book in which the only words were animal noises. He remarked that he was very good at that (and this had, in fact, been previously noted in his permanent school record). He read his book to his "little buddy" and later to several others. Incidentally, he did begin to read—just enough to understand that it was within his grasp (a giant step toward hope).

Another group of students, accompanied by their teacher, planted donated poinsettia plants at important crossroads in their town, not far from their middle school. Their pictures appeared in the newspaper and on the evening television news. They were recognized for doing something good.

The evaluations of these activities contained many positive comments about the appropriate behavior of the students and the pleasure of their parents, who saw their own children in a new light—working together for the good of the community. Such experiences do teach hope.   ∎

recommended altruistic experiences as a means of fostering hope (Brendtro, Brokenleg, & Van Bockern, 1990; Curwin, 1993; Gallagher, 1997). Curwin (1992, 1993) listed guidelines for teachers to use in planning activities focused on helping others:

- Select opportunities that are genuine.
- Provide a variety of possibilities.
- Have students help others with problems similar to their own.
- Make sure those being helped want to be helped.
- Choose tasks that match the abilities of the students (reasonable expectations).
- Make the opportunities optional.
- Do not praise the helpers, especially in public.
- Do not worry about rewarding negative behavior.
- Provide enough time for positive results to occur.

Examples of helping activities suggested by Curwin (1993) include: tutoring younger students, performing for other students, serving as monitors, carrying out administrative or secretarial tasks, serving as task-force leaders, raising money for school programs or charity, being a Big Brother or Big Sister, and assisting disabled youngsters or nursing home residents. I have also suggested that expectations for student involvement in helping activities should be flexible and tailored for each individual student. When students fail to meet expectations and removal from the activity becomes necessary, they should be removed from the helping situation for only a short period (no more than a day or two). It may also be necessary to protect certain students from the negative attitudes of other teachers and administrators.

Establishing a Continuum of Caring

A child's earliest experiences in helping others should begin within the family or "close to home" (e.g., bringing in a neighbor's newspaper, helping the family prepare food for an older relative, or collecting trash items for the home recycling bin). As children grow and their scope of understanding broadens (from family and home to neighborhood, school, community, state, nation, and world), the nature of the helping experiences should change accordingly. Youngsters will learn that helping behaviors can have a positive and far-reaching effect on others—not only in the immediate environment but in the rest of their world. An example of service with a broad scope is that of a high school student who recently led the organization of a local delegation of mothers to participate in the "Million Mom March" in the nation's capital.

Such activities—and many more—are reported throughout the educational literature. Programs that focus on community service range in scope from a highly successful therapeutic effort by one program manager with one student with E/BD (Panico, 1998) to participation in community service by all students in an entire school district (Hornbeck, 2000).

Discussion Questions

1. If Steven were in your classroom, how would you begin to give him a sense of hope?
2. Describe how you would plan a service learning project for your own classroom.
3. How would you convince a building administrator who is opposed to your taking students with emotional and behavioral disorders out in the community to do community service?
4. Given the information you have learned on providing hope to students, what input would you provide if your school was establishing a policy on which videos could and could not be shown?

References

American heritage college dictionary (3rd ed.). (1993). Boston: Houghton Mifflin.

Beck, A. T., Steer, R. A., Kovacs, M., & Garrison, B. (1985). Hopelessness and eventual suicide: A 10-year prospective study of patients hospitalized with suicidal ideation. *American Journal of Psychiatry, 142,* 559–563.

Billig, S. H. (2000, May). Research on K-12 school-based service-learning. *Phi Delta Kappan, 81,* 658–664.

Brendtro, L., Brokenleg, M., & Van Bockern, S. (1990). *Reclaiming youth at risk: Our hope for the future.* Bloomington, IN: National Educational Service.

Cloverdale students learn "habits of the heart" while volunteering. (2000, April 7). *Vancouver Sun,* p. B5.

Conrad, D., & Hedin, D. (1991, June). School-based community service: What we know from research and theory. *Phi Delta Kappan, 72*(1),743–749.

Curwin, R. (1992). *Rediscovering hope: Our greatest teaching strategy.* Bloomington, IN: National Education Service.

Curwin, R. (1993, November). The healing power of altruism. *Educational Leadership, 51,* 36–39.

Dyer, J. A., & Kreitman, N. (1984). Hopelessness, depression, and suicidal intent. *British Journal of Psychiatry, 144,* 127–133.

Ensminger, E. E., & Dangel, H. L. (1992, March). The Foxfire pedagogy: A confluence of best practices for special education. *Focus on Exceptional Children, 24*(7), 1–16.

Frederick, C. J. (1985). An introduction and overview of youth suicide. In M. L. Peck, N. L. Farberow, & R. E. Litman (Eds.), *Youth suicide* (pp. 1–16). New York: Springer.

Gallagher, P. A. (1997, May). Promoting dignity: Taking the destructive D's out of behavior disorders. *Focus on Exceptional Children, 29*(9), 1–19.

Guetzloe, E. (1989). *Youth suicide: What the educator should know.* Reston, VA: Council for Exceptional Children.

Guetzloe, E. (1997). Teaching hope to children and adolescents. Paper presented at the Annual Summer Institute of the Kentucky Council for Children with Behavioral Disorders, April 1997, Lexington, Kentucky.

Hornbeck, D. (2000, May). Service learning and reform in the Philadelphia public schools. *Phi Delta Kappan, 81*(9), 665.

Ingram, C. P. (1935). *Education of the slow-learning child.* New York: Ronald Press.

Katz, M. (1997). *On playing a poor hand well.* New York: W. W. Norton.

Kazdin, A. E., French, A. S., Unis, A. S., Esveldt-Dawson, K., & Sherick, R. B. (1983). Hopelessness, depression, and suicidal intent among psychiatrically disturbed inpatient children. *Journal of Consulting and Clinical Psychology, 51,* 504–510.

Kielsmeier, J. C. (2000, May). A time to serve: A time to learn: Service learning and the promise of democracy. *Phi Delta Kappan, 81*(9), 652–657.

Kilpatrick, W. H. (1918, September). The project method. *Teachers College Record,* pp. 319–335.

Lantieri, L. (1999). Hooked on altruism: Developing social responsibility in at-risk youth. *Reclaiming Children and Youth, 8*(2), 83-87.

Look at the bright side! It could help you live longer. (2000, March/April). *The Mayo Checkup.* (pp. 1–4). Jacksonville, FL: Mayo Clinic.

Meyen, E. L. (1981). *Developing instructional units: For the regular and special education teacher* (3rd ed.). Dubuque, IA: Brown.

Panico, A. (1998, Fall). Service learning as a community initiation. *Reaching Today's Youth, 3*(1), 37–41.

Seligman, M. E. P. (1991). *Learned optimism.* New York: Knopf.

Seligman, M. E. P. (1995). *The optimistic child.* New York: HarperCollins.

Skinner, R., & Chapman, C. (1999, September). *Service-learning and community service in K-12 public schools.* Washington, DC: National Center for Education Statistics, U.S. Department of Education.

Snyder, C. R. (1994). *The psychology of hope.* New York: Free Press.

Wigginton, E. (1985). *Sometimes a shining moment: Twenty years of foxfire.* Garden City, NY: Anchor/Doubleday.

Woehrle, T. (1993, November). Growing up responsible. *Educational Leadership, 51,* 40–43.

PART FOUR

Focus on Teaching

9

Engaged Time in the Classroom

A. J. is a very bright fifth grader who is enrolled in a regular classroom and now has been referred for emotional and behavioral disorders because of his acting out and aggressive behavior. The school psychologist observes A. J. in the classroom. The second-year teacher, who is struggling with lesson planning, provides lectures, during which A. J. is very attentive. The teacher then gives the students an independent practice sheet; she anticipates that the students will need 30 minutes to complete the sheet. A. J. completes the assignment within 5 minutes, has nothing to do, and starts to verbally pick on other students about how slow they are. The other students then call A. J. names. A. J. gets up and proceeds to "get in" the others' faces and yells at them.

The Importance of Engaged Time

Foremost in an effective curriculum for students with E/BD is a high level of engaged time—time spent doing meaningful learning activities. If A. J. had been busy, he would not have had time to get into trouble.

Winn, Menlove, and Zsiray (1997) stated that the link between time and learning is one of the most consistent findings in educational research. Wise allocation and the productive use of time increase the likelihood that greater student learning will take place. Unfortunately, schedules often control the school and drive the curriculum. In those situations, students and learning, which should be the focus of the school and the classroom, are often sacrificed to schedules. Kauchak and Eggen (1993) defined the following terms: allocated time, instructional time, engaged time (time-on-task), and academic learning time.

Allocated time is the amount of time that a teacher designates for a topic. For instance, the teacher may allow 55 minutes for social studies or 75 minutes for mathematics.

Instructional time is the amount of time that the teacher devotes to active teaching. It is often the time left for teaching after routine management and administrative tasks are completed. In all school programs, too much learning time is lost in counting lunch money, waiting for school buses, waiting to go to lunch, and taking restroom breaks. Although these nonengaged times often give teachers breaks, they also provide opportunities for students with behavioral problems to get into trouble. All teachers must look at the amount of "down time" that occurs during a school day and do all that is possible to reduce that time dramatically.

Engaged time (time-on-task) is the portion of instructional time that students spend directly involved in learning activities. Walker and Severson (1992) defined the following components of academic engaged time: (a) The student is attending to the material and the task; (b) the student is making appropriate motor responses (e.g., writing); (c) the student is asking for assistance in an acceptable manner.

Academic learning time combines engagement and success. It is the amount of time students are successful while engaged. Kauchak and Eggen (1993) summarized research that showed students in classes where success was the dominant pattern not only learned but also felt better about themselves and the material being learned.

Effective teachers of students with E/BD understand the importance of the time-on-task variable and realize that the time the students spend engaged in meaningful activities must provide them with a high degree of success. To assure that students can meet with a high degree of success, the teacher must engage in systematic planning and use academic materials that are appropriate for the students' performance level. Much of the research done on effective instruction has used academic engaged time as the measure of students' use of time and the appropriateness of the curriculum (Gunter & Denny, 1998). Gunter and Denny noted further that engagement is an important component of academic performance.

A recent study by Depaepe, Shores, Jack, and Denny (1996) noted the importance of a high degree of time-on-task coupled with effective instructional strategies that matched academic materials to students' performance levels. This high degree of time-on-task and appropriate instructional strategies may represent an additional means of decreasing disruptive behavior in the classroom and may promote gains in academic performance of students.

Carpenter and McKee-Higgins (1996) cited research that has shown that one of the essential components for the creation of a positive class climate is a high rate of student academic involvement and achievement in which the content of the curriculum and instructional delivery focus on high rates of student engagement during instruction and practice.

Engaged time-on-task is directly related to higher levels of student achievement. Reavis et al. (1996) reported that students should be spending at least 70% of their time on engaged academic tasks.

Mastropieri and Scruggs (1994) believe that the most important teacher-effectiveness variable is time-on-task. According to them, time-on-task can be broken down into allocated and engaged time. Allocated time refers to the 40-minute block of time that the teacher has scheduled for a reading activity. However, engaged time refers to the actual time that the students are engaged in instructional activities. During engaged time students are actively involved in areas that are directly relevant to instructional objectives. Involvement is evidenced by eye contact with the teacher, active attention to teacher presentation, direct responses to teacher questions, and active engagement with relevant and appropriate instructional materials. Nonengaged activities include those that do not require active student participation and that are not directly relevant to instructional objectives (transition activities such as sharpening pencils, making announcements, student conversation not directly relevant to instructional objectives, and time spent on disciplinary actions such as reprimands). Teachers should continually work toward keeping nonengaged time to a minimum.

A teacher can record engaged versus nonengaged time by creating a worksheet in which the day is divided into 15-minute segments and recording just how much time is devoted to engaged activities (see Figure 9.1).

Montague, Bergeron, and Lago-Delello (1997) suggested ways to increase the amount of academic engaged time: (a) Give explicit and direct instructions before the assignment of the task to ensure that students know what to do; (b) monitor progress by providing frequent positive reinforcement and corrective feedback during the activities; and (c) reward students for completing tasks.

Stewart, Evans, and Kaczynski (1997) reported on the importance of time and instructional management. They advocated that the teacher analyze the use of

Time of Day	Activities that reflect successful engaged time
8:30 a.m. – 8:45 a.m.	
8:45 a.m. – 9:00 a.m.	
9:00 a.m. – 9:15 a.m.	
9:15 a.m. – 9:30 a.m.	
9:30 a.m. – 9:45 a.m.	
9:45 a.m. – 10:00 a.m.	
10:00 a.m. – 10:15 a.m.	
10:15 a.m. – 10:30 a.m.	
10:30 a.m. – 10:45 a.m.	
10:45 a.m. – 11:00 a.m.	
11:00 a.m. – 11:15 a.m.	
11:15 a.m. – 11:30 a.m.	
11:30 a.m. – 11:45 a.m.	
11:45 a.m. – 12:00 p.m.	
12:00 p.m. – 12:15 p.m.	
12:15 p.m. – 12:30 p.m.	
12:30 p.m. – 12:45 p.m.	
12:45 p.m. – 1:00 p.m.	
1:00 p.m. – 1:15 p.m.	
1:15 p.m. – 1:30 p.m.	
1:30 p.m. – 1:45 p.m.	
1:45 p.m. – 2:00 p.m.	
2:00 p.m. – 2:15 p.m.	
2:15 p.m. – 2:30 p.m.	

FIGURE 9.1.   Daily Engaged Activities

academic and nonacademic time in the classroom and compare the results to a model schedule that allows for maximum efficiency.

Transition Times

Mastropieri and Scruggs (1994) summarized research that shows that transitions constitute a major source of off-task activities. Transition refers to intervals during which students move from one class or group or from one subject to another. During these times behaviors such as sharpening pencils, talking to classmates, or obtaining drinks at the water fountain may occur. Teachers should plan for these activities to occur at prespecified times during the day rather than during a specified engaged-time activity. Likewise teachers should establish an expectation that students move from one activity to another quickly, quietly, and efficiently. Students should be reinforced for making transitions smoothly.

Some suggestions for handling transitions include: (a) Adhere to a schedule so that students know when the transitions will occur; (b) announce to students in advance that there will be a change so that students know what to expect; (c) have materials ready before the transition begins; and (d) establish routines.

Practical Classroom Suggestion

Teachers should provide students who frequently ask to use the restroom or to sharpen pencils or engage in other off-task activities with a specified number of coupons for those activities. Each time the students wish to do the activity, they must forfeit a coupon. When all coupons are gone, the student can no longer request that activity. Such a system teaches students to budget their time and activities.

Accurate Teacher Scheduling

Being able to schedule properly and ensure that the task can be accomplished in the time allotted is very difficult for some beginning teachers. They will plan an activity that they think will take 30 minutes and discover that the students have completed the task in 10 minutes and now have 20 minutes left with nothing to do but get into trouble. Teachers must learn to gauge the approximate amount of time that the activity will take and then have contingency plans such as extra-credit or bonus work for students who finish early. It is important that the extra-credit or bonus work be related to the skill the teacher is trying to teach. It is also recommended that the additional activities utilize higher-level thinking skills. Busy work, such as coloring a picture about the topic or completing a simple word find, does little to challenge the student. Teachers will find it helpful to plan too many rather than too few lessons.

Analysis of Worksheets

For any worksheet assignment or group lesson, the teacher should determine the reason for teaching the material and the relevance for the particular student(s). In many classes, students are involved in busy work—worksheets that have little relevance to what they need to know or want to learn. In many classrooms, worksheets are assigned that are not even related to the topic. In this chapter, we show you multiple ways to increase engagement other than through the use of worksheets.

Students who find worksheets and assignments meaningless and view them as busy work become unmotivated to come to school. They often ask: "Why do I have to learn this, anyway?" or "How many more multiplication problems do I have to do on this sheet of paper?" Too many teachers have students do busy work because it requires less planning than appropriately developed activities. However, work that is not relevant to students can result in behavioral problems, which in turn will result in more work for the teacher.

Braukman (1995) outlined a hierarchy for the best way to teach the traditional curriculum through real life applications.

1. Being there—taking students to the natural environment where the application of the skill is immediate. Obviously, this approach would involve a high level of engaged time.
2. Immersion or simulation—creating the natural environment within the classroom.
3. Hands-on—students recreate natural learning through manipulatives or involvement in an experience.
4. Second-hand—use of television, videos or films of the material to be learned. Use of books that relate to the real life experience.
5. Abstract symbolic—teaching in a theoretical mode removed from real life application. Teachers must ask themselves how much of the school day is spent using the abstract symbolic method—the least effective way to teach.

Use of Videos as a Learning Tool

Some teachers allow students to earn the right to view videos. This practice may be appropriate on a limited basis provided it is not a substitute for teaching. We believe that video rewards should be limited to no more than 1-1/2 or 2 hours at the most per week, unless the video relates to a specific unit being taught and is integrated into the curriculum with planned activities prior to and after its showing. Videos encourage passive learning rather than active learning in which students are engaged in meaningful tasks.

Videos should not be used to simply fill the day. Likewise, only those videos should be shown that have been rated "G" or that have been approved by parents. Videos that depict violations of school or classroom rules should not be shown in the classroom. When teachers do so, they send a mixed message to students that although the school doesn't allow foul language, it is acceptable to show it on the screen. Obviously, videos that depict violence or inappropriate language should not be shown.

CHAPTER 9

The Dangers of Nonengaged Time

We know that the greater the amount of engaged time on tasks, the higher the achievement levels of the students. Kauchak and Eggen (1993) reported that high-achieving students are typically engaged for 75% of the time or more while low achievers have engagement rates that are often below 50%. Effective teachers produce on-task rates as high as 80% while less effective teachers exhibit on-task rates of 60%. If we want to assure higher achievement for our students, we must engage them in meaningful tasks.

According to Montague, Bergeron, and Lago-Delello (1997), research suggests that students who are not engaged academically most of the time frequently become passive learners, give up easily on tasks, become anxious, withdrawn, angry about school, and fail in future grades.

A low degree of engaged time also creates a vacuum in which students can and will exhibit behavior problems. When students have nothing to do or too much free time, behavioral problems will occur. Such was the case with A. J. Well-run classrooms with high rates of successful engaged time are places in which there are fewer behavior management problems.

Johns and Carr (1995) reported that many students who come to school are passive learners. They are used to watching television and expect to be entertained by the teacher. Although the teacher needs to be a performer, he or she must get students involved in the learning process.

Children learn better by doing than by being told. If we are to motivate students, decrease behavior problems, and ensure their academic success, then we, as educators, must engage them in meaningful tasks. The following section describes multiple ways through which we can engage students in meaningful and fun activities.

Ten Classroom Activities to Increase Meaningful Student Engagement

There are many ways that a teacher can increase engaged time for students within the classroom. The following represents some ideas for use with E/BD students.

1. Response Cards

Following an explanation of a concept, a teacher asks a variety of questions to determine whether the students have grasped the concept. The teacher asks students to raise their hands if they know the answer. The students who have grasped the concept, who are quick to respond, and who are not shy will immediately raise their hands. The students who do not grasp the concept, who have delayed processing times, or who are shy will not participate. Those students may even put their heads down and hope they are not called on to answer.

An activity that involves all students is the use of response cards. There are many variations of response cards. For young children, the teacher might give each child two popsicle sticks—one with yes on it, the other with no on it. The teacher asks a yes/no question, and each child raises the appropriate popsicle stick. The teacher may also give each child an index card and have each child write down the answer to a question. The teacher may have students stand up if they agree with a teacher statement or stay seated if they do not agree. The teacher might have each child do a thumbs up if he/she agrees or thumbs down if he/she disagrees.

2. Lecture Bingo

When a teacher is going to give a lecture, the teacher can pick out key terms he/she will be discussing in the lecture. The teacher can take a blank bingo card and in each square put one term until the bingo card is filled. Each student gets a bingo card with these terms. Students are instructed to listen closely to the lecture. When they hear one of the terms on the bingo card, they are to mark the bingo square. When a student has completed a line or the whole card (whatever is the teacher preference) the student yells, "Bingo!" This activity keeps the student focused on the key terms in the lecture.

3. Red Rubber Ball

A teacher can buy inflatable balls that have squares containing math problems, states, clocks with specific times, and so on. These balls are a great activity for engagement. The students throw the ball up in the air, catch the ball, answer the problem in the square where the left thumb is, and write the answer on paper. I prefer to make my own balls by buying a blank ball (preferably red) and writing questions about the topic being covered in class. Use a permanent marker to print the questions on the ball.

This activity can also be utilized in a team game. The teacher breaks the students into teams. The teacher throws the ball, and a student on the team catches it. The rest of the team has to answer the question, rather than the team member who catches the ball. Again, wherever the left thumb lands is the question that is answered by the team.

4. Pick Your Post

When the teacher has taught a given amount of material, rather than giving the students a worksheet or a test to measure how much has been learned, the teacher can post sheets of paper at various stations in the room. On one sheet it might state, write a poem; on another, write a song; on another, prepare a skit; on another, draw a picture; on another, make a game. Students then go around the room and "pick your post." Whatever post they pick is the activity that they do. Students can work together in a group on the project.

5. Carousel Brainstorming

The teacher puts up five large sheets of paper in locations around the classroom. The teacher writes on each sheet of paper some thought provoking questions on a topic. The teacher breaks the students into five groups and has each group start at one of the locations. The group is to "brainstorm" solutions to the problems and write down as many solutions as they can. When the teacher says, "Move to the next station," all groups move clockwise to the next sheet of paper. The brainstorming process begins again. The teacher does this until all groups have had a chance to brainstorm solutions to all of the problems. Music is sometimes helpful in the activity—when the music starts, the group moves.

6. Think-Pair-Share

In this activity, the teacher asks a thought-provoking question. Each student individually writes down what he or she believes is a possible answer. The teacher then breaks the class into pairs. This author breaks students into pairs in a variety of ways: using pairs of colored chips, and the student has to find another student who has the same color chip; using cards where a state is on one card and its capital is on another card, and students find the matching pair. When students have found their partner, they discuss what each one of them answered. After a short, specified amount of time, the teacher has each pair share their responses.

7. Games

Students love games, and teachers can increase engagement by developing learning games such as bingo, lotto, jeopardy, concentration, spelling baseball, and so on. If the teacher is going to play team games, he/she must be very careful to match skills on teams so that no child is embarrassed and no team has an unfair advantage over another team.

8. Dominoes

This gives students the opportunity to move around and is a great way to check basic understanding of facts. A student will be given a card with a question, and another student will be given a card with the answer to the question. Another student will be given a different question and another the answer to that question. Students have to go around the room to find the individual who has the answer to the question.

9. Crossword Puzzles and Word Finds

This is an excellent activity for spelling. The teacher may create the crossword puzzle or the word find, but it can be more fun and engaging for the students to create a puzzle or word find using their spelling words.

10. K–W–L

Bos and Vaughn (1991) discuss the use of KWL. KWL is an excellent way to activate student background knowledge, to find out what the student wants to learn about a given topic, and to check what the student has learned about the topic. The strategy is based on research that stresses the importance of background knowledge in giving meaning during reading. It can be used when a student is beginning to read about a topic, or it can be used when a teacher is introducing a new topic to the class.

The student is given a sheet of paper with three columns. The first column is K: What I know about the topic. The second column is W: What I want to learn about this topic. The third is L: What I learned about the topic. During the "K" step, the teacher and students engage in a discussion that assists students in thinking about what they already know about the topic being introduced. During the "W" phase, the teacher finds out what may be interesting to the student. In the "L" step, the students write down what they learned after reading about the topic or after it has been discussed in class.

Discussion Questions

1. How many time-wasters have you seen when you have observed classrooms?
2. Obtain and assess a worksheet in terms of value and relevance to a student.
3. What ways can you think of that teachers can assure successful transitions from one activity to another?

References

Bos, C., & Vaughn, S. (1991). *Strategies for teaching students with learning and behavior problems.* Boston: Allyn & Bacon.

Braukman, D. (1995). The best way to teach. Handout provided at the Learning Disabilities Association of Illinois Convention, October 1995.

Carpenter, S., & McKee-Higgins, E. (1996). Behavior management in inclusive classrooms. *Remedial and Special Education, 17*(4), 195–203.

Depaepe, P., Shores, R., Jack, S., & Denny, R. (1996). Effects of task difficulty on the disruptive and on-task behavior of students with severe behavior disorders. *Behavioral Disorders, 21*(3), 216–225.

Gunter, P., & Denny, R. (1998). Trends and issues in research regarding academic instruction of students with emotional and behavioral disorders. *Behavioral Disorders, 24*(1), 44–50.

Johns, B., & Carr, V. (1995). *Techniques for managing verbally and physically aggressive students.* Denver: Love.

Kauchak, D., & Eggen P. (1993). *Learning and teaching.* Boston: Allyn and Bacon.

Mastropieri, M., & Scruggs, T. (1994). *Effective instruction for special education,* (2nd ed.). Austin: Pro-ed.

Montague, M., Bergeron, J., & Lago-Delello, E. (1997). Using prevention strategies in general education. *Focus on Exceptional Children, 29*(8), 1–12.

Reavis, H., Kukic, S., Jenson, W., Morgan, D., Andrews, D., & Fisher, S. (1996). *BEST practices: Behavioral and educational strategies for teachers.* Longmont, CO: Sopris West.

Stewart, S., Evans, W., & Kaczynski, D. (1997). Setting the stage for success: assessing the instructional environment. *Preventing School Failure, 41*(2), 53–56.

Walker, H., & Severson, H. (1992). *Systematic screening for behavior disorders.* Longmont, CO: Sopris West.

Winn, D., Menlove, R., & Zsiray, S. (1997). *Rethinking the scheduling of school time.* Bloomington, IN: Phi Delta Kappa Educational Foundation.

10

Student Self-Management

Amanda, 16 years old, receives high school resource services for students with emotional and behavioral disorders. Although her academic skills are adequate, she is unable to budget her time and has to be reminded frequently by the resource teacher to take her books and necessary materials to class. Is Amanda going to be able to survive in the real world if someone is not around to help her manage herself?

o prepare our students for the real world, we must teach them how to manage themselves, their learning, their time, and their behavioral and social skills. Teachers, parents, and other adults will not always be available to guide them. Students must learn to guide themselves.

According to Carpenter and McKee-Higgins (1996), behavioral interventions and social skills training should foster skills that will enable students to function not only successfully but also independently in the school and community setting.

Self-management—the application of behavior-change processes to modify or maintain one's behavior—empowers students to be independent performers. Through self-management, students become their own teachers. Kaplan and Carter (1995) stressed the reasons for teaching students how to manage their own behavior.

1. Research shows that self-management strategies are effective in changing academic and social behavior among students of differing ages and ability levels.
2. Students who manage themselves save teacher time and energy.
3. The ability to self-manage may lead to enhanced generalization and maintenance of behaviors.
4. Self-management provides a bridge, or transition, between extrinsic control and self-control.
5. Self-management changes the student's locus of control from external to internal.
6. Self-management skills are more relevant than many other skills we teach our students.

Todd, Horner, and Sugai (1999) believe that self-management procedures are a particularly encouraging intervention for students with behavior problems and have been associated with improved academic performance and reduction in those problems. Self-management skills may also be used effectively with minimal demands on the time and skills of the teacher.

King-Sears and Cummings (1996) offered these recommendations to encourage students in the area of self-management.

1. Reinforce students when they use self-management skills appropriately.
2. Alter the self-management techniques as necessary.
3. Use self-management techniques in conjunction with other behavior management techniques.
4. Chart data to determine the effectiveness of self-management.
5. Supervise the use of self-management.
6. Involve students in the development of self-management techniques.

The following are important self-management techniques for us to teach to students:

1. Goal-setting is an important first step. According to Mitchell and McCollum (1987), 87% of people do not have goals, 10% of people have goals—but not written goals, and 3% of people have written goals. The 3% of the people who have written goals accomplish 50 to 100 times more than the others. The key to accomplishing what we strive to achieve is the setting of goals; we need to teach children at an early age how to set goals for themselves and that they can achieve the goals they set. When teaching students to set goals, teachers are advised to begin by urging students to set one, two, or three daily goals and then by having the students monitor their success in meeting the goals. Next, teachers can have students set weekly goals and monitor whether the goals are met by using daily or weekly goal sheets (see Figure 10.1 and 10.2):

2. Student monitoring of their ability to follow rules is an important self-management technique. According to Hoover and Oliver (1996), self-monitoring involves putting students in charge of their own behavior. Students can monitor their appropriate and inappropriate behaviors related to bullying, for example, by having those who bully tally aggressive words or actions they make. A positive technique would have students record each positive, prosocial response they give—such as greeting others appropriately. Another might be to teach students to record the passage of time intervals during which no bullying behaviors occurred.

Kaplan and Carter (1995) discussed using a tape recorder to teach students to monitor their own behavior—particularly on-task behavior. A tape recorder on

---

Student name _____

Today is _____

My goal(s) for today   Did I meet my goal(s)?

_____   Yes/No

_____   Yes/No

_____   Yes/No

FIGURE 10.1.   Daily Goal Sheet

Student name _____

Dates: From _____to _____

My goals for the week	Mon.	Tues.	Wed.	Thurs.	Fri.
_____	Yes/No	Yes/No	Yes/No	Yes/No	Yes/No
_____	Yes/No	Yes/No	Yes/No	Yes/No	Yes/No
_____	Yes/No	Yes/No	Yes/No	Yes/No	Yes/No

FIGURE 10.2.   Weekly Goal Sheet

the teacher's desk beeps at regular intervals. When the tape beeps, students who are on-task put a check mark on a card. Students who receive a designated number of check marks receive a reward.

Another self-monitoring technique, which was developed for first graders and described by Montague, Bergeron, and Logo-Delello (1997), consists of teacher cues, a student checklist, and a systematic reinforcement chart. The checklist is established for each subject and is completed by the student who answers the following questions:

Am I *listening* to the teacher?
Do I *know* what to do?
Did I *finish* my work?

The teacher assists students having difficulty staying on-task by providing verbal and visual cues that correspond to the three questions that are on the checklist. Children monitor their own progress and receive rewards of stickers and positive notes to take home.

3. Our society demands people do many tasks in a short time. Learning to manage time is critical. One valuable activity teaches students to estimate the amount of time it will take them to complete a task. This technique is very effective for those students who get off-task easily or do not want to complete assignments within the designated time period given. Students also begin to see this device as a game and they try to beat their own time. Provide students with time cards like the one in Figure 10.3.

CHAPTER 10

Date: _____

Student name: _____

Task to be done:_____

Before starting the task:
The time I estimate it will take me to do this task:_____

After completing the task:
The time it took me to do this task: _____

FIGURE 10.3.   Time Card

4. Teachers should help students plan to complete long-term assignments by using the WATCH strategy (outlined in *Teaching Self-Management Strategies to Adolescents* by Young, West, Smith, and Morgan [1995]. A summary follows:

W: Write down the assignment, the date it is due, and any special requirements for the assignment.

A: Ask yourself if you understand the assignment; if not, ask for clarification.

T: Task analyze the assignment and schedule the various tasks over the days that are available.

CH: Check each of the tasks as you do them for completeness, accuracy, and neatness.

According to Young and colleagues, students are usually more successful with long-term assignments (for example, book reports, term papers, and speeches) if they organize their approach and plan ahead. The WATCH strategy assists students in doing this planning.

5. Students should learn to proofread their own work. They often rush to complete an assignment and will not bother to check the quality of the work or even if their name is on the paper. Teach students to proofread their work by providing them with a checklist (Figure 10.4) for use prior to turning in an assignment.

McNaughton, Hughes, and Ofiesh (1997) offered a proofreading strategy, known as INSPECT, that can be used by students who use a word processor or computer with a spell check to do their assignments. The steps are as follows:

Before I turn this assignment in, I have:

_____   Put my name on my paper

_____   Put the date on the paper

_____   Read through all of my responses to see if they are what I meant

_____   Checked my punctuation

_____   Checked my spelling

FIGURE 10.4.   Student Checklist for Proofreading

In your document:
Start the spelling checker
Pick correct alternatives
Eliminate unrecognizable words
Correct additional errors
Type in your corrections

6. Learning strategies should be taught to students from a very young age. (In Chapter 12, such strategies are discussed in detail.) According to Cole and McLeskey (1997), this approach is not designed to teach specific content but focuses on teaching students the skills, of how to learn. Cole and McLesky have compiled much evidence that indicates students with disabilities lack learning skills. Thus, learning strategies such as those researched by Deshler, Ellis, and Lenz (1996) are a critical part of the curriculum for E/BD students and are important self-management techniques for students.

7. Problem-solving strategies empower students to make responsible decisions that impact their lives. Gallagher (1997) stressed the importance of giving students the opportunity to make choices and to recognize the outcomes of the choices. Such strategies include: recognizing the problem, defining the problem and the goal, generating alternative solutions, evaluating the solutions, and designing a plan. One such strategy Gallagher recommends is:

S: Situation. Discuss the problem situation.
O: Options. Share options for a solution.
C: Consequences. Describe the possible consequences for the options.
S: Select solution. Select the appropriate solution from the identified options.

Gallagher recommends using this strategy during class meetings. A series of problems that students can relate to are introduced and students use the process. After students learn the strategy, the teacher can then use it individually with a student who is having difficulty handling a situation.

8. Reflection activities are vital tools for teaching students to learn from their experiences—their successes and failures. According to Henley (1997), troubled students are unable to apply lessons from the past to current interpersonal situations. They are often unable to move beyond unpleasant events and focus on current concerns. Reflection can assist a student in moving forward. One activity to encourage reflection is the use of journals. We have found this technique especially effective with students involved in community service projects. Students who have volunteered at a nursing home or an animal shelter, for example, are asked to write down two thoughts or lessons they learned from the activity. The students can then share their thoughts.

9. Students should learn to graph and post their own progress. Advertising for success (public posting) is an intervention delineated by Jenson and Reavis (1996). It primarily involves the display of academic progress or behavioral measures on a bulletin board or blackboard. It could include such items as scores on papers, test scores, number of assignments completed, being on time for class, being prepared to work, and so on. It is important to post positive information if possible. The more negative the information, the less effective the system will be. The basic components of this system include some type of visual feedback system that students can see from their desks, accurate and meaningful information that can be displayed, and lastly, the engineered reaction to the information—those reactions from teachers, aides, the principal, and peers.

10. Students need to learn how to organize themselves. Students with E/BD often have difficulty organizing their time and their belongings; yet, we spend little time at school teaching them how to become organized. Simple activities that can be implemented in the classroom include the use of checklists for what needs to be done and by when, the use of individual folders for each subject, folders with pockets, cleaning out desks at the end of each day while determining what should and should not be saved, using separate compartments in desks for pencils, books, papers, and so on.

An excellent technique that can be used for students with attention deficit disorder is to have them keep their books in storage tubs (each marked by name) away from their desks. When the students need a book, they can retrieve it from their tub, which gives them the opportunity to move frequently with permission. Similarly, small cardboard mailboxes can be used by students to put work from each subject in a different compartment.

11. In order to function in the real world, students must be able to see that a task needs to be done and that they should do it—that is, to be independent self-starters. An excellent way to teach students the importance of being self-starters is to provide reinforcement for seeing tasks that need to be done and doing them without being told. For example, a student in a janitorial work program did a good job of doing exactly what he was told to do but he did not look to see if another item needed to be dusted or if the windows needed to be washed. I gave him a list of jobs that he was to do and then left blank spaces in which he could write down other chores that he had seen needed to be done and had done them without being told to do so. The student's evaluation for the day was dependent not only upon how well he did with the jobs that he was told to do but also with the tasks that he saw needed to be done and did.

12. Students should be encouraged to exercise individual independent judgment. They need to be encouraged to think for themselves—to explore all sides of an issue and make a decision after seeing all sides. We must teach students how to gather knowledge and to form opinions of their own rather than doing something because everyone else is doing it. Gangs are made up of young people who do not think for themselves. An activity such as putting up a statement each morning and having students gather information and express their own opinions is an excellent vehicle for self-expression.

13. Students should be taught responsibility for their own behavior. It is critical to continually teach children that throughout the day they make choices—some good and some bad—and that they must live with the results of those choices. Likewise, assessing an event after its occurrence helps students to process their role in it. Students should be encouraged to ask themselves questions such as:

What happened?
What did you do?
What do you need to do the next time it happens?

14. Students need to be taught to engage in self-talk in order to deal with difficult situations or to control their anger. In *Anger Management for Youth: Stemming Aggression and Violence,* Eggert (1994) provided some examples of self-talk and suggested a strategy, known as COPING, to teach students how to cope with anger while using self-talk phrases:

C: Calm down. Say, "calm down" or "stop."
O: Overcome the negative; opt for control. Say, "overcome, easy does it, I am in control."
P: Prepare, problem solve, plan. Say, "think, problem solve, remember your plan."

I: Identify, invite alternatives rather than use insults. Say, "Imagine success. Don't use insults."

N: Name the anger feelings and negotiate. Say, "I'm angry, I need to think about negotiation."

G: Go, get on with the plan, give praise to self and others. Say, "Way to go!! Good job!" (p. 114)

Bos and Vaughn (1991) outlined ways to encourage students to use self-talk. They stressed that teachers should model self-talk and self-statements as they perform a task. Students should be encouraged to develop and use cue cards to help them remember the steps to take in resolving a problem.

Corral and Antia (1997) discussed the importance of attribution theory, which indicates that people who experience frequent success often attribute their success to their own effort or ability and attribute failure to their own lack of effort or ability level. They summarized research that indicates that teaching students learning strategies alone may not be enough to consistently increase effort and persistence because the attributional state of the student determines whether the learning strategy will be used. They contend that when people feel success is possible, they will exert greater effort and attribute a greater proportion of success to the effort they exerted than someone who does not expect success. Thus, there is a strong need to combine learning strategies with the teaching of positive self-talk.

Corral and Antia outlined six steps to positive attribution, using math as an example: (a) model correct strategy applications, (b) model positive attribution statements often, (c) model positive self-talk when discovering errors in your own work, (d) allow students to reflect on class math tasks and reasons for their success or failure through the use of self-report journals, (e) encourage students to keep records of positive attribution statements that they make when working, and (f) encourage students to set goals.

15. To be successful in the real world, students must be able to advocate for themselves. To do so, students must be able to identify their needs and express those needs appropriately to those who can meet them. Often, parents and teachers intervene, as they should, to see that students receive the services to which they are entitled. However, at the same time that we advocate for our students, we must also prepare them for a world in which we will not be at their side to assure that their needs are met. Students must learn to speak up, to voice their opinions in an appropriate manner, and to let their needs be known.

Sands and Doll (1996), referring to the importance of self-determination, noted that: "Self-determination is best conceptualized as an adult outcome of earlier experiences that enhance and support self-sufficiency" (p. 58). In addition, there is accumulating evidence that students with special education needs are more likely than nondisabled students to exhibit an external locus of control in situations that require choice or decision-making. They believe that it is important to empower students to advocate for themselves. In order to self-advocate, students must have accurate perceptions of their own performance—strengths and weaknesses—and must know the conditions that enhance their performance.

Hoy and Gregg (1997) wrote: "A critical component of job success is the ability of consumers to express their own service needs, to be self-advocates" (p. 14). Self-advocacy strategies can help individuals be more aware of their own strengths and weaknesses as well as the requirements for job success.

16. Conflict resolution is a critical self-management skill that we must teach students with behavioral disorders. Students need to be able to solve their own problems and resolve conflict in a peaceful manner. According to Johnson and Johnson (1995), violence prevention programs alone are not enough. Conflict resolution is a key component in any effective curriculum for students with emotional and behavioral disorders. Johns and Keenan (1997) believe that if we can teach students that skillful conflict resolution can result in more positive relationships with peers and can result in peace of mind for the student, students will want to use the techniques increasingly in their everyday life.

They outline numerous advantages of the conflict resolution process, including:

1. It brings students who have conflicts together in a neutral setting.
2. It resolves a conflict with open communication.
3. It teaches cooperative decision-making.
4. It provides consistency and fairness with students.
5. It makes students responsible for their own actions.
6. It directly teaches negotiation skills and higher level thinking. Life is full of situations that require negotiation. Through conflict resolution, students learn how to negotiate.
7. It brings closure to a problem.
8. It opens the lines of communication.
9. It provides respectful treatment of students.
10. It is more effective than suspensions and detentions in shaping appropriate behaviors. Rather than being removed from a situation and escaping from the problem, the student is taught to face and resolve the conflict peacefully.

The basic process used by us (adapted from the work of Schrumpf [1991]) is:

A. Bring the two parties who have the conflict together.
B. Have the parties sit facing each other with the mediator at the head of the table.

C. The mediator opens the session, introducing himself or herself as the mediator and each disputant introduces himself or herself. The mediator then provides the ground rules:

(1) The mediator is neutral and does not take sides.

(2) The session is confidential; nothing leaves the room.

(3) Each party is to respect the other party by listening and by not interrupting when the other is speaking.

(4) It is important that both parties cooperate in order to resolve the dispute.

The mediator should obtain a commitment for the parties to follow the ground rules.

D. The mediator then begins the process of gathering necessary information by doing the following:

(1) Each disputant is asked to tell his or her side of the story. "Will you each tell me what happened?"

(2) The mediator listens, summarizes, clarifies—repeats statements made, rephrases to check accuracy, sums up the statements of the disputants.

(3) The mediator then repeats the process by asking for additional information. "Is there anything you want to add?"

(4) The mediator then restates both sides of the situation.

(5) Then the mediator focuses on common interests asking such questions as: What do you want? If you were in the other person's shoes, how would you feel? If you could ask the other person to do one thing, what would it be?

(6) After gaining insight into the students' interests, the mediator states what the interests are.

(7) Then the mediator asks the disputants to brainstorm possible solutions that might satisfy both parties.

(8) The mediator then asks the disputants to evaluate options and choose solutions.

(9) The mediator then writes the agreement and closes by asking each participant to sign it.

17. Students need to learn how to deal with stress. I spend time teaching stress-reduction techniques to adults but hardly ever find them being taught to children. Children indeed seem to be more susceptible to stress and yet are less equipped to handle it than adults. Kaplan and Carter (1995) reported that suicide rates continue to increase for 10- to 14-year-olds. There is more stress in the home—higher rates of divorce, children accepting more responsibility, and pressure to grow up faster. There is increased stress at school—peer pressure, deadlines for completing assignments, and pressure to achieve. Is it any wonder that children are feeling stress! Kaplan and Carter pointed out that childhood stress is correlated with childhood maladjustment and that much of the maladaptive

behavior we see in the schools is the result of life stress events that children experience in and out of school. They outlined the key concepts that should be taught to students prior to teaching them stress management strategies.

1. Define the terms—stress, stressor, distress.
2. Teach students that not all stress is bad.
3. Teach students the physiological changes that occur during times of stress.
4. Teach students that they can't always escape from stress by running away from it.
5. Teach students that effective stress management requires a holistic approach.
6. Teach students that stress is cumulative and that people are often better able to deal with one big stressor than with the cumulative effect of several small stressors.
7. Teach students that it is not the event that produces stress but it is what we say to ourselves about the stressors that produce stress.

Conclusion

The checklist in Figure 10.5 can be used to determine if you are teaching your students self-management strategies.

Do you teach your students how to set goals for themselves?
Do you have your students monitor their compliance with classroom rules?
Do you teach students how to manage their time?
Do you teach your students how to manage long-range assignments?
Do you teach your students how to proofread their work?
Do you teach a variety of learning strategies?
Do you teach your students how to reflect on experience?
Do you use graphs and charts for monitoring each student's progress?
Do you teach students how to organize their materials?
Do you encourage your students to be self-starters?
Do you encourage students to be independent thinkers?
Do you encourage students to take responsibility for their behavior?
Do you encourage students to self-talk to handle a difficult situation, do their assignments, and control their anger?
Do you encourage students to advocate for themselves?
Do you teach your students how to manage conflict?
Do you teach your students how to manage stress?

FIGURE 10.5.   Teacher Checklist for Determining Use of Student Self-Management Techniques in the Classroom

Discussion Questions

1. After reading this chapter, can you think of self-management techniques, other than those mentioned in the text, that you might utilize for students 8 years of age and under?
2. Can you think of opportunities within and outside of the classroom through which you could teach students how to advocate for themselves?
3. At what age do you believe it is important to teach stress reduction to students and why?

References

Bos, C., & Vaughn, S. (1991). *Strategies for teaching students with learning and behavior problems.* Boston: Allyn and Bacon.

Carpenter, S., & McKee-Higgins, E. (1996). Behavior management in inclusive classrooms. *Remedial and Special Education, 17*(4), 195–203.

Cole, C., & McLeskey, J. (1997). Secondary inclusion programs for students with mild disabilities. *Focus on Exceptional Children, 29*(6), 1–16.

Corral, N., & Antia, S. (1997). Self-talk: Strategies for success in math. *Teaching Exceptional Children, 29*(4), 42–45.

Depaepe, P., Shores, R., Jack, S., & Denny, R. (1996). Effects of task difficulty on the disruptive and on-task behavior of students with severe behavior disorders. *Behavioral Disorders, 21*(3), 216–225.

Deshler, D., Ellis, E., & Lenz, B. K. (1996). *Teaching adolescents with learning disabilities: Strategies and methods.* Denver: Love.

Dev, P. (1997). Intrinsic motivation and academic achievement: What does their relationship imply for the classroom teacher? *Remedial and Special Education, 18*(1), 12–19.

Eggert, L. (1994). *Anger management for youth: Stemming aggression and violence.* Bloomington, IN: National Educational Service.

Gallagher, P. (1997). Promoting dignity: Taking the destructive D's out of behavior disorders. *Focus on Exceptional Children, 29*(9), 1–19.

Henley, M. (1997). *Teaching self-control: A curriculum for responsible behavior.* Bloomington, IN: National Educational Service.

Hoover, J., & Oliver, R. (1996). *The bullying prevention handbook: A guide for principals, teachers, and counselors.* Bloomington, IN: National Educational Service.

Hoy, C., & Gregg, N. (1997). Consumer-led empowerment training. *LDA Newsbriefs, 32*(2), 14–15.

Jenson, W., & Reavis, H. K. (1996). Advertising for success: improving motivation. In H. K. Reavis et al., *BEST practices: Behavioral and educational strategies for teachers.* Longmont, CO: Sopris West.

Johns, B., & Carr, V. (1995). *Techniques for managing verbally and physically aggressive students.* Denver: Love.

Johns, B., & Keenan, J. (1997). *Techniques for managing a safe school.* Denver: Love.

Johnson, D., & Johnson, R. (1995). *Reducing school violence through conflict resolution.* Alexandria, VA: Association for Supervision and Curriculum Development.

Kaplan, J., & Carter, J. (1995). *Beyond behavior modification: A cognitive-behavioral approach to behavior management in the school.* Austin, TX: Pro-Ed.

Kauchak, D., & Eggen, P. (1993). *Learning and teaching.* Boston: Allyn and Bacon.

King-Sears, M., & Cummings, C. (1996). Inclusive practices of classroom teachers. *Remedial and Special Education, 17*(4), 217–225.

Mastropieri, M., & Scruggs, T. (1994). *Effective instruction for special education.* Austin, TX: Pro-Ed.

McNaughton, D., Hughes, C., & Ofiesh, N. (1997). Proofreading for students with learning disabilities: Integrating computer and strategy use. *Learning Disabilities Research and Practice, 12*(1), 16–28.

Mitchell, M., & McCollum, M. (1987). *Learning to be positive.* Birmingham, AL: EBSCO Media.

Montague, M., Bergeron, J., & Lago-Delello, E. (1997). Using prevention strategies in general education. *Focus on Exceptional Children, 29*(8), 1–12.

Reavis, H. K., Kukic, S., Jenson, W., Morgan, D., Andrews, D., & Fisher, S. (1996). *BEST practices: Behavioral and educational strategies for teachers.* Longmont, CO: Sopris West.

Sands, D., & Doll, B. (1996). Fostering self-determination is a developmental task. *Journal of Special Education, 30*(1), 58–76.

Schrumpf, F. (1991). *Peer mediation.* Champaign, IL: Research Press.

Todd, A., Horner, R., & Sugai, G. (1999). Self-monitoring and self-recruited praise. *Journal of Positive Behavioral Interventions, 1*(2), 66–76.

Young, K. R., West, R., Smith, D., & Morgan, D. (1995). *Teaching Self-management strategies to adolescents.* Longmont, CO: Sopris West.

11

Higher-Level Thinking Skills

Ryan, a 15-year-old student with significant behavioral problems, had recently enrolled at a new school. Ryan was reported to have above-average ability but his social skills were very delayed. He was impulsive, and when he was angry, he became both verbally and physically aggressive. One day shortly after his enrollment, the teacher gave Ryan a social studies worksheet. Some of the questions were concrete—Ryan had to read a short selection and answer questions whose answers were found in the text. Other questions asked for Ryan's opinion on an issue. I was in the classroom, checking his work. I noticed that Ryan had completed all the answers that were easily found in the reading passage. However, the questions that required Ryan to express his opinion were left blank. After I praised him for answering the factual questions correctly, I asked Ryan why he left the other questions blank. He looked up and said: "Those questions asked for my opinion—I can't do that."

I wondered if Ryan was pulling my leg or was not used to formulating an opinion. It became apparent that Ryan was simply not used to expressing his opinion. I speculated and suspected that in Ryan's previous schools he was given rote work that required little thinking and that he was not asked for his opinion very often. In fact, most curricula reinforce the premise that the task of a successful student is to learn the content of the course. Most of the content, according to Barrickman (1997), is "knowledge-based information" (p. 6).

ohnson (1992) reported that most teachers are stimulating low-level thinking—recall and comprehension—about 80% of the time. Most school curriculum is by nature fact-oriented rather than thought-oriented; if teachers want their students to learn the curriculum, then they will naturally focus on factual questions.

In this chapter, we discuss what can be done to assure that the Ryans of the world have an opportunity to express opinions and are encouraged to evaluate and synthesize—to develop higher-level thinking skills. As we have stated throughout this text, students with emotional and behavioral disorders need a highly challenging, motivating, and relevant curriculum in order to stimulate their thinking. According to Barrickman (1997): "The realities of today's society require citizens who can be problem solvers—people who can think" (p. 5).

Means, Chelemer, and Knapp (1991) have done research on curricula for educationally disadvantaged students, focusing on the knowledge, skills, and abilities that the child brings to school rather than taking a deficit view of the learner. Coincidentally, the latest IDEA reauthorization calls for a focus in the IEP on the strengths of the student. Means and colleagues believe that we should dismiss the assumption that students cannot meaningfully engage in activities involving advanced skills of comprehension, composition, and reasoning unless they have mastered those so-called basic skills. They recommend that teachers should explicitly and repeatedly model the higher-order intellectual processes they are trying to encourage in their students.

A colleague of an alternative school in an inner city teaches seventh- and eighth-grade students with severe behavioral problems. Students in her class read at the second- and third-grade level. However, every day she puts up a thought-provoking statement or question and asks the students to write an opinion about it. She finds this activity highly motivates the students. Some typical questions are:

Do you think that all schools should require students to wear uniforms? Defend your opinion.

Do you think that newspapers should print the names of juveniles who commit crimes? Defend your opinion.

Do you believe that individuals who are not U.S. citizens should be able to get jobs in this country? Defend your opinion.

The Importance of Critical Thinking

According to Paul (1993), critical thinking is the essential foundation for education because it enables an individual to adapt to the everyday personal, social, and professional demands of the 21st century.

Paul (1993) defined critical thinking as that which is responsive to and guided by intellectual standards such as relevance, accuracy, precision, clarity, depth, and breadth. He names these components as important to critical thinking: (a) purpose, or goal; (b) question at issue, or problem to be solved; (c) point of view, or frame of reference; (d) the empirical dimension of reasoning; (e) the conceptual dimension of reasoning; (f) assumptions; and (g) inferences. He advocates that critical thinking (using these components) be built into all subject areas of the curriculum.

O'Tuel and Bullard (1993) also advocated that the most practical approach to teach thinking skills is to do so in the context of subjects and disciplines that the students in the classroom are studying.

As early as 1977, Dr. Joseph S. Renzulli developed the Schoolwide Enrichment Model referred to by Burns (1990) in *Pathways to Investigative Skills.* This model addresses the needs of a broad group of students who can benefit from enrichment activities and systematic growth in thinking processes.

Bloom's Taxonomy of Thinking

Every day teachers should look closely at the activities that they have planned to assure that they provide more activities in the evaluation and synthesis hierarchy of Bloom's taxonomy of thinking. In Bloom, Englehart, Furst, Hill, and Krathwohl (1956), *Taxonomy of Educational Objectives: The Classification of Educational Goals. Handbook I: Cognitive Domain,* a six-step taxonomy describes the progression of higher levels of cognitive activity:

Knowledge—tell, recite, list, memorize, remember, define, locate. Activities may include doing workbooks, taking quizzes and tests, building vocabulary, and connecting facts in isolation.

Comprehension—restate, give examples, explain, summarize. Activities may include drawing, diagramming, responding to questions, and revising.

Application—demonstrate; use guides, maps, and charts; build; cook. Activities may include using recipes and models, creating artwork, giving demonstrations, and making crafts.

Analysis—investigate, classify, categorize, compare, contrast, solve. Activities may include doing surveys, creating questionnaires, making plans, coming up with solutions, preparing reports, and writing a prospectus.

Evaluation—judge; give opinion or viewpoint; prioritize; recommend; critique. Activities may include making decisions, debating, giving ratings, and writing editorials, and critiques.

Synthesis—compose, design, invest, create, hypothesize. Activities may include lesson planning, writing a song, writing a poem, writing a story, designing an ad, or creating an invention.

Teachers should look at their lesson plans to measure which levels of thinking are required for each activity and analyze what percentage of the day is spent on activities requiring the two highest levels of thinking. The goal for teachers should be to increase that percentage.

Young children are making order out of their world and are learning to classify. Observing or collecting data, describing the data, and classifying that data are important. Young children should be taught to plan, monitor, and evaluate the choices they are given. How can teachers teach them to do these tasks? In all subject areas, teachers should use themes that are general and inclusive rather than specific and limited. For example, rather than creating a unit on bears, the teacher might create a unit on animals that hibernate. The teacher should then decide on important generalizations that the students need to learn—key concepts—and determine which learner outcomes or grade-level competencies the students should experience during the unit. Lastly, the teacher should design instructional activities to be encompassed in the unit and assure that those instructional activities incorporate the highest levels of thinking.

We often read to children and follow the story with questions about what was read. However, there are many activities we could provide for children that would encourage higher-level thinking. Modest and Cymerman (1988) provide examples of activities students might do after the teacher has read *Goldilocks and the Three Bears.*

1. What type of story is *Goldilocks and the Three Bears?*
2. List other fairy tales.
3. Describe Goldilocks.
4. Compare and contrast Goldilocks with the heroine of another fairy tale.
5. Construct a diorama of a scene from the story.
6. Suppose Goldilocks left the house before the three bears came home. How would that have affected the ending? Write a new ending.
7. Debate: Was Goldilocks justified in doing what she did: breaking into someone's home?
8. Construct a mobile showing scenes from the story.
9. Write a diary as if Goldilocks were writing it.
10. Design a board game based on the Goldilock's story.
11. Draw a flow chart tracing the storyline of Goldilocks.
12. Do an improvisational skit.
13. Prepare two newspaper editorials: one defending Goldilock's actions, one criticizing them.

14. You are a reporter: Interview Goldilocks and the bears.
15. Write a commercial advertising the book.
16. Make a filmstrip of the story.
17. If Goldilocks was hungry and lost, what other solutions could she have found to her problems (p. 45).

At the intermediate level, students are developing work and study habits that will last a lifetime. Students at this level should be conceptualizing, inferring, analyzing, organizing, problem solving, and evaluating their decisions. In all subject areas, teachers should once again use themes that are general and inclusive rather than specific and limited. (For example, themes like "marvelous machines" or "Native Americans" can be used.) VanTassel-Baska (1992) offered examples of activities on the topic of marvelous machines:

1. Redesign a machine of today to show how it might look in the year 2010.
2. Develop an idea sheet for a story about being invisible. List five characters, five events, and five settings that you could use in the story.
3. Research the microscope.
4. List advantages and disadvantages of "invisibility" machines.
5. Select a science fiction book to read about a marvelous machine.
6. List three machines (inventions) that are most important to you. Why? How would you change them? What did the three machines look like in 1889? What will the machines look like in 2089.

"Shoe Game" is another example of an activity appropriate for intermediate age students (taken from Kornelly (1990) in *Mind Maneuvers*). Students can work in pairs for the exercise, in which they learn to give precise directions. One student in the pair takes off a shoe. The other student gives directions for putting the shoe back on. The first student, who may ask questions, must follow the directions without watching what he or she is doing. The second student needs to give specific directions and responses. In a follow-up class discussion, students should observe that the more questions were asked, the shorter the time required to complete the task. A similar activity could involve making a peanut butter sandwich.

At the junior and senior high level, students are developing the ability to deal with abstract ideas. They need to focus on expanding their abilities to conceptualize, infer, analyze, create, organize, and evaluate. They need many opportunities to solve problems and make decisions in a broad context. They should develop metacognitive strategies in complex ways and have an increasing awareness of their own mental functioning.

O'Tuel and Bullard (1993) provided a list of activities that can be used in connection to the novel *All Quiet on the Western Front:*

1. Examine the novel's symbols that reflect the effects of the war.

2. Have each student pick a major character and compose a question about each character.
3. Have students compare and contrast two characters of their choice.
4. Have students write a short essay in which they decide which character in the book would make the best or worst friend.
5. Have students work in small groups to develop a commercial about the book.

Kornelly (1990) advocated teaching students the Future Problem Solving Program, an adaptation of a creative problem-solving process developed for business and industry. Students are divided into teams of four, each of which is assigned a problem by the teacher. The team must follow these steps:

1. Research the topic thoroughly.
2. Brainstorm problems related to the situation.
3. Identify an important underlying problem.
4. Brainstorm solutions to the underlying problem.
5. Select criteria for evaluating the solutions.
6. Evaluate solutions to determine the best solution.

Kornelly provided sample problems: acid rain, hazardous waste, AIDs.

Problem-Based Learning

Checkley (1997) described problem-based learning as "an instructional method that uses a real-world problem as the context for an in-depth investigation of core content" (p. 3). She suggests that the problems students tackle are ill-structured, including just enough information to suggest how the students should proceed with an investigation, but never giving enough information to the student to solve the problem. Medical schools have been using such an approach since the 1970s. In that setting, simulations are created that allow students to act as practicing doctors when confronted with a medical question. For example, instead of hearing a lecture on the brain stem, students are presented with a patient who has symptoms that would indicate something was wrong with the brain stem. Before the students are able to give a diagnosis, they have to generate several possibilities, determine what they know about the brain stem, and then search for additional needed information.

Checkley lists examples of problem-based learning activities for students as young as those in the second grade. Her example for older students comes from Indian Trail Junior High School in Addison, Illinois. A video depicting a prom night auto accident is shown to students. Each student is given a folder containing accident reports and a name card identifying them as an inspector. The students have five days to review existing evidence and investigate further. They must then recommend an indictment to the state's attorney's office and notify the press of their findings. Another example Checkley provides came from a teacher at Cary Grove High School in Cary, Illinois. Students receive a letter stating that a volcano in Yellowstone Park is showing signs of activity. If the volcano erupts, the middle third of the United States could be wiped out. Students work in groups to determine the probability that such an event would occur, and they also describe the effect that a major natural disaster would have on jobs and politics in the region. Students could be encouraged to locate information on the Internet.

Ketterling, Ljung, Willis, and Torp (1997) wrote that problem-based learning shatters the vision of the teacher as the dispenser of knowledge and stresses that the teacher provides opportunities for students to construct meaning for themselves. Through problem-based learning, students must define the problem and the criteria for a good solution, research the problem, generate potential solutions, identify the solution that appears to best fit the criteria, and then present the solution to an audience. Summer Sleuths, a program they described, was presented by the Center for Problem-Based Learning at the Illinois Mathematics and Science Academy. A typical problem is reprinted in their article:

> During an assembly a student worker is arrested for tobacco possession and possible sales. This violates school policy. Students and teacher receive a letter and position paper from the ATAC (Aurora Tobacco Action Council), a group urging the adoption of strong—nearly offensive—policies and consequences against tobacco usage among middle grade students by school districts. They also receive a newsletter from the CTU (Citizens for Tobacco Use) championing their view (p. 25).

Assuming they were middle-grade students, the pupils attempted to solve the problem. They became very engaged in the process because, according to the authors of the article, the students saw the problem as real; they owned the problem; they were coached; they worked as a team and collaborated; they used multiple and varied resources; they generated numerous solutions; and they also interacted with others.

Literature Discussion Groups

Methods advocated by Romero and Young (1997) include literature discussion groups and journaling, both of which help students develop inquiry skills by generating questions about what they have read. Literature discussion groups for primary grade students can meet once or twice a week. Intermediate students can meet two or three times each week to discuss a book.

The teacher provides a list of books for the students in order to ensure that the books are age- and grade-appropriate; teachers should look for books in which the primary characters are about the same age as the students in the class. Likewise, it is beneficial to select books that add depth to a current unit. Several books can be introduced by the teacher, and the students can choose one that they wish to read. The students, who read the book independently or ask their parents to assist, record questions they may have. In the group the teacher, as coach and facilitator, demonstrates how to function in a group and how to contribute to the discussion. Romero and Young advocate this approach to teach students to develop responsibility for their own learning.

They also believe that reader-response journals can be a part of the process and can enhance higher-level thinking. Keeping a journal is an excellent writing opportunity that allows students to evaluate what they have read instead of simply repeating knowledge to show comprehension. Students can be encouraged to write about their reactions to important events in the story. This entire approach "highlights the difference between recitation and discussion, helps build inquiring minds, and promotes life-time readers" (p. 16).

DiPillo and Leone (1997) provided another approach to reading that might motivate students with E/BD. They have adapted a strategy originally used for adults in business and industry: "Six Viewing Visors" (p. 18). Students are asked to read controversial nonfiction material from an assigned perspective according to the color of the visor they are given.

1. White visor considers the information read from a factual and objective point of view.
2. Red visor takes into account emotional considerations, responding about feelings involved.
3. Black visor reads in a critical manner (negative but fair and logical).
4. Yellow visor reads in an upbeat and positive manner, finding positive value in the material.
5. Green visor is innovative and creative, looking for a novel perspective.
6. Blue visor oversees the work of other visors.

This excellent activity can be used to analyze articles in newspapers or magazines.

Using Literature for Critical Thinking

Often, as educators, we read to students or have them read a selection and follow-up with questions. Too often our questions concern who, what, where, and how. There are, however, many questions that we could ask beyond these simple ones to encourage students to think critically.

What do you think about . . . ? Why do you say that?

How do you think you would have reacted if you were . . . ? Why?

Does this situation remind you of a similar experience you've had? In what ways?

Do you agree with the outcome of the story? Why or why not?

What did you learn from this story? Why?

Compacting

Winebrenner and Berger (1994) reported that effective teachers find that students differ in the ways they learn best and therefore learn better when teachers vary approaches to learning.

Compacting, a technique recommended for gifted students, can also be an interesting educational opportunity for students with emotional/behavioral disorders. According to the technique, "students who demonstrate previous mastery spend less time with the regular curriculum and more time with extension and enrichment opportunities" (p. 1). I was reminded of the importance of this technique in a classroom for students with E/BD. It became quickly apparent that one student already knew how to do what was being requested and finished very quickly and ahead of the other students. That student became bored and then disruptive.

In such a situation, Winebrenner and Berger (1994) offer the following guidelines. At the beginning of a unit, provide opportunities for interested students to demonstrate mastery through pre-testing. Students who show mastery are then given a list of required concepts, enrichment option, and specified working conditions. For material that cannot be pretested, the teacher should prepare a study guide that includes the same concepts for which all students will be held responsible. Students who have exhibited easy mastery of previous topics will be expected to learn the study guide material but will spend the majority of their time working on extension tasks. The students can then demonstrate to the rest of the class their competence with the required concepts.

Contracts

Winebrenner and Berger (1994) defined contracts as "written agreements between teachers and students that outline what students will learn, how they will learn it, in what period of time, and how they will be evaluated" (p. 1). Contracts give students the opportunity to direct their course of study, which is highly motivating to students with E/BD.

In one part of the contract, the teacher lists the concepts that the whole class will learn. In another section of the contract, the teacher lists a variety of alternative or extension activities from which the students may choose. The student could also develop some suggested activities with teacher approval. Students then work on the alternative activities during the time that the class is learning concepts that the student has already mastered. Students have to document their time by keeping a log of their activities or another means that the teacher may choose. Students then present their project to the class.

Media Literacy

Lantieri (1997) wrote about media violence and methods of teaching media literacy skills. She believes that images from the media bombard children so rapidly that they do not have time to sort through the real messages behind the images. According to Lantieri, we should teach children to think about the messages that are conveyed. She points to activities that can be used to generate higher-level thinking skills in this area. These activities are based on a videotape the teacher makes of three commercials seen on TV. Ask the students to write the methods that are used by advertisers to entice people to buy their products. Discuss their lists. Ask them to consider the allure of the objects seen on TV and why they seem so appealing. She also suggests discussing inferences after viewing advertisements.

Encouraging Higher-Level Thinking Through Questioning

John Dewey (as quoted by Johnson (1992)) said: "To Think is to Question." Johnson summarized the previous work, stating that only 20% of teachers' questions require students to think while approximately 60% of the questions require factual recall, and 20% are procedural in nature. She stated that most teachers stimulate low-level thinking. She believes that one good question can trigger a fascinating chain reaction in the human brain—a reaction that stimulates the production of many more ideas, then more questions, more ideas, and so on. Questions teach effective communication, which then stimulate more questions, which then enhance a positive self-concept, which then stimulates more questions that promote intellectual curiosity, which then stimulates more questions. Johnson provides a hierarchy of questions, beginning with those that require high-level thinking and ending with those requiring low-level thinking.

> Level 5: What would happen if . . . ?
> Level 4: Predictions/projections for the future.
> Level 3: How come . . . ?
> Level 2: Why . . . ? I wonder why . . . ?
> Level 1: Who? What? Where? When?

She reported that students believe that the higher-level questions are fun. When such questions are asked, the student can let go of rigid thinking patterns and open their minds. Johnson (1990) provides some examples:

What if humans had x-ray eyes?
What would happen if all of a sudden you could not speak English?
What would happen if your sneakers had wings?
What would happen if you could trade places with your parents?
What would happen if human beings had to sleep standing up? (p. 27)

A self-monitoring technique that she offers for the teacher to use in determining the types of questions he or she asks during a lesson is to place a tape recorder on the desk and actually record the lesson. Play the tape recorder back and record the number of questions that were asked at each level.

Our goal in education should be to teach students to be lifetime thinkers. By following some of the suggestions provided in this chapter, the teacher can meet this critical goal. As stated well by Means, Chelemer, and Knapp (1991), educators must consider the world onto which their students will emerge. That world requires the kind of advanced skills that are discussed in this chapter.

Discussion Questions

1. Think back to the last classroom you observed. Estimate the percentage of time that was spent in higher-level thinking activities.
2. Why do you think that many teachers do not utilize higher-level thinking activities in their classrooms?
3. Think of at least five questions that could be used to engage higher-level thinking processes.

References

Armstrong, T. (1994). *Multiple intelligences in the classroom.* Alexandria, VA: Association for Supervision and Curriculum Development.

Barrickman, D. (1997). Challenging all students to THINK. *The Delta Kappa Gamma Bulletin, 63*(2), 5–11.

Bloom, B., Englehart, M., Furst, E., Hill, W., & Krathwohl, D. (1956). *Taxonomy of educational objectives. The classification of educational goals. Handbook I: Cognitive domain.* New York: Longmans Green.

Burns, D. (1990). *Pathways to investigative skills.* Mansfield Center, CT: Creative Learning Press.

Checkley, K. (1997, Summer). Problem-based learning: The search for solutions to life's messy problems. *Association for Supervision and Curriculum Development Curriculum Update,* 197179, 1–8.

Curry, J., Samara, J., & Rogers, W. (1990). *Gifted education unit.* Atlanta, GA: Georgia Dept. of Education.

Dantonio, M. (1990). *How can we create thinkers.* Bloomington, IN: National Educational Service.

DiPillo, M. L., & Leone, S. (1997). Meeting the standards: Strategies for developing critical thinking. *The Delta Kappa Gamma Bulletin, 63*(2), 17–21, 28.

Johnson, N. (1990). *Questioning makes the difference.* Beavercreek, OH: Pieces of Learning.

Johnson, N. (1992). *Thinking is the key.* Beavercreek, OH: Creative Learning Consultants.

Ketterling, G., Ljung, E., Willis, Y., & Torp, L. (1997). Summer sleuths: Investigating problem-based learning and scientific literacy. *Illinois School Research and Development Journal, 33*(2), 25–29.

Kornelly, D. (1990). *Mind maneuvers.* Longmont, CO: Sopris West.

Lantieri, L. (1997). Waging peace in our homes: Battling media violence. *Reaching Today's Youth: The Community Circle of Caring Journal, 1*(3), 50–53.

Means, B., Chelemer, C., & Knapp, M. (1991). *Teaching advanced skills to at-risk students.* San Francisco: Jossey-Bass.

Modest, D., & Cymerman, S. (1988). *Sage teacher training and implementation manual.* Longmont, CO: Sopris West.

O'Tuel, F., & Bullard, R. (1993). *Developing higher order thinking in the content areas K-12.* Pacific Grove, CA: Critical Thinking Press and Software.

Paul, R. (1984). Critical thinking: Fundamental to education for a free society. *Educational Leadership, 42*(1), 4–14.

Paul, R. (1993). *Critical thinking.* Santa Rosa, CA: Foundation for Critical Thinking.

Renzulli, J. (1977). The enrichment triad model: A plan for developing defensible programs for the gifted and talented. *Gifted and Talented Quarterly, 21*(22), 227–233.

Romero, L., & Young, Susan. (1997). Promoting higher-level thinking skills through the use of literature discussion groups and journaling. *Delta Kappa Gamma Bulletin, 63*(2), 12–16.

VanTassel-Baska, J. (1992). *Planning effective curriculum for gifted learners.* Denver: Love.

Winebrenner, S. (1992). *Teaching gifted kids in the regular classroom.* Minneapolis, MN: Free Spirit.

Winebrenner, S. and Berger, S. (1994). Providing curriculum alternatives to motivate gifted students. *ERIC Digest.* Reston, VA: Council for Exceptional Children Clearinghouse on Disabilities and Gifted Education.

12

Learning Strategies and Study Skills

Gerald is a bright nine-year-old boy who is highly impulsive, distracted, disorganized, and irritable as well as physically and verbally aggressive. Upon entering the classroom, I immediately noticed messy clothes and a disorganized desk area. One hour after his arrival in the classroom, he had already packed his coat, balled up pieces of writing paper, his lunch, and more into the storage area of his desk. He seemed to have no idea that coats are hung on the hooks in the back of the classroom and that discarded paper is put in the wastepaper basket. He fumbled to find things in his desk and frequently failed to find what he was looking for. He often became frustrated and angry.

Kevin is a bright seven-year-old boy who knows the concepts and basic facts of addition and subtraction. Despite his ability in this area, when given an addition problem, such as 25 + 23, he writes 12 (2 + 5 + 2 + 3); for 45 + 24, he writes 15 (4 + 5 + 2 + 4). Kevin has serious problems with spatial relationships. Despite his intelligence, left and right mean nothing to him and neither do north, south, east, and west. Upon finding out that he has made errors in math or when confused about his orientation in space, he becomes agitated, angry, and at times even out of control.

Susan is a bright twelve-year-old girl who has a good sight-word vocabulary but understands less than half of what she reads of even simple text. She seems to read without knowing that textual understanding by a reader and an audience is to be expected. When asked comprehension questions on the text she has just read, she answers only the most elementary ones correctly. She becomes anxious and agitated about reading and often refuses to complete her assignments.

he academic and behavioral problems of children and adolescents with emotional and behavioral disorders go on and on. What can an observant and astute teacher do to teach Gerald, Kevin, and Susan? The answer does not lie in giving them more and longer assignments, somehow expecting that practice will make perfect. For these children, it will not. Placing these students in strict behavior management programs, which require them to cooperate in the classroom, at best will serve to teach compliance and at worst will fail to provide the students with the strategies and skills they really need in order to learn.

Many students with learning disabilities and behavioral disorders lack organizational skills that are essential to learning. These deficits become evident when students cannot engage in such self-organizing tasks as checking, monitoring, planning, testing, revising, and evaluating their academic and social behaviors. Learning and solving problems in the school setting, therefore, poses great difficulties for them. Some students may become so discouraged that they stop trying to learn. School failure often results.

The Database of Learning Strategies

Many teachers have been successful in teaching students how to use learning strategies. The database in support of the use of learning strategies by students with learning disabilities and behavioral disorders is extensive (Day & Hackett, 1996; Forness, Kavale, Blum, & Lloyd, 1997; Harris & Pressley, 1991; Lambert, 2000; Leal & Rafoth, 1991; Leon & Carretero, 1995; Swanson & Hoskyn, 1998). Data support the use of learning strategies for students with a variety of characteristics, for a variety of purposes, as well as a variety of age groups. For example, recent literature indicates support for the use of learning strategies to develop the math skills of adolescents with learning and behavioral problems (Jolivette, Wehby, & Hirsch, 1999; Mastropieri, Sweda, & Scruggs, 2000), to facilitate the inclusion of middle school students into general education classrooms (Rose, 1999), and to teach reading skills to first graders (Mathes, Grek, Howard, Babyak, & Allen, 1999). Strategies have been used to head off learning and behavioral problems of some students (Kamps, Kravits, Stolze, & Swaggart (1999) as well as remediate the problems of others (Lebzelter, & Nowacek, 1999). Teachers who use learning strategies may be confident that the intervention they are using rests on a solid and highly respected database, which began in the 1970s and continues to be developed today.

How to Teach Learning Strategies

During learning strategy instruction teachers act as models for students by assisting them in the development of a structure for their thinking. Learning strategy instruction focuses on what is modifiable and on the development of conscious and active rule creation and rule following (Bos & Vaughn, 1998; Deshler & Lenz, 1989). Learning strategies involve the use of a carefully organized sequence of steps. For example, when teaching students about standards for written papers a teacher might use the HOW strategy. The HOW strategy focuses a student's attention on:

H: Heading
O: Organized
W: Written neatly

Each step in the strategy is taught specifically and step-by-step. When organizing assignments, students learn what is included in the heading: their name, date, title, and page numbers. They then focus on what is involved in being organized, such as rules about margins, spacing, and writing on one side of the paper, and so on. Writing neatly involves writing on the line and neatly erasing or crossing out. When given a learning strategy like HOW, students have a tool that guides them on how to begin a task as well as a tool for understanding and addressing the standards for its successful completion.

When using learning strategies, students learn by posing questions to themselves and by challenging their own assumptions. Disorganized learners begin to approach learning tasks in an organized manner. Teachers act as models and interrogators of students' thinking, and they plan for and use activities that develop and strengthen students' learning. As students self-regulate, control eventually becomes more internalized, and the teacher's level of participation diminishes.

When planning learning strategies, it is important to begin each step of a learning strategy with a verb. This facilitates the students' accurate and active response at each step of the strategy. The wording of learning strategies must be simple and brief. The first letters of key words in learning strategies make a mnemonic, which focuses students on the desired behavior. The steps in a strategy are task-specific and not situation- or content-specific.

Gerald's problems with disorganization carry over into other areas of his life. In order to maximize his potential in school and beyond, he needs to learn organization skills. He needs to learn a strategy that will help him to put things in their own place. He needs a strategy that will help him to stop and think before he pushes his coat, books, lunch, and more into his desk storage area. He needs a strategy that will help him to think about where the wastepaper and other items belong. A strategy that might be useful for Gerald is Stop, Think, and Place (STP). He could be taught to stop when he is about to put personal items away. Then he could be taught to think about the best place to put the particular item. Following this, he could be taught to place the item where it belongs. For example, clothes are stored in closets or on coat hangers, books may be stored in the desk storage area, and wastepaper belongs in the wastepaper basket. A teacher who teaches Gerald organization strategies will give him tools that he will benefit from now and in the future.

Likewise, Kevin needs strategies to help him orient himself in space. He knows his math facts but he often gets a zero on his assignments. Giving him more exercises in mathematics or rewarding or punishing him will fall short of what Kevin really needs in order to learn. An astute teacher will note his difficulty with left and right and with directions and may point out that the answers Kevin provides are correct if addition of the numbers were the only priority. However, he must learn to add the units and the tens and refrain from adding all the digits together. A strategy that Kevin might use is to draw a line between the tens and the units and ask himself, "Where do I start?" Following this strategy, Kevin would then add the units first and proceed to add the tens. By teaching Kevin strategies, a teacher will give him tools for coping with the demands of learning in the school setting and tools for coping with life beyond the school setting.

Despite her knowledge of vocabulary, Susan has major trouble with reading. She already dreads reading lessons and expects to fail when asked reading comprehension questions. Like Gerald and Kevin, Susan needs a strategy such as

R: Read a paragraph
A: Ask yourself, "What is the main idea and details?"
P: Paraphrase the content of the paragraph

This strategy, known as RAP, helps students to glean meaning from text. RAP has been used successfully by Deschler, Ellis, & Lenz (1996) at the University of Kansas to teach students to become more efficient readers. After learning how to use the RAP strategy, Susan has a life skill that she will benefit from, not only in the classroom but whenever she reads within and outside of the classroom environment.

Teaching Learning Strategies

Teaching students with emotional and behavioral disorders to use learning strategies designed to address their academic and social deficits requires an organized and concerted effort. Teachers must employ a sequence of steps in order to develop the students' ability to use the strategy.

The four core teaching procedures that constitute strategy development are modeling, role-playing, performance feedback, and generalization training. Modeling is a demonstration of the use of a strategy. During role-playing, the teacher acts out the strategy to teach the student how it is used. Performance feedback is offered by the teacher after the student learns the strategy. Finally, during generalization training, teachers show students how to use specific strategies beyond the training setting.

A sequence of eight stages of instruction are involved in teaching a learning strategy. (These steps will be illustrated with an example.) This strategy will assist students when they need to memorize or study something carefully. A teacher can teach this and other learning strategies to a single student in a one-on-one setting or to a group of students. We will call it the RCRC learning strategy:

R: Read
C: Cover
R: Recite
C: Check

Stage 1: Give Pretest and Make Commitments

Phase 1: Orientation and pretest
Phase 2: Awareness and commitment

By using a pretest, teachers establish the needs of a particular student or group of students. The results of the pretest will indicate the level of difficulty the student or students are having. A student might have correct answers to 20% or 30% of questions asked by the teacher. It is very important to show the student the outcome of the pretest in order to build the student's awareness that indeed this is an area of difficulty. A discussion between the teacher and the student about the difficulty of the task may follow. Then having done the pretest and shared the results, the teacher and the student make a commitment to work on this problem. This commitment is very important as it serves to motivate and focus the student's energy to learn the new strategy.

Stage 2: Describe the Strategy

Phase 1: Orientation and overview
Phase 2: Present strategy and remembering system

When describing the strategy, the teacher provides an overview of the strategy, which is designed to address the specific learning needs of a student or group of students. In our example, the teacher might have a card with RCRC written on it along with the words each letter introduces. At this point the students will understand the strategy and will comprehend the purpose of each step in the sequence. The teacher will discuss the remembering system employed in this strategy and thereby facilitate the students' recall of the four letters in the strategy.

CHAPTER 12

Stage 3: Model the Strategy

Phase 1: Orientation
Phase 2: Presentation
Phase 3: Student enlistment

At stage three the teacher models the use of the strategy by actually taking a piece of text and reading one, two, three, or four sentences. The teacher may read the sentences more than once. The students observe the teacher use the first part of the learning strategy, and the teacher may point this out to the students. The teacher may say, "Now let me show you how to use the RCRC learning strategy. First, the R says read, read a certain amount of text and reread it if necessary." The teacher proceeds to cover the sentences with a hand and recites what has been read. Finally, the teacher demonstrates checking to make sure that he or she has remembered the content in the text accurately. Next, the teacher asks the students if they are willing to learn this strategy and use it when they need to memorize something or study something carefully. It is important that the students are clearly eager to learn the strategy and that they appreciate its potential as a learning tool for them.

Stage 4: Verbal Elaboration and Rehearsal

Phase 1: Verbal elaboration
Phase 2: Verbal rehearsal

In the verbal elaboration and rehearsal stage, the teacher and students talk at length about the strategy in search of full understanding of the meaning and use of it. They discuss the meaning of words, specific areas that pose difficulty for them, and they affirm the importance of each step in the strategy. For example, the teacher explains the importance of the purpose of the strategy by such statements as, "When reading it is often important to know the precise meaning of some words and to use the text to learn this meaning." Other such statements can be made. Furthermore, the teacher and students will then rehearse the steps in the strategy RCRC. The teacher leads this phase by asking such questions as, "What is the first step in the RCRC strategy?" Continue on until each step is rehearsed as many times as the student might need in order to understand the strategy fully.

Stage 5: Controlled Practice and Feedback

Phase 1: Orientation and overview
Phase 2: Guided practice
Phase 3: Independent practice

At this stage the teacher and students are focused on the memorization of the learning strategy. The teacher and students again discuss the purpose of the learning strategy. The teacher makes it clear to the students that the strategy will be useful when engaging in specific academic tasks. The students indicate their understanding of the contribution of this strategy to their academic efforts and guided practice will begin. The teacher is focused on teaching the students to remember what RCRC prompts them to do while reading text. Memorization of the strategy is the goal.

Stage 6: Advanced Practice and Feedback

Phase 1: Orientation and overview
Phase 2: Guided practice
Phase 3: Independent practice

At this stage the teacher and students continue to work on understanding the purpose of the strategy and memorizing each step in its use. The students and teacher continue to talk about the strategy and practice its use. The students are growing in understanding, use, and familiarity with the strategy. They may even change the strategy to fit their own purposes. They may add a new step; they may delete one.

Stage 7: Confirm Acquisition and Make Generalizations

Phase 1: Confirm and celebrate
Phase 2: Forecast and commit to generalization

At this point the students know the strategy and clearly indicate that they do. They can use the strategy, and they can communicate the value of knowing this set of steps when learning. Together the student and teacher forecast and commit to the use of the learning strategy in other areas of the curriculum. For example, the RCRC strategy can be useful in reading comprehension and when studying science, social studies, and other subject areas. By using this strategy, students understand that text comprehension, concepts, and vocabulary are more accessible to them.

Stage 8: Generalization

Phase 1: Orientation
Phase 2: Activation
Phase 3: Adaptation
Phase 4: Maintenance

In this final stage, students focus on the task at hand and link it to the appropriate learning strategy. That is, they are aware of the task demands and can recall the strategy that will address the requirements of the task. They will also be aware that the task may require changing the strategy by adding to it or deleting from it. For example, they may add a step, such as W: Write, which requires students to write down vocabulary or short definitions. Thus, the strategy then becomes RCRCW. Likewise, a student may decide to shorten the strategy to RCR when it will suffice to read, cover, and recite the content just read. At this stage the students are making their own versions of the strategies they are learning, using them across settings, adapting them, and maintaining them over time.

Tips for Maximizing Learning Strategy Instruction

Before instruction, it is important that the teacher carefully select the skill or strategy that will be taught. The academic or social task the student is trying to accomplish and the strategy must match in a clear and logical manner. At this point the teacher provides the students with a clear rationale for why and how the skill or strategy will be useful. It is important for the teacher to discuss, in a direct manner, when and where the strategy can be employed by students. Finally, it is important for the teacher to gain a commitment from students that they are interested in learning the strategy. Open dialog about the use, role, and importance of learning strategies is important with students who have learning disabilities and behavioral disorders. The teacher cannot assume that the students will understand, appreciate, or use learning strategies unless this issue is addressed in a direct manner.

During instruction it is important that students really understand and fully master the learning strategy. Talk about why, when, and where the skill can be applied. Many students with learning disabilities and behavioral disorders will not understand the usefulness of learning strategies unless it is clearly presented to them. During instruction, the teacher may also facilitate the students' learning by pointing out cues that signal the use of a particular strategy. For example, the word "memorize" might indicate the use of the RCRC strategy, whereby a student reads a piece of text once, twice, or even more often, then covers the text while reciting specific aspects of what has been read and finally, checks for accuracy.

After instruction, it is important that a teacher tell students they are expected to use the newly learned strategy. It may be necessary for the teacher to remind the students to use the strategy when completing their academic tasks. Following instruction, it is also important for a teacher to review the strategies that the students have learned periodically in order to ensure accurate use of each step in the sequence. Teachers might also provide opportunities for students to use and practice the strategies they are learning. They might check students' use of specific strategies in other environments and continue to discuss why, when, and where specific strategies may be useful. Teachers must not assume that the students want to and actually do use the strategies they have acquired. Therefore, teachers must continue to receive such evidence from students.

After students use a specific learning strategy, it is important that teachers provide them with feedback on their performance. Students might also be guided by teachers to engage in self-evaluation and self-monitoring of their strategy use. Finally, when teachers have an opportunity to work in collaboration, it might be very helpful to inform other teachers about the strategies that students have been taught. In this way, teachers can reinforce the strategies that they know students have been taught.

Conclusions

The words used and the steps outlined in learning strategies are largely governed by the unique individual learning needs of children and adolescents. Learning strategies are the products of teachers' and students' creativity. For example, a learning strategy for completing daily assignments might be:

Plan it
Complete it
Check it
Turn it in!

The teacher and the student will learn the steps involved in each step of the strategy. The teacher will show students how to use the strategy by instructing them while using the eight stages described above. It is important for teachers to know that students must be taught to use learning strategies in a step-by-step manner. Describing the strategy to a student alone will not bring about its use.

When teachers instruct a student or a group of students on how to preview the content of an expository chapter, they may use the Warm-Up strategy, which involves teaching students to read the title and introduction of a chapter. Then students could be instructed to examine the chapter headings and subheadings. Next, students can be taught to read the chapter summary and the questions following the chapter. The last step would involve saying to oneself, "This chapter will talk about _____." By using the Warm-Up strategy, students will have a plan for how to approach a reading task and thereby increase the probability that the content of the chapter will make sense. Again, the Warm-Up strategy must be taught by teachers and learned by students. It will not suffice merely to tell students about the strategy and expect them to use it.

A final example is a strategy for proofreading that can be used by students before they turn in assignments. They can examine each sentence by using these four checking steps. First, check to make sure the sentence makes sense. Second, check the capital letters. Third, check the punctuation, and finally, check the spelling. When teaching this strategy, explain how to conduct each step. For example, some students will need specific instructions on how to check spelling. They may need to look for the correct spelling of a word in the assignment, in the textbook, or in the glossary of the textbook. If they cannot find the word, they may be instructed to underline the word and ask for assistance with the word when the assignment is complete.

Learning strategies give students tools for learning. They help them create order where there is disorder. They give them a way to approach a task that otherwise might be impossible for them to accomplish. Learning strategies make explicit for some students what is implicit for others. They might be the only hope some students have for accomplishing tasks that inherently expose their greatest weaknesses in the school setting and beyond.

Discussion Questions

1. Describe learning strategies. Provide an example of a learning strategy a teacher might use in a classroom for students with emotional and behavioral disorders.
2. Explain the steps involved in teaching a learning strategy to one student or to a group of students. Provide an example to illustrate each stage in the teaching process.
3. What is the underlying rationale that supports the use of learning strategies? How might you explain the use of learning strategies to someone who never heard of teaching students in this manner?
4. What additional resources, materials, knowledge might you use to develop your understanding and use of learning strategies?

References

Bos, C. S., & Vaughn, S. (1998). *Strategies for teaching students with learning and behavior problems* (4th ed.). Boston: Allyn & Bacon.

Day, V. P., & Hackett, G. S. (1996). LEARN to succeed. *Teaching Exceptional Children, 29,* 70–71.

Deshler, D. D., Ellis, E. S., & Lenz, B. K. (1996). *Teaching adolescents with learning disabilities: Strategies and methods.* Denver, CO: Love.

Deshler, D. D., & Lenz, B. K. (1989). The strategies instructional approach. *International Journal of Disability, Development and Education, 36,* 203–224.

Forness, S. R., Kavale, K. A., Blum, I. M., & Lloyd, J. W. (1997). Meta-analysis of meta-analyses: What works in special education and related services. *Teaching Exceptional Children, 29,* 4–9.

Harris, K. R., & Pressley, M. (1991). The nature of cognitive strategy instruction: Interactive strategy construction. *Exceptional Children, 57,* 392–404.

Jolivette, K., Wehby, J. H., & Hirsch, L. (1999). Academic strategy identification for students exhibiting inappropriate classroom behaviors. *Behavioral Disorders, 24,* 210–221.

Kamps, D., Kravits, T., Stolze, J., & Swaggart, B. (1999). Prevention strategies for at-risk students and students with E/BD in urban elementary schools. *Journal of Emotional and Behavioral Disorders, 7,* 178–188.

Lambert, M. A. (2000). Tips for teaching: Using cognitive and metacognitive learning strategies in the classroom. *Preventing School Failure, 44,* 81–82.

Leal, L., & Rafoth, M. A. (1991). Memory strategy development: What teachers do makes a difference. *Intervention in School and Clinic, 26,* 234–237.

Lebzelter, S., & Nowacek, E. J. (1999). Reading strategies for secondary students with mild disabilities. *Intervention in School and Clinic, 34,* 212–219.

Leon, J. A., & Carretero, M. (1995). Intervention in comprehension and memory strategies: Knowledge and use of text structure. *Learning and Instruction, 5,* 203–220.

Mastropieri, M. A., Sweda, J., & Scruggs, T. E. (2000). Putting mnemonic strategies to work in an inclusive classroom. *Learning Disabilities Research & Practice, 15,* 69–74.

Mathes, P. G., Grek, M. L., Howard, J. K, Babyak, A. E., & Allen, S. H. (1999). Peer-assisted learning strategies for first-grade readers: A tool for preventing early reading failure. *Learning Disabilities Research and Practice, 14,* 50–60.

Rose, T. D. (1999). Middle school teachers: Using individualized instruction strategies. *Intervention in School and Clinic, 34,* 137–142, 162.

Swanson, H. L., & Hoskyn, M. (1998). Experimental intervention research on students with learning disabilities: A meta-analysis of treatment outcomes. *Review of Educational Research, 68,* 277–321.

PART FIVE

Focus on Partnerships

13

Access to the General Curriculum

Jamie is a sixth grader in an instructional classroom for students with emotional and behavioral disorders. He has a significant learning disability in the area of auditory memory. He loves to do social studies in his E/BD classroom. His teacher wants to integrate him into the regular sixth-grade classroom for social studies but she is undecided because she knows that the sixth-grade teacher likes to lecture and that Jamie requires additional visual cues. She is not sure what she should do.

he focus of IDEA 97 and its accompanying regulations is access to the general curriculum. At the same time the law continues to define special education as specially designed instruction. The E/BD teacher must strike a balance between access to general curriculum when it is appropriate for the student and provision of specialized instruction to meet the individualized needs of the student.

The Mandates of IDEA 97

IDEA 97 states: "Over 20 years of research and experience has demonstrated that the education of children with disabilities can be made more effective by having high expectations for such children and ensuring their access in the general curriculum to the maximum extent possible" (20 U.S.C. Chapter 33, part A, Section 1400[c][5][A]. In the evaluation process, Section 1414(a)(2) states that

> school personnel . . . shall (A) use a variety of assessment tools and strategies to gather relevant functional and developmental information, including information provided by the parent, that may assist in determining whether the child is a child with a disability and the content of the child's individualized education program, including information related to enabling the child to be involved in and progress in the general curriculum or, for preschool children, to participate in appropriate activities.

Once the evaluation is conducted and the child has been identified as in need of special education, the IEP is developed. The IEP must include a statement of how the child's disability affects the child's involvement and progress in the general curriculum. Goals and benchmarks, or short-term objectives, are then developed and designed to enable the child to be involved in and progress in the general curriculum. Although IDEA 97 does not define the general curriculum, the accompanying regulation, Sec. 300.347 of the IDEA Regulations (Federal Register, 1999), defines the general curriculum as the same curriculum as for nondisabled children.

Special education is defined in Section 1401(25): "The term 'special education' means specially designed instruction, at no cost to parents, to meet the unique needs of a child with a disability, including (A) instruction conducted in the classroom, in the home, in hospitals and institutions, and in other settings; and (B) instruction in physical education."

Does access to the general curriculum mean that the instruction must be delivered in the regular classroom? The law clearly delineates that access is to content, not necessarily placement.

The least restrictive environment is defined by 20 U.S.C. 1412(a)(5)(A) as: "To the maximum extent appropriate, children with disabilities, including children in public or private institutions or other care facilities, are educated with children who are not disabled, and special classes, separate schooling, or other removal of children with disabilities from the regular educational environment occurs only when the nature or severity of the disability of a child is such that education in regular classes with the use of supplementary aids and services cannot be achieved satisfactorily."

Implementation of Access

In a tribute to Sam Kirk, often called the "Father of Special Education," Minskoff (1998) referred to his answer to the question "What's special about special education?" Kirk always identified the use of individualized instruction in which methods and materials were adapted to a child based on a thorough diagnosis of the child's abilities and disabilities. Kirk's view of the special education approach, according to Minskoff, is the opposite of the general education approach in which all children, despite their individual learning characteristics, are taught the same content at the same level using the same instructional methods and materials. As Minskoff stated: "He believed that all children have the same right to an education, but not to the same education. Children deserve the education that best suits their unique needs" (p. 20). Fuchs and Fuchs (1995) answered the question "What's special about special education?" by referring to its "intensive data-based focus on individual students" (p. 528).

As we investigate the requirement for students with disabilities to have access to the general curriculum, the "I" in the IEP must be the priority. The balance is between homogenization seen most often in the general education classroom and individualization based on the diagnostic-prescriptive approach seen in special education.

The following are the possible options to be considered in balancing the general curriculum with individualized needs.

1. Can the student utilize the general curriculum in some or all subject areas and do so with no accommodations in the regular classroom setting? For example, the student with E/BD may have a strength in math, may be able to do math work with no accommodations, and may be able to function during that time in the regular classroom setting. We must address a student's strengths and therefore would want to assure that the student must be provided the opportunity to "shine." This is an opportunity for success for the student.

2. Can the student benefit from the content of the general curriculum within the regular classroom but need accommodations to be successful in that

environment? For instance, a student may be able to participate in the general education social studies classroom, is able to do the written work, and benefits from the verbal classroom instruction. However, the student has a deficit in auditory memory and needs to have the lecture material taped so that he can hear it more than once. The classroom teacher may utilize learning strategies within the context of the regular classroom. Strategies such as SLANT, PIRATES, and PACER may be taught by the classroom teacher or by both the classroom teacher and the E/BD teacher. SLANT is a strategy for class participation (Edge Enterprises, 2000, p. 2):

S it up
L isten
A ctivate your thinking
N od
T rack the talker.

PIRATES is a test taking strategy (Deshler, Ellis, & Lenz, 1996):

P repare to succeed
I nspect the instructions
R ead, remember, reduce
A nswer or abandon
T urn back
E stimate
S urvey. (p. 251)

PACER is another test taking strategy (Lapansky, 1991):

P: Preview the test
A: Arrange your time
C: Look for Clue words
E: Do the Easy questions first
R: Review the test before turning it in.

3. Can the student benefit from the content of the general curriculum but need that content provided through direct, specialized instruction within a smaller setting and with one-on-one instruction? For instance, if the regular classroom teacher uses lecture material, which the student is unable to benefit from because of a significant auditory memory deficit and a high degree of distractibility, then the special educator may provide specialized instruction, utilizing visual aids, decreased work at one time, and additional hands-on activities to learn the content. Another student, for example, may have a significant visual memory deficit and needs to learn multiplication facts. It may be appropriate to teach the student to utilize a calculator to do problems that involve multiplication.

A recent study of IEPs for students with mild disabilities in resource and inclusive programs (Espin, Deno, and Albayrak-Kaymak, 1998) suggested that programming for students in resource models is more individually designed than it is for students in inclusive models. Those IEPs allocated more time for service and included more long-range goals than did the IEPs written for students in inclusive programs. Smith and Simpson (1989) and Smith (1990) found that placement in less restrictive settings led to less individualized programming. Given all these findings we must recognize the importance of specialized instruction.

4. Does the student need a "parallel" curriculum? Suppose a student is in the eighth grade and the content of social studies at the eighth grade level is the U.S. Constitution. Some of the concepts are too complex for the student to grasp. The student can in fact learn the basics of the U.S. Constitution but needs a different set of materials to cover the content of the material. A wide variety of high-interest, low vocabulary materials are available from publishers.

Although the subject matter curriculum parallels the general education curriculum, instruction must be differentiated to meet the student's individual needs for pacing of instruction, amounts of guided practice tests, and grading standards. The teacher utilizes specialized instruction with different texts and provides different ways of presenting the information.

5. Is the content of the general curriculum inappropriate for the student and does the student need a functional alternative curriculum? For example, the content of a high school world history class may not be a priority for a particular student; rather, that student may need to learn how to get around in the community, utilizing the public transportation system. Or a student may have a significant memory deficit and be unable to learn multiplication facts. It may be appropriate for that student to learn to utilize a calculator to complete multiplication operations.

Remember that a purpose of IDEA is to prepare students for employment and independent living. Section 1400(d)(1)(A) states that the purposes of this title are "to ensure that all children with disabilities have available to them a free appropriate public education that emphasizes special education and related services designed to meet their unique needs and prepare them for employment and independent living." Using these five options, teachers should have high expectations for achievement, should teach for generalization, provide appropriate feedback, and teach students to become independent learners.

Likewise because of the word "individualized" in the IEP, student needs will vary according to specific courses. For example, Bill (a fifth grader) may have a significant reading disability but may like math and excel in math facts and concepts. He may be successful in math in the general classroom with accommodations—specifically, word problems are read to him by an aide in the classroom. However, his language arts must be provided to him in a specialized setting with direct specialized instruction.

Universal Design for Learning

A very promising practice designed to assure students with special needs access to the general curriculum is universal design for learning (UDL). This term was originally used in the field of architecture and is based on the premise that rather than redesigning something after it is in existence, it is better to assure accessibility by design from the very beginning. As Pisha and Coyne (2001) state: "Just as the curb cut improves access for everyone, curricula and materials that embrace elements of UDL can be expected to improve outcomes for all learners" (p. 198).

Universal design for learning suggests that with technology, flexible curricula and materials that accommodate each student's idiosyncratic patterns of styles, strengths, weaknesses, interests, and background knowledge can be designed. While using text on paper—where one size has to fit all—makes many tasks impossible, emerging multimedia technologies allow students to construct and monitor their own learning. The classroom computer, for example, can hold a complete textbook in electronic form and has software that allows for adaptations.

According to Orkwis and McLane (1998), the curriculum must provide three essential qualities of universal design for learning: (1) multiple means of representation, (2) multiple means of expression, and (3) multiple means of engagement (p. 11). Digital format is the most flexible means for presenting curricular materials because material can be customized, easily changed and recordable.

CAST is the Center for Applied Special Technology, which has been developing materials over the past several years. In a cooperative agreement with the U.S. Department of Education's Office of Special Programs, CAST has established the National Center on Accessing the General Curriculum. The Center provides a vision of how new curricula, teaching practices, and policies can be put together to create practical approaches for access to the general curriculum for students with disabilities.

Teachers wanting to keep up with the latest materials developed utilizing universal design principles should access the following website: http://www.cast.org/ncac.

Learning Standards

With the push toward academic standards throughout the country, teachers have the additional challenge of focusing on standards for students within special education—exhibiting that our goals and objectives on the IEP address the access to the general curriculum via the statewide goals and learning standards. During the IEP process, goals and objectives are written to address the deficit areas of the student. Jane, a sixth grader with emotional and behavioral disorders, has a significant written expression deficit but has strengths in the entire auditory area. The special education teacher is working with Jane to verbally relate her ideas into a tape recorder and then to type those ideas by computer after listening to the tape as many times as needed. The learning standard for all students at the sixth grade level is to compose well-organized and coherent writing for specific purposes and to communicate ideas in writing to accomplish a variety of purposes.

Let's take another example. Joey, a third grader with emotional and behavioral disorders, also has significant visual and auditory memory deficits. His special education teacher wants to teach him to use mnemonic devices to learn facts. One of the goals on Joey's IEP is to teach Joey to use mnemonic devices to learn the earth's physical systems. The state standard is to analyze and explain characteristics and interactions of the earth's physical systems. The teacher of students with emotional and behavioral disorders will need to work collaboratively to assure that the content of the general curriculum is addressed while meeting the individualized needs of the student. The general education teacher brings to the IEP the knowledge of the general curriculum and the learning standards expected of students at particular grade levels; the special education teacher brings to the IEP the specific individualized needs of the students and the specialized techniques and strategies to meet those needs.

In regard to planning for academic instruction and necessary instructional modifications for a student with a disability in a regular classroom, Hogan (1999) stated "The match between the learning characteristics of the student and the demands of the classroom setting is the key consideration." The general educator and the special educator together plan adaptations by obtaining a view of the student as a learner, a view of the classroom, and a view of how that student might function academically within the classroom.

Let's take the example of Jamie described in the beginning of this chapter. Through the diagnostic work of the special education teacher and the school psychologist, the special education teacher knows that Jamie has a significant auditory memory problem. He is able to grasp social studies concepts as long as he has visual cues such as maps, pictures, and the textbook. He reads with comprehension at grade level. However, when a lecture approach only is used, Jamie is inattentive because it is hard for him to remember; he then becomes a behavior problem. We know that the sixth-grade teacher prefers and utilizes the lecture approach in social studies. The special educator sits down with the sixth-grade teacher to determine whether it is appropriate to even consider integrating Jamie in the regular sixth-grade social studies class. The general education teacher has been very accommodating with other students in the special education classroom and has voiced a willingness to take Jamie for social studies. However, she does not want to change her primary mode of instruction. She is, however, willing to give a copy of her lecture notes to Jamie the day before so he can review the material prior to class. The special education teacher assists in the review of the material by providing visual aids such as maps and pictures. When Jamie then goes into the classroom for the lecture, he feels well prepared and is attentive during social studies.

Figure 13.1 contains a checklist to assist the teacher in determining appropriate access to the general curriculum.

Discussion Questions

1. With the push toward inclusion, how can schools ensure that specialized instruction (the heart of special education) is maintained?
2. At the secondary level, how can the special education teacher assure that students with emotional and behavioral disorders have access to the general curriculum and have a curriculum that prepares them for independent living?

---

1. Is the student able to function in any general education classes without accommodations? If yes, please list classes.
2. Is the student able to function in any general education classes with accommodations? If yes, please list the appropriate classes and the accommodations needed in each.
3. Is the student able to meaningfully benefit from the content of the general curriculum but need to be provided specialized instruction in a small group or on an individualized basis with a qualified special education teacher?
4. Is the student able to meaningfully benefit from the content of the general curriculum but need to have the material modified such as being given fewer spelling words to study or shortened assignments?
5. Does the student need a "parallel" curriculum where other materials (such as those with high-interest and low-vocabulary) are utilized?
6. Does the student need an alternative to the general curriculum for any specific course of study—specifically, a functional curriculum?
7. Do the individualized goals and objectives on the student's IEP address the state's learning standards? If so, which individualized goals do so?

FIGURE 13.1.   A Checklist for Implementing the Provision for Access to the General Curriculum

3. How can we assure that regular classroom teachers have been provided adequate diagnostic information about a student who is in the regular classroom?

References

Dashler, D., Ellis, E., & Lenz, B. K. (1996). *Teaching adolescents with learning disabilities.* Denver, CO: Love.

Edge Enterprises, (2000). *Strategic instruction.* Lawrence, KS: Edge Enterprises.

Espin, C., Deno, S., & Albayrak-Kaymak, D. (1998). Individualized education programs in resource and inclusive settings: how "individualized" are they? *Journal of Special Education, 32*(3), 164–174.

Federal Register, March 12, 1999 (Volume 64, Number 48). 34CFR Parts 300 and 303.

Fuchs, D., & Fuchs, L. S. (1995). What's special about special education? *Phi Delta Kappan, 76*(7), 522–530.

Hogan, T. (1999). Academic modifications for students with learning disabilities: Questions and considerations for planning. *Learning Disabilities Association of Illinois Scope, 33*(3), 1, 4–5.

Lapansky, A. (1991). *Learning strategies and teaching techniques.* Lockport, IL: Innovative Learning Strategies.

Minskoff, E. (1998). Sam Kirk: The man who made special education special. *Learning Disabilities Research and Practice, 13*(1), 15–21.

Orkwis, R., & McLane, K. (1998). *A curriculum every student can use: Design principles for student access.* Arlington, VA: ERIC/OSEP Special Project, Eric Clearinghouse on Disabilities and Gifted Education, Council for Exceptional Children.

Pisha, B., & Coyne, P. (2001). Smart from the start. *Remedial and Special Education, 22*(4), 197–203.

Smith, S. W. (1990). Comparison of individualized education programs (IEPs) of students with behavioral disorders and learning disabilities. *Journal of Special Education, 24,* 85–100.

Smith, S. W., and Simpson, R. L. (1989). An analysis of individualized education programs(IEPs) for students with behavioral disorders. *Behavioral Disorders, 14,* 107–116.

20 U.S.C. 1400 et seq. (1997). Amendments to the Individuals With Disabilities Education Act.

14

Effective Inclusion of Students With Emotional and Behavioral Disorders

Mario is a 13-year-old seventh grader whose parents have fought to keep him mainstreamed as much as possible. He has been in regular classes with one regular education teacher and a resource teacher, who provides direct services for up to half the day and consultation with the regular classroom teachers on appropriate behavior management techniques. The junior high school is departmentalized and Jamie has seven teachers throughout the day and also sees the resource teacher part of the day. Mario has had difficulty adjusting to the new setting (and to adolescence). He is reported to be sexually harassing other students and has become very defiant in class, talking back to teachers and refusing to work. As a result, Mario has been suspended for 10 days, and an IEP and manifestation determination are to be held. The school personnel want Mario to be in a self-contained class; the parents don't know what to do.

Note: Portions of this chapter have been adapted from Moving Toward Inclusion: Meeting the Needs of Students with Emotional/Behavioral Disorders, by Eleanor Guetzloe. In L. M. Bullock and R. A. Gable (Eds.) *Monograph on Inclusion: Ensuring Appropriate Services to Children and Youth With Emotional/Behavioral Disorders—II*. Copyright 1994 by Council for Children with Behavioral Disorders, Reston, Virginia. Adapted by permission.

his sort of dilemma is frequently faced in schools. Many educators have proposed that students with emotional and behavioral disorders should live and learn under conditions similar to those made available for normal peers. In 1950, the Children's Charter issued by the White House Conference on Child Health and Protection proclaimed that "every child who is in conflict with society had the right to be dealt with intelligently as society's charge, not society's outcast; with the home, the school, the church, the court, and the institution, when needed, shaped to return him whenever possible to the normal stream of life" (Deno, 1978, p. 5). In his 1956 presidential address to the Council for Exceptional Children, Francis Lord expressed the concepts of inclusion when he urged that educational systems be structured to provide normalizing learning experiences to every handicapped child to the maximum extent possible (Deno, 1978). There were very few public school programs for students with E/BD at that time, so his comments were directed primarily toward those running programs for children with sensory impairments, physical disabilities, and mental retardation.

Inclusion is obviously not a new idea. What is new in this decade is that school systems across the continent are placing ever-increasing numbers of children with disabilities in the regular classroom, sometimes without the careful preparation of the student, the student's peers, the faculty, and the environment. School administrators, legislators, and other public officials have been exhorted by very vocal advocacy groups to place all children with disabilities in the regular classroom. These groups use as their battle cries such statements as, "All means all!" and "What part of all do you not understand?" They might well include, "Here we come, ready or not," because many regular school programs are not prepared to deal with students with disabilities—particularly those with E/BD (Guetzloe, 1994a, 1994b, 1994c).

E/BD—The Unwanted Population

Students with E/BD are still considered undesirable in the regular school program. General education teachers and nondisabled students regard these youngsters more negatively than students from any other disability category (Safran & Safran, 1984, 1985; Vidoni, Fleming, & Mintz, 1983). Those who exhibit assaultive behavior are the most rejected peer group of all (Parkhurst & Asher, 1992). Even those individuals who advocate "full" inclusion do not want their children placed in the same classes with students with E/BD, particularly those who exhibit aggressive behaviors (Guetzloe, 1994c). In this case, "All means all except students with E/BD."

The Meaning of Inclusion

The interpretation of the term *inclusion* may vary considerably from district to district in regions in North America. In some districts, inclusion has been defined as the provision of an educational program for students with mild disabilities (mild learning disabilities or mild mental retardation) in the regular classroom with little or no assistance from a special educator. In other districts, students with severe disabilities are placed in the regular classroom for the entire school day, each student accompanied by a full-time instructional aide. It is evident that (a) inclusion means different things to different educators, even those in neighboring school districts, and (b) there may be a "continuum" of inclusion, even in school districts that ostensibly embrace a philosophy of full inclusion of all students with disabilities.

Kauffman (1999) noted that the term *inclusion* is "virtually meaningless" (p. 246). "Perhaps the most startling example of the term's incomprehensibility to date is a news report in which Vermont school officials describe a special, separate school as part of their full-inclusion plan" (Kauffman, 1999, p. 246).

Placement in the regular classroom (whether it consists of maintaining a student with behavior problems in the regular classroom or reintegrating a student who has been served in a more restrictive setting) has always been a goal of special education for children with E/BD. Knowledgeable professionals clearly understand, however, that (a) the regular classroom is not an appropriate placement for all students, and (b) a full continuum of educational options must be maintained, as required by federal law. There are many youngsters (and the number seems to be growing) whose behavior and affect are such that they cannot receive an education in a regular school. For these students (particularly those who exhibit violent behavior), more restrictive options are not only desirable but absolutely necessary. For some youngsters with E/BD, the least restrictive environment may be a special class, a special school, or a residential institution.

Elements of Inclusion

Among the most important elements of inclusion are (a) attending the home school—the same school that neighbors, siblings, or nondisabled peers attend; and (b) being placed in regular education classes with classmates of the same chronological age. At the same time, inclusion of students with disabilities means (a) having an individualized education program, as required by federal law; and (b) being provided with the special education and related services necessary for success in that environment.

CCBD Position on Inclusion

The Council for Children with Behavioral Disorders (CCBD) sponsored several national forums for purposes of gathering information from the field regarding successful inclusion programs. CCBD has led the field of special education in (a) presenting the issues related to the inclusion of children and youth with E/BD, and (b) asking practitioners for their input regarding what works, what doesn't, and what barriers to effective inclusion exist (Bullock & Gable, 1994a, 1994b).

The CCBD Executive Committee (1994) promulgated a position statement on inclusion of students with E/BD. Among the important points included in the statement are:

■ For some, but not all, students with emotional and behavioral disorders, successful integration into the regular classroom is a reasonable expectation.

■ We should look at educational options for students with emotional and behavioral disorders separately from options for students with other disabilities.

■ Alternative (more restrictive) arrangements are necessary for students whose behavior is so disruptive that the learning of nondisabled students is significantly impaired.

■ Successful integration of the E/BD student depends upon special preparation of both the student and the setting and the availability of an array of support services for the student, the student's family, and the regular classroom teacher.

■ A full continuum of educational services must be maintained.

Components of an Effective Program for Students With E/BD

The current task for special education professionals is not to continue to debate the appropriateness of inclusion, but rather to determine the conditions under which inclusion will be successful for students with E/BD. The following discussion will focus on strategies for planning and implementing appropriate inclusive school programs for these students. The first section is devoted to the components of an effective program; the second section addresses an appropriate curriculum for students with E/BD.

One product of the National Needs Analysis Project at the University of Oregon is a resource handbook for administrators of programs for students with E/BD (Grosenick, George, & George, 1986). In this handbook, the components that must be considered in planning effective programs for students with E/BD are listed and discussed, including (a) the program philosophy, (b) student needs and identification procedures, (c) program goals and objectives, (d) instructional methods and curriculum, (e) community involvement, (f) program design and operation, (g) procedures for program exit, and (h) program evaluation. All of these components should be addressed, as they relate specifically to inclusion, *long before the implementation of program changes.* In one school district in which inclusion of students with E/BD has been successful, the planning began three years before the actual integration of students with E/BD (S. Keenan, personal communication, March 25, 1994).

Initial Planning for Inclusion. Fostering the sense of "ownership," which is vital to the success of an inclusive program, requires the commitment and collaboration of all individuals and agencies who will work with students with E/BD and their families. An important first step in planning for inclusion is the establishment of a number of committees and teams to assist in the process. Some of these groups may be assigned specific short-term tasks, but some may have responsibilities over a long period of time.

Establishment of a District-Wide Task Force

A district-wide task force, or planning committee, should be established, with representatives of all institutions, organizations, agencies, and groups that may be affected by the inclusion of students with E/BD (e.g., parents of students with E/BD and those without, teachers, administrators, mental health professionals, community organizations, volunteer groups, law enforcement agencies, and the business community). It is important to include members of diverse ethnic, linguistic, or cultural populations represented in the community. Community involvement and support are essential to the success of an inclusive program.

Other Teams or Committees. Other teams or committees may already exist or may be selected as specific needs emerge. These may include (a) interagency councils of service providers, (b) building teams (e.g., child study or case management committee, multidisciplinary assessment teams, parent advisory committees, crisis intervention teams), (c) content area or grade-level instructional teams, (d) co-teaching teams (each consisting of a regular education teacher and a special education teacher), and (e) grant proposal committees.

All planning committees should include individuals who possess a great deal of knowledge about students with E/BD, the needs of their families, and the services that are available. It is necessary to involve effective teachers, administrators, and clinicians; concerned parents; people who are active in national and international organizations; and individuals who read and understand the literature and are therefore aware of current trends, issues, and best practices. If such individuals are not available in the district, knowledgeable consultants should be brought in to help.

Communication Procedures. Early in the process, the various committees should decide on the communication procedures (formal and informal, verbal and written) that will be used between and among all the individuals and groups involved in the planning. These may include memoranda, letters, news releases, brochures, program policy statements, program handbooks, and newsletters. Progress reports and other information can be made available for meetings of parent organizations, professional societies, interagency councils, building teams, faculty and staff, parents and teachers, and community organizations and agencies. It is essential to keep all participants in the school and community informed of progress and possible changes in the program.

Program Philosophy

The program's philosophy, or mission statement, should be promulgated early in the planning process. For example, the following statements were suggested by Grosenick et al. (1986):

- We believe that all children can learn and benefit from an education.
- We declare that all children have the right to an education in the least restrictive environment.
- We believe that families should participate in the educative process.

Program Goals

Program goals should also be written and operationalized, including (a) the intended long-term goals of the total program, and (b) specific purposes and directions for individual students' programs. A goal statement for an inclusive program might be "to maintain E/BD students in the regular school program to the maximum extent possible."

Goals for an inclusive program in Westerly, Rhode Island, included the following:

- Gradually, over 3 years, incorporate change and success that would lead to more inclusive programs
- Provide teachers and school personnel with support and resources that would improve the programs
- Rebuild trust and communication with students, teachers, administrators, parents, and the community (S. Keenan, personal communication, March 23, 1994).

Student Characteristics and Needs

Careful consideration must be given to the characteristics and needs of the individual students to be included in the program. A committee assigned to this task should (a) find all students with E/BD in the district, (b) visit and observe them in their current placements and their homes, and (c) study their permanent school records and individualized education programs. This committee should also review teacher referrals over the past year to determine if other students (still in the regular school program without special education) are in the process of referral and identification. Students who may be eligible for a change in placement, whether or not the current IEP includes that recommendation, should be brought to the attention of the appropriate multidisciplinary assessment team. Federal law in the United States requires that all placements of students with disabilities must be individually determined according to the student's needs and abilities. Placement of any student in a less or more restrictive setting must be made according to local, state or province, and national laws, rules, and regulations.

Instructional Methods and Curriculum

In determining an appropriate curriculum for a student with E/BD, the following issues must be considered.

The curriculum should provide for the unique needs (social, emotional, physical, behavioral, and academic) of each student, as well as the traditional educational demands of the regular school. The curriculum should focus on the specific factors that caused an individual student to be eligible for special education services. These factors should be addressed as goals and objectives in the student's IEP.

Instructional methods, which should also be individually determined and written in the student's IEP, include (a) the ways in which information will be presented and modified (e.g., individualization, direct instruction, lectures, workbooks, role play, and videos), and (b) behavioral change techniques (e.g., behavior modification, counseling, and cognitive strategies). Any of these methods must be matched to the student's cognitive, social, and emotional developmental levels. Curriculum and instructional practices that are particularly suitable for the regular classroom are further discussed below.

Program Design and Operation

A careful review of all the current program offerings for students with E/BD should be conducted, which should result in precise statements of (a) needs or problems, (b) recommendations for action, and (c) written policies and procedures. All planning committees, as well as the entire program faculty and staff, should be involved in and kept informed about this program review. Specific suggestions for program review are included in the handbook from the National Needs Analysis Project (Grosenick, George, & George, 1986).

Program Design

A study of the program design will reveal components that are already in place, those that are needed, and those that must be changed to accommodate students with E/BD in the regular school program. The review should also detail the community services (individuals and agencies) that are already available and those that must be developed. It will be necessary to maintain the full continuum of service options (special education and related services), even if the program itself is housed in the regular school. These services may be provided directly by the school program or purchased through joint agreements with other districts or public or private providers. The program for E/BD must continue to reflect the requirements of federal law, state or province statutes and rules, and local regulations and guidelines.

Some program policies and procedures must be rewritten to accommodate students with E/BD in the regular school (e.g., preferral and referral procedures, discipline, reinforcers, transportation, transition, and program exit), and the need for new policies may emerge. For example, there is often a problem in determining equitable case loads for teachers and ancillary personnel who are working with E/BD students in the regular classroom. Maher (1987) reported on a high school program for students with E/BD that limits (to two) the number of students with disabilities assigned to any one classroom at one time. Another possibility is a "weighting" system, which assigns a number to each student as an indicator of the severity of disturbance. One teacher might have three "ones" (with mild problems) during a class period, while another might have one "three" (with severe problems) and a reduced class load.

Program Operation

A review of program operation will address both (a) the adequacy of material and fiscal resources (e.g., facilities, transportation, materials and supplies, and funding), and (b) the availability and caliber of personnel assigned to the program (including the amount and quality of administrative and supervisory support). Modifications of facilities may be necessary to accommodate students with E/BD. For example, there will always be a need for a "safe space" within the school (for those times when the student must leave the regular classroom for a period of time) as well as trained personnel to supervise that space and offer crisis counseling. Appropriate space and equipment, which might previously have been provided in only one school setting, must be available in every facility in which a student with E/BD is included.

The Need for Collaboration

Inclusion of students with E/BD will also require increased collaboration between and among regular and special educators, parents, administrators, ancillary personnel, multiple service providers, and business professionals who may be involved with the program. Time must be provided during the school day for communication, networking, inservice training, and planning between and among all individuals involved. This will necessitate the hiring of more personnel—both part-time or temporary (e. g., substitutes for inservice training days and planning periods) and full-time (e.g., instructional aides and additional teachers).

The Costs of Inclusion

Planners of inclusive programs should be aware that these programs will cost more, not less, than a more traditional special education program. The director of a federally funded project that is investigating the integration of students with disabilities has commented that even more special education personnel, rather than fewer, are needed when students with disabilities are served in general education (Alberg, cited in Behrmann, 1992). Although children with severe developmental disabilities or serious medical conditions may need medical services as adjuncts to their school program, children with emotional and behavioral disorders will need case management, mental health services, and crisis intervention. The provision of these additional services in all regular schools will be costly. Inclusion is not a money-saving proposition.

Funding Sources

In some districts, collaborative efforts have been funded through a combination of regular and special education resources. Planning committees should also consider other possibilities for fiscal support (in addition to local tax money), such as grants from the Office of Special Education Programs (OSEP), National Institute of Mental Health (NIMH), and Adolescent Social Services Programs (CASSP), and private foundations. Subcommittees could be assigned specifically to the task of developing proposals for such funding.

Personnel Training

The characteristics, beliefs, knowledge, and skills of all individuals involved in the inclusive program must be addressed in both the self-study and subsequent planning. Surveys, observations, and discussions may be used to identify the education and training needs of teachers, administrators, parents, and ancillary personnel, and inservice training in areas of need should be begun as soon as possible. There will be a need for a variety of training options, as faculty and staff will have to assume new responsibilities related to providing support for students with E/BD in the regular school program.

It is extremely important to include the building administrator in the inservice training, as the effectiveness of the program may well depend on this individual's attitudes, knowledge, and leadership ability. The support of the principal is of paramount importance to the success of the inclusive program. Regular education teachers are probably already knowledgeable about some teaching techniques used in special education settings, such as direct instruction and cooperative learning. They will need training in (a) nature and needs of students with E/BD, (b) special education procedures and requirements (e.g., IEPs, due process, and evaluation), (c) classroom management of disturbed and disruptive students, (d) learning strategies and social skills instruction, (e) therapeutic group procedures and affective education, and (f) crisis intervention. Experienced and skilled teachers of E/BD, who should already possess these skills, will need training in regular education policies, procedures, and curriculum. For both regular and special education teachers, specific training in team-building and collaboration is essential. Schools should also offer support groups and education for families of students with E/BD (Guetzloe, 1994b).

Inservice training components should focus on such topics as (a) student profiles and case studies, (b) functional behavior analysis, (c) reality therapy, (d) avoiding power and control issues, (e) crisis intervention, and (f) physical restraint. Options for inservice training should include (Guetzloe, 1994c):

- a "menu" of offerings, rather than the same training requirements for all personnel
- long-term offerings, rather than a "one-shot-dog-and-pony show"
- teacher support groups and mentors
- a professional library of books
- instructional materials, videos, and audiocassette tapes
- university courses, workshops, and consultants
- national, international, and regional forums, institutes, conferences, and conventions.

Many different kinds of training programs that have proved helpful to teachers and administrators involved in inclusive programs for students with E/BD are commercially available (Bullock & Gable, 1994a, 1994b). It appears that all of these programs were well received by the participants—if (a) inservice training was provided, and (b) the administrators, faculty, and staff were committed to their use.

Exit and Transition Procedures

Criteria for Program Exit

Students should be allowed to exit the special education program when they no longer meet the criteria for eligibility, whether the students are receiving services in a regular classroom or in a more restrictive placement. Criteria for both transition to a less restrictive environment and decertification should (a) parallel the criteria for identification or eligibility, (b) be written in the student's IEP, and (c) be used as goals and objectives for the individual student's program. The following are examples of such criteria:

- The student demonstrates social skills in interactions with peers and teachers that allow for satisfactory interpersonal relationships.
- The severity, frequency, and duration of the interfering behavior or affect no longer impedes the educational progress of the student or of other students in the classroom.
- The student exhibits adequate academic performance in terms of quantity and quality of work, which allows for success in the regular classroom.

A criterion statement for a student with E/BD who will be placed in the regular classroom might be: "The student exhibits the ability to achieve in the regular school environment with only the assistance available to students without disabilities." Terms used in criterion statements should be operationalized so they are clearly understood by everyone involved in the evaluation process. For example, the phrase "success in the regular classroom" might be operationalized as "the achievement of at least 'C' grades." Further, in programs for students with E/BD, we should include a criterion of being able to generalize learnings to community settings as well as the regular school environment. Many years ago, special education professionals became aware that a student might be labeled "retarded" only during the school day and considered "normal" after school hours. Students with E/BD might exhibit the reverse—being included within the school program but not in the community. We need to ensure that we do not have a "seven-hour-normal-child" at the time of program exit (Guetzloe, 1994a).

Planning for Transition

Transition to a less restrictive environment should be gradual and unobtrusive rather than "cold turkey." It will also be necessary to increase rather than decrease support services for both the student and the family during transition from more restrictive settings to the regular school. It may be helpful to have a transition checklist to follow, such as the transition plan promulgated for the Lane School in Eugene, Oregon (George & George, 1993), which includes the following steps:

1. Notify appropriate persons that the student is approaching the transition period.
2. Specify anticipated dates for the beginning of transition.
3. Try to time transition according to "windows of opportunity" such as spring break, semester break, or a job opening.

4. Assess the receiving environment: teachers and other receiving personnel, types of services available (e.g., remedial reading, counseling, and vocational education) and extracurricular offerings (e.g., sports, music, clubs, etc.).
5. Invite receiving personnel to observe the student in the present school setting and to examine samples of the student's work.
6. Introduce the student to the new environment by carrying out the following: (a) conference meeting with the receiving teacher (or job supervisor), (b) a peer-guided tour of the new setting, (c) job-shadowing, (d) a meeting with the principal, counselor, and other personnel, and (e) a trial or part-time placement.
7. Plan for continuous monitoring and tracking in the new environment, including the procedures to be followed (what, when, how often) and the person(s) responsible.

Program Evaluation

Program evaluation is an ongoing process of inquiry, data-gathering, and decision-making, which is extremely important in inclusive programs. Program evaluation should answer the question, "Are we meeting the goals for both individual students and the total program?" Specific procedures for planning and carrying out a program evaluation are included in the adminstrator's guide from the National Needs Analysis Project (Grosenick, George, & George, 1986).

Curriculum and Instructional Strategies

The curriculum for a student with E/BD in any educational setting should be designed to meet that student's individual cognitive, social, and emotional needs as determined by a comprehensive individual assessment. In the United States, the individualized education program is mandated by federal law. In other countries around the world, it is still the best educational practice.

The curriculum in an inclusive setting is based on the same goals and objectives that should be met by the students without disabilities. It should follow, as closely as possible, the regular curriculum for nonhandicapped youngsters of the same grade level or chronological age. It should also provide, as is the case for students without disabilities, for remediation, maintenance, and enhancement of basic academic skills.

Often, however, there must be modifications in the instructional materials, schedule, teaching techniques, assignments, grading criteria, and physical environment in order to ensure the success of the student with E/BD. These adaptations must be made according to the characteristics and needs of the individual student (although they would be good practice for any student who is exhibiting academic difficulties). In addition to normal learning problems encountered by every student at one time or another, students with E/BD often exhibit such characteristics as short attention span, frustration, anxiety, aggressive behavior, or withdrawal from peers, any of which will make completion of classroom assignments difficult. Lewis and Doorlag (1991) applied the concept of intensity of intervention to the adaptation of instruction, suggesting that adaptations may be made in the following:

- instructional materials and activities (e.g., clarifying or shortening directions, adding prompts or cues, and addressing specific student errors).
- teaching procedures (e.g., additional presentations of concepts or skills, additional guided practice, slowing the pace, and using more desirable reinforcers).
- task requirements with the same task (e.g., changing requirements for completion or successful performance, breaking the task into smaller subtasks).
- selecting an alternate task from the general curriculum (e.g., substituting a prerequisite or easier task related to the same material).
- selecting a similar task from a different curriculum.

Lewis and Doorlag (1991) stressed that the task being considered must be at the appropriate level of difficulty for the individual student. If the standard curriculum is suitable for the instructional level of the student, shortening the assignment can be accomplished easily by circling the numbers of a few questions or problems to be completed (instead of the entire page).

My favorite technique was to cut a commercial workbook sheet into fourths and assign one small piece at a time or to assign a single problem or question on an index card. Teaching practices that contribute to the success of an inclusive program include (a) co-teaching (by a regular classroom teacher and a special education teacher) of the classes in which students with E/BD are included, (b) a commitment on the part of the co-teaching team to adaptations and modifications of both what is taught and how it is presented (for the entire class and not just the student with E/BD), (c) the use of student peer facilitators (e.g., in mentoring, tutoring, mediation, and conflict resolution), (d) carefully planned cooperative learning activities, with special attention to the social skills and dynamics of the group, (e) flexibility in scheduling and grading for individual students and whole classes, and (f) integration of social skills instruction into the curriculum. Methods and materials that have proved to be effective with both students with disabilities and those without should be used throughout the program.

Larrivee (1985), in a study of students with mild disabilities in regular classrooms, identified teacher behaviors that were positively related to students' academic, social, and emotional gains. Consistent with findings of research with students without disabilities, these behaviors included:

- maintaining an organized and efficient learning environment.
- maximizing student time spent on academic tasks and minimizing time spent on noninstructional activities. (Time-on-task is treated in Chapter 9.)
- providing students with tasks at which they could be successful.
- using direct and active teaching procedures with groups of students.
- being responsive to students who needed support because of learning or behavioral difficulties.
- holding high expectations for student achievement and behavior.

Choate (1997) suggested guidelines for planning and modifying instruction for students with E/BD in the inclusive setting:

- Planning highly structured instruction; using consistent routines, stimulus-response formats, and positive reinforcement.
- Involving students in planning activities that they can accomplish, gradually phasing in interactive activities.
- Contracting with students for learning certain skills (and charting progress).
- Accommodating students' attention and frustration-tolerance levels.
- Directly teaching social skills and conflict resolution.
- Selecting bibliotherapeutic themes for lesson content.
- Directly teaching and coaching students in the use of learning strategies suitable for addressing each assigned task.

About Teacher Expectations

According to Morgan and Jenson (1988), an appropriate expectation for all students (including those with E/BD) would be that they progress at a realistic pace through an instructional program specifically designed to meet their individual needs. Many students with E/BD are achieving at a lower level than would be expected of students with their chronological ages or intelligence quotients; they will need extra help in many academic areas. Further, they will exhibit more inappropriate behavior (to a greater degree, much more often, and for a greater length of time) than would a student without E/BD if their needs are not effectively addressed.

Morgan and Jenson (1988) offered several practical guidelines for teachers of classes in which students with E/BD are included:

- Involve all students during group instruction (not avoiding the student with E/BD).

- Seat students with academic or behavioral problems near the center of active teaching (e.g., middle row, center of semicircle, or near the teacher).
- Give clear directions before beginning any activity, using both visual and auditory cues. Be sure all students clearly understand the directions.
- Use a variety of instructional arrangements for organizing the classroom.
- Do not assign too much independent seatwork. According to Hewett and Taylor (1980), 15 minutes is an appropriate length of time for an instructional activity; Morgan and Jenson (1988) suggest 20. An hour is too long.
- Instead of focusing on disruptive behaviors, work on strengthening academic performance (Ayllon & Roberts, 1974). When academic responses are reinforced, disruptive behaviors decrease.

In *The Special Education Teacher's Book of Lists* by Pierangelo (1995), there are instructional considerations of the student with E/BD that would be useful in the regular classroom. Although many of these suggestions focus on behavior management, the following are related more directly to curriculum:

- Planning a special activity in the morning hours.
- Teaching an "emotional vocabulary" (p. 225) so the child is able to label feelings.
- Giving shorter but more frequent assignments.
- Encouraging the use of a word processor or typewriter.
- Ensuring that the materials being presented are compatible with the student's learning style.
- Using a variety of visual and auditory techniques (e.g., overhead projector, tape recorder, or computer).

Siegel (1973) has suggested many curriculum-related techniques for solving basic problems of students with E/BD who are placed in the regular classroom, including failure-free activities—with no right or wrong answers: limited use of timed activities; short assignments; concrete (manipulable) materials; activities aimed at helping others; games; and therapeutic activities, such as humor, creative writing, skits, group discussions, and role-playing with puppets).

The Need for Research: Evaluation of Inclusive Programs

There is a tremendous need for accurate information regarding the short- and long-term impact (on students with and those without E/BD) of the inclusion of students with E/BD in the regular classroom. Recent reviews of research have revealed a lack of empirical evidence regarding the efficacy of including students with E/BD (MacMillan, Gresham, & Forness, 1996). Future investigations should address the social and emotional development, as well as the academic progress, of *all* students in the inclusive educational setting.

Conclusion

A critical current responsibility of both special and regular education professionals is to determine, to the best of our collective ability, the policies, procedures, facilities, and services that must be in place to ensure the educational success of all children—with and without disabilities—that will be included in the regular school program. This discussion has focused on educational components that must be addressed in the development of appropriate inclusive programs for students with E/BD.

Discussion Questions

1. What would you advise Mario's parents to do when they attended the conference for formulating his IEP?
2. Do you believe the inclusion movement has resulted in more exclusion—suspension—of students with disabilities? Why or why not?
3. What are the key components for training of classroom teachers to meet the needs of students with emotional and behavioral disorders?
4. How would you deal with a classroom teacher who believes that confrontational techniques are effective methods for working with students with emotional and behavioral disorders within the regular classroom?

References

Ayllon, T., & Roberts, M. D. (1974). Eliminating discipline problems by strengthening academic performance. *Journal of Applied Behavior Analysis, 7,* 71–76.

Behrmann, J. (1992). Study explores how to's of integration. *Counterpoint, 13*(1), 6.

Bertness, H. J. (1976). Progressive inclusion: The mainstream movement in Tacoma. In M. C. Reynolds (Ed.), *Mainstreaming: Origins and implications* (pp. 55–58). Reston, VA: Council for Exceptional Children.

Bullock, L. M., & Gable, R. A. (1994a). *Monograph on inclusion: Ensuring appropriate services to children and youth with emotional/behavioral disorders—I.* Reston, VA: Council for Children with Behavioral Disorders.

Bullock, L. M., & Gable, R. A. (1994b). *Monograph on inclusion: Ensuring youth with emotional/behavioral disorders—II.* Reston, VA: Council for Children with Behavioral Disorders.

Choate, J. S. (1997). *Ways to detect successful inclusive teaching; Proven correct special needs* (2nd ed.). Boston: Allyn and Bacon.

CCBD Executive Committee. (1994). Position paper on inclusion. (Available from Council for Exceptional Children, 1920 Association Drive, Reston, VA 22091–3660).

Deno, E. N. (1978). *Educating children with emotional, learning, and behavior problems.* Minneapolis, MN: Leadership Training Institute/Special Education, University of Minnesota.

George, M. P., & George, N. L. (1993). Lane School transition checklist. (Available from Michael George, Lane Educational Service District, 1200 Highway 99N., P. O. Box 2680, Eugene, OR 97402)

Grosenick, J. K., George, N. L., & George, M. P. (1986). *Designing and evaluating quality programs for seriously emotionally disturbed children: A guide for administrators.* Eugene, OR: University of Oregon: National Needs Analysis Project.

Guetzloe, E. (1994a). Inclusion of students with emotional/behavioral disorders: The issues, the barriers, and possible solutions. In L. M. Bullock & R. A. Gable (Eds.), *Monograph on inclusion: Ensuring appropriate services to children and youth with emotional/behavioral disorders—I* (pp. 20, 21–24). Reston, VA: Council for Children with Behavioral Disorders.

Guetzloe, E. (1994b). Moving toward inclusion: Meeting the needs of students with emotional/behavioral disorders. In L. M. Bullock & R. A. Gable (Eds.), *Monograph on inclusion: Ensuring appropriate services to children and youth with emotional/behavioral disorders—II* (pp. 29–32). Reston, VA: Council for Children with Behavioral Disorders.

Guetzloe, E. (1994c). Inclusion of students with emotional and behavioral disorders: Program considerations for designing appropriate services. In L. Bullock & L. Ellis (Eds.), *Designing effective services for students emotional problems: Perspectives on the role of inclusion* (pp. 1–12). Denton, TX: University of North Texas.

Hewett, F. M., & Taylor, F. D. (1980). *The emotionally disturbed child in the classroom: The orchestration of success* (2nd ed.). Boston: Allyn and Bacon.

Kauffman, J. M. (1999). Commentary: Today's special education and its messages for tomorrow. *Journal of Special Education, 32*(4), 244–254.

Larrivee, B. (1985). *Effective teaching for successful mainstreaming.* New York: Longman.

Lewis, R. B., & Doorlag, D. H. (1991). *Teaching special students in the mainstream* (3rd ed.). New York: Merrill.

MacMillan, D. L., Gresham, F. M., & Forness, S. R. (1996). Full inclusion: An empirical perspective. *Behavioral Disorders, 21*(2), 145–159.

Maher, C. A. (1987). Involving behaviorally disordered adolescents in instructional planning: Effectiveness of the GOAL procedure. *Journal of Child and Adolescent Psychotherapy, 4*(2), 204–210.

Morgan, D. P., & Jenson, W. R. (1988). *Teaching behaviorally disordered students: Preferred practices.* New York: Merrill.

Parkhurst, J. T., & Asher, S. R. (1992). Peer rejection in middle school: Subgroup differences in behavior, loneliness, and interpersonal concerns. *Developmental Psychology, 28,* 231–241.

Pierangelo, R. (1995). *The special education teacher's book of lists.* West Nyack, NY: The Center for Applied Research in Education.

Safran, S. P., & Safran, J. S. (1984). Elementary teachers' tolerance of problem behaviors. *Elementary School Journal, 85,* 237–243.

Safran, S. P., & Safran, J. S. (1985). Classroom context and teachers' perceptions of problem behaviors. *Journal of Educational Psychology, 77,* 20–38.

Siegel, E. (1973). *Special education in the regular classroom.* New York: Day.

Vidoni, D. O., Fleming, N. J., & Mintz, S. (1983). Behavior problems of children as perceived by teachers, mental health workers, and children. *Psychology in the Schools, 20,* 93–98.

15

Working With Families of Students With Emotional and Behavioral Disorders

Mike, a student at a therapeutic day school, was being raised by his mother. Two siblings were in the home. During the time Mike was in the school, he did very well and thrived on positive reinforcement. His mother also received a lot of positive encouragement. She was recognized at awards assemblies and in the school newsletter and often called by the school personnel, who told her how well her son was doing. When Mike received the good citizen badge for the year, she was taken out to lunch along with him. Mike continued to do well and was slowly integrated into a high school of 1,200 students. Within three months of his total integration, he started doing poorly. Eventually, it was discovered that his mother had been sabotaging the integration by negatively commenting on the new school because her needs for positive reinforcement and encouragement were not being met in the large school setting.

Note: Portions of this chapter have been adapted from training materials by Eleanor Guetzloe, copyright 1996 by Behavioral Institute for Children and Adolescents, Arden Hills, Minnesota. Adapted by permission.

ver the past several decades, the school-related roles and activities of families of students with disabilities have changed dramatically—from observers of the education process and passive recipients of information from school personnel to equal partners and active participants in the education of their children. A positive working relationship with the family of a student with E/BD is generally viewed as one of the most important components of an effective school program. This chapter will provide information to the teacher of students with emotional and behavioral disorders regarding the needs of the families of these children and ways of working closely and cooperatively with families in the provision of an appropriate education program.

The Value of Parent Involvement

Parents are the first—and most important—teachers for any child (with or without disabilities). They can be valuable adjuncts to those in the instructional program in many ways: discussing the day's activities with the student; assisting with, signing, and returning homework assignments; reading aloud to the student; watching and discussing media presentations with the student; tutoring; and participating in behavior management programs.

A number of studies have shown that active parent involvement in the school program results in increased academic and behavioral gains (Allen, 1978; Henderson, 1988; Imber, Imber, & Rothstein, 1979). Smith, Finn, and Dowdy (1993) found that parents could increase a student's progress in reading by (a) providing a conducive atmosphere for reading, (b) modeling reading behaviors, and (c) carrying out remedial activities at home. In other studies, the inclusion of a home-based component in which parents delivered consequences for behavior resulted in decreases in both noncompliant behavior and symptoms of depression (Johnson & Zemitsch, 1988; Rosen, Gadardi, Miller, & Miller, 1990).

As Dettmer, Dyck, and Thurston (1999) noted, children are not the only beneficiaries of family involvement. Family members have the opportunity to learn helpful skills (e.g., behavior management techniques and communication skills); teachers can learn more about their students' backgrounds, interests, and needs; and school systems benefit from improved attitudes toward schools and advocacy for school programs. "Reaching the family is as important as reaching the child" (Rich, 1987, p. 64).

Parents' Rights as Mandated in Federal Law

The right to be active participants in their child's special education program is ensured by certain procedural safeguards included in federal law. Teachers of students with E/BD must be aware of the parents' rights, as mandated by federal law, and be able to assist in informing parents about these rights in an understandable manner. Among major safeguards guaranteed to parents are (Friend & Bursuck, 1999):

- The right to be members of any group that makes decisions about educational placement.
- The right to consent for initial formal evaluation and assessment and written notice in advance of any subsequent evaluation.
- The right to written notice before the school initiates, changes, or refuses to initiate or change the identification or placement of a student.
- The right to participate directly in the development of their child's individualized education program and the periodic (at least annually) review of the IEP.
- The right to inspect and review educational records maintained by the school district or other agency providing service under IDEA.
- The right to request mediation as a means of resolving conflicts with a school district.
- The right to request a hearing by an impartial hearing officer.
- The right to be fully informed of their rights and the procedural safeguards related to special education.

Despite the mandates of federal law, a cooperative and collaborative partnership between teachers and parents is by no means guaranteed. The success of the family-school relationship often depends upon the classroom teacher's commitment to that process. Most teachers recognize the importance of successful family-teacher collaboration, but some may not have the knowledge, skills, or persistence necessary to establish a positive working relationship with the family. The desire to form an effective partnership is not sufficient; specific knowledge and skills related to working with families are also necessary.

What Teachers Need To Know About Working With Families

The Behavioral Institute for Children and Adolescents, a not-for-profit corporation located in Minnesota, promulgated a checklist of teacher knowledge and skills necessary for working effectively with parents of students with E/BD. The checklist, which is intended for use in teacher training programs, includes the following statements of things teachers need to know:

- Major functions and evolving role of families.
- Special needs of families of students with E/BD, including the impact of E/BD on parents and siblings and the needs of nontraditional families.

- Parental rights and responsibilities (e.g., access to information, participation in decisions, confidentiality of data).
- The social, medical, mental health, and legal resources available in the community; roles and responsibilities of community resources; and procedures for referral to community agencies.

Further, a teacher of students with E/BD should be capable of exhibiting the following observable skills:

- Developing and maintaining open lines of communication.
- Planning and conducting parent conferences.
- Planning and implementing a daily or weekly report system to communicate with parents regarding student progress.
- Developing, implementing, and evaluating a home-school intervention program.
- Planning and conducting parent training sessions related to a student's educational program.
- Identifying appropriate agencies for provision of related services, making appropriate contacts and referrals, and maintaining collaborative communication.

Developing and Implementing the Individualized Education Program

Of all the interactions between and among parents, families, and education professionals, the most crucial are related to the development and implementation of the individualized education program or the individual family service plan (IFSP), as mandated by federal law. It is extremely important that teachers (a) assist parents in understanding the process, and (b) secure their full participation as members of the multidisciplinary team.

Dettmer and associates (Dettmer, Dyck, & Thurston, 1999; Dettmer, Thurston, & Dyck, 1993) outlined ways in which families can be involved in the development and implementation of individualized plans before, during, and after the team conference. These items can become a checklist for families to follow as they collaborate with educational personnel.

First, throughout the year, families can (a) read about educational issues and concerns; (b) study the structure of the local school system; (c) observe the student, paying attention to work habits, play patterns, and social interactions; and (d) record information about special interests, talents, or accomplishments as well as areas of concern.

Second, before the IEP planning conference, parents can (a) visit the school, (b) converse with the student about school activities, (c) talk with other families about what happens at a conference, (d) write down questions or points for discussion, (e) review notes from previous conferences; (f) prepare a file of information, observations, and samples of the student's work; and (g) invite other knowledgeable persons of their choosing to attend the conference.

Third, during the conference, family members can (a) be active participants; (b) ask questions about anything that is unclear; (c) insist that educational jargon (e.g., "alphabet soup") be avoided; (d) contribute information, ideas, and recommendations; (e) comment on positive things the school has provided; (f) ask for a copy of the IEP if one is not provided; and (g) ask for a follow-up contact time for purposes of comparing notes about progress.

Finally, after the IEP has been developed, families should (a) discuss the conference proceedings with the student, (b) continue to monitor the student's progress and add to their own information file, (c) follow up according to their agreement with the other members of the IEP team, (d) reinforce the school staff for positive outcomes of the planned program, and (e) actively attempt to help improve the school in any way possible.

Parent Involvement in School and Classroom Activities

Parents can be involved in the school program in less formal ways, such as observing and volunteering in the classroom, meeting with teachers, participating in out-of-class activities, providing transportation, attending parent groups, providing support to other parents, acting as advocates, raising funds, working with administrators, and sharing program information with other agencies (Cone, Delawyer, & Wolfe, 1985). Parents can also give valuable input to the planning of curriculum and school-sponsored activities outside the school. Information about family histories, occupations, avocations, and cultures can provide the foundation for such curricular components as (a) topics for thematic units, (b) choices of literature and other materials (e.g., readings for bibliotherapy), and (c) activities based on strengths of individual students and/or family members.

Barriers to Family Involvement

In many instances, despite supportive legislation, parents are not fully involved in the planning and implementation of the educational program. In particular, for parents of students with emotional and behavioral disorders, it is often not sufficient to provide information regarding the mandates for parent involvement or remind them of their responsibilities in this regard. School personnel must work to eliminate barriers to parent participation (e.g., lack of transportation or child care) and provide tangible ways in which parents can become involved in the school program. (Some suggestions for addressing these barriers will be found below.)

Special Needs of Families of Students With E/BD

The stages of grief experienced by a survivor after the death of a loved one (Kubler-Ross, 1969) have been adapted by Duncan (cited in Kroth & Edge, 1997) to help educators understand the feelings of parents when they learn that their child has a disability. Many disabilities are detectable at birth or shortly thereafter. In the event of later discovery of a child's disability (after the newborn stage, as is the case with most E/BD), parents become gradually aware of the condition (Turnbull & Turnbull, 1990). The stages of grief related to the discovery may still occur, but in a slightly different pattern: (a) denial, (b) anger, (c) bargaining, (d) depression, and (e) acceptance or coping.

Special education teachers may find themselves in the position of helping parents to (a) understand that their child actually has a disability, and (b) deal with the grief associated with that discovery. Suggestions for helping parents through this difficult time have been offered by a number of special educators (Healey, 1996; Ramp, 1999; Turnbull & Turnbull, 1990, 1997).

Some parents may continue to exhibit what some authorities have termed "chronic sorrow," a situation in which grieving continues throughout the lives of both the child and the parents (Kroth & Edge, 1997). These parents will need continuing support—from school personnel during the student's school years and from other public or private providers after the student has reached adulthood.

Parents of students with emotional and behavioral disorders often experience even greater difficulties than parents of students with other disabilities. They deeply love their children, but have an intense dislike for the children's behavior. They may feel guilty. They may experience problems in controlling aggressive, violent, or noncompliant children; they may describe their home lives as being "out of control." They are often embarrassed by their children's behavior and find it difficult to explain the behavior to others. They need to know that they can look to school personnel for understanding and support.

Providing Support to Parents

Shea and Bauer (1991) proposed a hierarchical model for the support of parents of students with disabilities. These authors suggest that as parents' needs at each level are met, they will be more comfortable in participating at the next higher level. The levels of this model are:

1. *Crisis assistance.* The first level addresses both (a) help in making referrals to crisis services and (b) the concept of "doing no harm," as described in the physician's Hippocratic oath (Johnston, 1998, p. 197). Teachers must (a) be alert and sensitive to signs of serious emotional distress, (b) offer in a sympathetic way to assist in securing services if needed, and (c) assist in referring the parents to trained professionals when the situation warrants.

Regarding "doing no harm," teachers and administrators need to be aware that some school policies and practices may actually exacerbate family crises. Johnston (1998) cited examples of (a) an attendance policy that punished a student for staying home to care for a seriously ill member of the family, or (b) a grading policy that did not allow a student to complete work missed when the student was in an emergency care facility. Teachers must be alert to the possibility of such situations and be willing to advocate for the student and family in need.

2. *Providing information and resources for parents.* The information that parents find most helpful is specifically related to the school program and their child's performance. They often need assistance in fully understanding their rights, as guaranteed by federal law (more than just a single sheet of printed material). They also want to know how they can help their child become more successful in school.

3. *Supporting parent engagement.* Parents can become involved in planning and delivering parent education on topics of interest (e.g., federal law, behavior management, or ways to gain access to community service agencies). Support groups may be most beneficial when they are organized by the parents themselves, but the school may support this effort by providing a meeting place, refreshments, or transportation. Barriers to parent participation can be removed by scheduling conferences that take into consideration the needs of working parents, providing telephone access to teachers, running school buses on "back-to-school night," providing child care during meetings, and conducting meetings in other locations besides the school (e.g., churches, or community centers).

4. *Securing support for school programs.* After other crises have been resolved, parents are well informed, and they feel supported in their tasks of parenting students with E/BD, they are ready to support the school's programs and operations by volunteering, helping to provide resources for school and classroom programs, and sharing responsibility for school governance (e.g., serving on school advisory committees).

What Parents Want From Professionals

Jordan and Richardson (n.d.) of Parent Advocacy Coalition for Educational Rights (PACER) in Minneapolis, Minnesota, discussed what parents of students with E/BD want from professionals, including respect and dignity, information, choices, practical skills, and support services.

At the head of the list of particulars, parents want equal status relationships on issues related to their child. They would like to work with professionals who deal with them honestly, who will listen and act on their recommendations, and who acknowledge that parents have expertise about their own children.

Next, parents would like information about such issues as their legal rights, their child's behavior, programming based on individual needs, choices of educational program options, and effective alternatives to punishment. They would also like help in learning practical skills, such as behavior management techniques.

Third, parents would like to have information about national, state or province, and local community agencies and support groups; support networks (including those available on the internet); and ways to contact other parents of students with E/BD.

Most of all, parents want teachers for their children who are knowledgeable, skillful, and compassionate, who will advocate for students with E/BD. Parents need to know that they are not alone in their quest for appropriate services—that the teacher is an ally and not an adversary.

Parent Education

Parent education is not a new development; it has been an important component of the special education program for students with E/BD since the 1960s. The general emphasis in the 1960s, in keeping with the psychodynamic approach in acceptance at that time, was on helping parents to develop psychological insight into the needs of their child, the rest of the family, and themselves. Parent meetings were often therapeutic in nature, facilitated by a psychologist, social worker, or psychiatrist, with parent change as a major goal (Swanson & Reinert, 1984).

During the 1970s, parent education emphasized a behavioral approach to behavior management. A number of commercial programs were developed for the purpose of encouraging parent involvement in the educational program of their children with E/BD. For example, the Systematic Training for Effective Parenting program (Dinkmeyer & McKay, 1976) included audiotapes and written materials designed to promote both parent growth in understanding their child and parent-professional interaction. There are now a multitude of commercially available materials for parent education, many of which include both written materials and videotapes.

Parent advocacy groups (e.g., Federation of Families for Children's Mental Health and PACER) offer well-planned and executed programs of parent education on topics ranging from the federal law to medication. These programs can be used directly by parents, and teachers can also select from a variety of materials and approaches to offer education on topics of interest to parents of students with E/BD.

Teachers must be aware that not all parents will need "education." Many parents are extremely knowledgeable about their child's disability, the federal law, their rights, and appropriate educational programs. They may be very skillful in carrying out behavioral change programs. Further, as Walker and Shea (1991) noted, "Parents with problem children are not necessarily problem parents" (p. 247). They are often normal individuals who are responding in a normal way to the unexpected trauma associated with having a child with E/BD.

When parents ask for training or education, however, or when they respond positively to an offer of such assistance, it is extremely important for the school to provide this service. In several instances, courts have ordered residential placement for students who required consistency and support that was not available at home. A district court in Texas held that an appropriate placement could be made available within the public school setting if training and counseling were provided to the child's parents (Osborne, 1996). An Alabama district court ordered a school district to provide training and counseling to the parents of a student who exhibited academic and behavioral problems. Finding that the student's IEP was not appropriate, the court held that "school officials had ignored a crucial component of a behavioral control program by failing to counsel and instruct the parents in how to reinforce at home the training the student received at school" (Osborne, 1996, p. 149).

Respite Care

In the early 1980s, I collaborated with the local chapter of the National Society for Autistic Citizens to provide respite care for families of children with autism. With partial funding from a grant awarded by the state of Florida, parents of children and adolescents with autism were able to pay trained university students to provide day care (and night care) for their children. In the early days of the project, the parents themselves provided the necessary training by meeting with the students in weekly practicum seminars. After a period of group orientation, students were matched with the families for whom they would provide respite care. Parents provided extensive information about their families, including such things as food preferences; medications taken; house rules about eating, bathing, and bedtime; physician's telephone numbers and locations; insurance cards;

signed forms giving permission to procure medical treatment for the children; and other routine matters.

One male student was able to teach a 19-year-old to bathe himself, a task the young person had never mastered. Another student stood firm and taught a twelve-year-old to go to bed at the appointed hour. Many students used their time with the youngsters to engage in educational activities suggested by the young-sters' teachers. For many parents, this project provided their first opportunity to go out together without worrying about their child's well-being. One mother reported that she had never, since the birth of her child, been able to leave him long enough to go to the beauty salon.

As the program continued, all of the participants—families, university stu-dents, and the professor—learned a great deal about youngsters with autism. Parents began to use some of the strategies that worked for the university stu-dents. Formative and summative evaluations completed by both the parents and the students revealed high levels of satisfaction with the program. Every student was successful in providing quality care, there were no serious crises, and every parent was delighted with the opportunity (Guetzloe & DiNapoli, 1981).

Recreation for Students

In a federally funded project for the purpose of fostering and enhancing intera-gency collaboration, the first step in planning was to simply ask the parents of students with E/BD what they needed or wanted for their children. A great major-ity of the parents indicated that they were reasonably satisfied with the school program, but that their children needed recreational opportunities—places to play after school hours and other children with whom they could interact—in settings in which they would be both safe and accepted. Through arrangements with recreational and environmental programs (e.g., Boys and Girls Clubs, Little League, and local environmental agencies) and by furnishing assistants who were knowledgeable about both the characteristics of the children and appropriate behavior management techniques, students with E/BD were "included" in after-school and weekend activities (Guetzloe, 1992).

Making Families Welcome at School

The school should establish a place in which parents who visit may gather on an informal basis. Ideally, this would be a separate room (a parent lounge) with toi-let facilities; attractive furniture; a coffeepot and cookies; drink machine; journals and magazines; videotapes, audiotapes, and necessary equipment; information about the school curriculum; paper, pens, and pencils; photographs of students engaged in school activities; and examples of student work. If an entire room is not available, teachers can designate a small section of a classroom as a "Family Corner," making the amenities mentioned above available on a smaller scale.

If the school community includes families from diverse linguistic backgrounds, having "Welcome" signs at the school entrance in every language represented in the school is very encouraging to both families and students. Reading materials and other media should be made available in the languages spoken by the families.

Maintaining Positive Communication With Families

Authorities in the field of special education generally agree that the most important component of an effective relationship between parents and teachers is positive communication (Kroth & Edge, 1997; Turnbull & Turnbull, 1990, 1997). Families need to know what is expected of their children, and teachers need to know what children are doing at home. School personnel should make every effort possible to ensure that communicating with the school is an enjoyable experience for parents and families.

Being Aware of Cultural Differences in Patterns of Communication

Cultural backgrounds dictate patterns of communication that may differ from those of the ethnic majority (Sue & Sue, 1990). Among the ethnicity-based values and behaviors that affect collaboration between and among parents, members of the community, and teachers (and which extend to student relationships with peers and adults) are:

- Proxemics (personal space), which affects an individual's feelings about appropriate physical distance between people or the arrangement of furniture during a conference.
- Kinesics (body movement), which affects personal interpretations of posture, facial expression, and eye contact.
- Time orientation, which can increase or decrease an individual's thinking regarding the importance of being on time for meetings or other events.
- Paralanguage (vocal cues beyond actual words), such as loudness, inflections, hesitations, and speed.

Teachers and other educational personnel must make every effort to become aware and knowledgeable about the ethnic, linguistic, and cultural differences in the families of their students. School staff, volunteers from diverse communities, or outside consultants can assist in determining the appropriateness of the conference setting, topics to be discussed, or any other facets of the communication process. Cultural sensitivity and competence are essential to a productive relationship with families of students with E/BD.

Starting the Year on a Positive Note

Teachers can initiate a positive working relationship with parents by contacting parents as soon as the school term begins (or as soon as a student is assigned to the school or class). Parents should be given information about the school and classroom program as well as ways in which they can participate in the program. Every possible effort should be made to welcome parent participation.

Ways To Communicate With Families

Among the many ways in which teachers can communicate with families are conferences, telephone calls, e-mail, a class web page, parent handbooks, notes, class newsletters, and interactive journals. Several authors suggested the use of "traveling notebooks" (notebooks that are carried by the students between home and school) as effective ways to maintain continuous communication with parents (Cronin, Slade, Bechtel, & Anderson, 1992; Hallahan & Kauffman, 2000).

Parent preferences with regard to communication with teachers have been investigated by a number of researchers. Ammer and Littleton (1983) asked 217 parents of exceptional students to check the methods they preferred for getting regular communication from the school. Letters were the most preferred (selected by 69% of the parents), followed by parent-teacher conferences (51%) and telephone calls from teachers (45%). Home visits were the least preferred (selected by only 19%). Similar results were reported by McCarney (1986), who asked a large geographically diverse sample of parents and teachers to rate their preferences among 20 types of parent-teacher communication. The five most preferred by the parents were telephone calls from teacher to parent (90.4%), report cards (90.4%), parent-teacher conferences at school (88.5%), telephone calls from parent to teacher (86.5%), and student's work sent home by the teacher (84.9%). The parents' five lowest-ranked choices were parent-teacher meetings in a place other than school or home, PTA meetings, parent-teacher conferences that include other adults, parent group meetings, and parent-teacher conferences at home (the lowest-ranked of all).

Early in the school term, teachers can explain the various ways in which they will be normally communicating with all of their students' families (e.g., newsletters, traveling notebooks, a class website, etc.). Parents can select those methods that they would prefer when the teacher needs to contact them individually.

Planning Conferences To Support Effective Communication

Teachers can use a variety of techniques in planning conferences that support effective communication with parents, including (Rizzo & Zabel, 1988; Simpson, 1982):

- Offering scheduling options, including before-school and evening appointments.
- Encouraging parents, guardians, or child-care workers who are involved with the student to attend conferences. Outcomes of the conference should be shared with individuals who are invited but do not attend.
- Inviting parents (or other adults) to observe the student in the classroom and encouraging them to leave a note on the student's desk regarding something positive that was said or seen during the conference (e.g., "I saw your neat writing paper." "Your teacher said you have done good work in mathematics.").
- Making arrangements for supervision of younger children who come with parents (or providing activities for the children to do independently while the adults are in conference). Parents should be asked in advance if younger children will be coming.
- Providing adult-sized, comfortable furniture for all adults and arranging chairs informally.
- Having refreshments available.
- Preparing an outline of discussion topics (if the conference is teacher-initiated).
- Preparing a conference form on which to record conference dates, names of individuals attending, major topics covered, and actions to be taken.
- Following through on plans and suggestions agreed upon during the conference.

Special Conference Techniques for Parents Who Are Upset

The same authorities (and others) also suggested special conference techniques for conferring with parents who are angry or emotionally upset (Rizzo & Zabel, 1988; Simpson, 1982):

- Listen to parents. Do not try to "talk them out of their feelings." Allow them to talk about, fully explain, and exhaust their concerns without interruption or response. To the extent possible, avoid offering solutions. Let them talk.
- Avoid arguing.

- Request clarification on points you do not understand, but avoid constantly interrupting or asking more than one question at once.
- Maintain an acceptable listening posture, but try to remember the parents' major concerns so they can be recorded later (or explain in advance that you need to record these issues as they are mentioned).
- Be aware of your own anxieties and possible reactions (e.g., avoiding eye contact, shifts in body posture, and body movements) when talking with emotionally overwrought adults. Concentrate on keeping your voice low and relaxed; avoid defensive or intimidating gestures.
- Avoid any attempt to discount or belittle parents' feelings (e.g., You couldn't possibly feel . . ." "You should not overreact.").
- As much as possible, avoid responding to generalized allegations or threats (e.g., "If you were in control of your classroom, this wouldn't have happened." "You'll be hearing from my attorney.").
- Avoid strong emotional reactions and insensitive responses (e.g., sarcasm, disbelief, pain, anger, or disapproval).
- Be sensitive to parents' problems without assuming ownership or responsibility for those problems.
- Be aware that emotionally upset parents are in a highly vulnerable position. You must be able to (a) communicate a sense of understanding, (b) offer verbal support (e.g., "It's all right for you to cry."), and (c) physically offer assistance (e.g., touching or offering tissues).
- Avoid being critical or impatient ("Come on, pull yourself together.") or intolerant of emotional responses ("As a teacher, I can talk only about your child's school performance.").
- Do not discount or belittle the descriptions of feelings or situations discussed by the parents. The emphasis should be on understanding their perceptions.
- Remember that a teacher is not a therapist. If the parents need counseling, consider including other knowledgeable, skilled, and carefully selected staff in the conference.
- When confronted by parents with a confirmed history of being physically abusive toward professionals, get a colleague to sit in on the conference.

A Final Word From a Parent

Naseef (1999), a psychologist who is also the father of a son with autism, offered the following suggestions for educators who seek to work more effectively with parents:

- Respect the skills and knowledge that parents bring to the process.
- Maintain open and clear two-way communication.

TABLE 15.1.   Effective Parent Conferences: What To Do and What Not To Do

Do	Don't
Make "happy-calls" and send "happy-grams" to parents of difficult students	Dwell on student's mistakes when reporting to parents
Prepare reports summarizing student's progress	Allow parents to focus on student's mistakes
Emphasize strengths	Argue with parents
Explain and seek agreement with parents on your action plan	Ask parents to monitor or consequate school teacher-student behavior issues or in-school assignments
Ask parents to let you know of changes in student behavior that they notice	
Meet with student before parent-teacher conference	Keep student "in the dark," fostering suspicion or fear
Protect student self-esteem in parent-teacher conferences	Permit parents to attack student
	Think you have to handle every difficult situation yourself
Request presence of counselor or principal if you think you expect a difficult conference	Rush toward quick solutions
	Overlook parents' strengths
Use reflective listening, especially when parents are upset	Make assumptions about nontraditional families before getting to know them
Consult parents as resources	
Understand the unique concerns of single parents	

- Try to understand and have empathy for the family's individual circumstances.
- Respect differences of opinion.
- Share planning and decision-making.
- Be aware of the family's unique strengths and needs.
- Offer unconditional positive regard for the students and family.

Discussion Questions

1. Given what you have learned from this chapter, outline the steps you would take at the beginning of the school year to establish a communication system with the parents of students with E/BD.
2. How would you resolve the issue discussed at the beginning of the chapter and keep Mike's mother from sabotaging her son's integration?
3. How would you approach a parent who refuses to attend any IEP meetings because he is intimidated by the number of people present?

References

Allen, K. F. (1978). The teacher therapist: Teaching parents to help their children through systematic contingency management. *Journal of Special Education Technology, 2,* 47–55.

Ammer, J. J., & Littleton, B. R. (1983, April). Parent advocacy: Now more than ever, active involvement in education decisions. Paper presented at the 61st Annual International Convention of the Council for Exceptional Children, Detroit, MI.

Cone, J. D., Delawyer, D. D., & Wolfe, V. V. (1985). Assessing parent participation: The parent/family involvement index. *Exceptional Children, 51,* 417–424.

Cronin, M. E., Slade, D. L., Bechtel, C., & Anderson, P. (1992). Home-school partnerships: A cooperative approach to intervention. *Intervention in School and Clinic, 27,* 286–292.

Dettmer, P., Dyck, N., & Thurston, L. P. (1999). *Consultation, collaboration, and teamwork for students with special needs* (3rd ed.). Boston: Allyn and Bacon.

Dettmer, P., Thurston, L. P., & Dyck, N. (1993). *Consultation, collaboration, and teamwork for students with special needs.* Boston: Allyn & Bacon.

Dinkmeyer, D., & McKay, G. (1976). *Systematic training for effective parenting.* Circle Pines, MN: American Guidance Service.

Gallagher, P. A. (1988). *Teaching students with behavior disorders* (2nd ed.). Denver: Love.

Guetzloe, E. C. (1992). The Manatee Community Services Coordinating Council: Research and development in the community. In K. Kutash, C. J. Liberton, A. Algarin, & R. M. Friedman (Eds.), *A system of care for children's mental health: Expanding the research base* (pp. 307–311). Tampa, FL: Florida Mental Health Institute, University of South Florida.

Guetzloe, E., & DiNapoli, A. (1981, April). The family friend: In-home respite program and case management service. Paper delivered at a conference of the Florida Mental Health Institute, Tampa, FL.

Hallahan, D. P., & Kauffman, J. M. (2000). *Exceptional learners: Introduction to special education* (8th ed.). Boston: Allyn and Bacon.

Healey, W. C. (1996, November). Helping parents deal with the fact that their child has a disability. *CEC Today,* pp. 12–13.

Henderson, A. T. (1988). Parents are a school's best friends. *Phi Delta Kappan, 70*(2), 148–153.

Hester, P. P., & Kaiser, A. P. (1998). Early intervention for the prevention of conduct disorder: Research issues in early identification, implementation, and interpretation of treatment outcomes. *Behavioral Disorders, 24*(1), 57–65.

Hunt, N., & Marshall, K. (1995). *Exceptional children and youth* (2nd ed.). Boston: Houghton Mifflin.

Imber, S. C., Imber, R. B., & Rothstein, C. (1979). Modifying independent work habits: An effective teacher-parent communication program. *Exceptional Children, 46,* 218–221.

Johnson, A. C., & Zemitsch, A. (1988). Family power: An intervention beyond the classroom. *Behavioral Disorders, 14,* 69–79.

Johnston, H. J. (1998). Family involvement models in middle schools. In M. L. Fuller & G. Olson (Eds.), *Home-school relations: Working successfully with parents and families* (pp. 191–207). Boston: Allyn and Bacon.

Jordan, D., & Richardson, V. (n.d.). *Keys to working with parents and families.* (Available from PACER, 4826 Chicago Avenue South, Minneapolis, MN 55417)

Kroth, R., & Edge, D. (1997). *Strategies for communicating with parents and families of exceptional children* (3rd ed.). Denver, CO: Love.

Kubler-Ross, E. (1969). *On death and dying.* New York: Macmillan.

McCarney, S. B. (1986). Preferred types of communication indicated by parents and teachers of emotionally disturbed students. *Behavioral Disorders, 12,* 118–123.

McLean, M., Sandell, E. J., & Johnston, J. H. (1998). Family involvement models. In M. L. Fuller & G. Olson (Eds.), *Home-school relations: Working successfully with parents.* Needham Heights, MA: Allyn & Bacon.

McLoughlin, J. A., Edge, D., & Strenecky, B. (1978). Perspective on parental involvement in the diagnosis and treatment of learning disabled children. *Journal of Learning Disabilities, 13,* 295–300.

Meese, R. (1996). *Strategies for teaching students with emotional/behavioral disorders.* Pacific Grove, CA: Brooks/Cole.

Naseef, R. (1999). An insider's view of the invisible challenges: Understanding parents of children with mental, emotional, and behavioral disorders. *Healing, 4*(1), 36–40.

Osborne, A. G. (1996). *Legal issues in special education.* Boston: Allyn and Bacon.

Ramp, A. (1999). How to tell parents their child has a disability. *CEC Today, 5*(8), 6.

Rich, D. (1987). *School and families: Issues and actions.* Washington, DC: National Education Association.

Rizzo, J. V., & Zabel, R. H. (1988). *Educating children and adolescents with behavioral disorders: An integrative approach.* Needham, MA: Allyn and Bacon.

Rosen, L. A., Gadardi, L., Miller, C. D., & Miller, L. (1990). Home-based treatment of disruptive junior high school students: An analysis of the differential effect of positive and negative consequences. *Behavioral Disorders, 15,* 227–232.

Seifer, R., & Dickstein, S. (1993). Parental mental illness and infant development. In C. H. Zeanah (Ed.), *Handbook of infant mental health* (pp. 21–142). New York: Guilford.

Shea, T. M., & Bauer, A. M. (1991). *Parents and teachers of children with disabilities* (2nd ed.). Boston: Allyn and Bacon.

Simpson, R. L. (1982): *Conferencing parents of exceptional children.* Rockville, MD: Aspen.

Smith, D. D. (1998). *Introduction to special education: Teaching in an age of challenge* (3rd ed.). Boston: Allyn and Bacon.

Smith, T. E., Finn, D. M., & Dowdy, C. A. (1993). *Teaching students with mild disabilities.* Fort Worth: Harcourt Brace Jovanovich.

Sue, D. W., & Sue, D. (1990). *Counseling the culturally different: Theory and practice* (2nd ed.). New York: Wiley.

Swanson, H. L., & Reinert, H. R. (1984). *Teaching strategies for children in conflict* (2nd ed.). St. Louis, MO: Mosby.

Turnbull, A. P., & Turnbull, H. R., III. (1990). *Families, professionals, and exceptionality: A special partnership* (2nd ed.). New York: Macmillan.

Turnbull, A. P., & Turnbull, H. R., III. (1997). *Families, professionals, and exceptionality: A special partnership* (3rd ed.). Upper Saddle River, NJ: Prentice-Hall.

Walker, J. E., & Shea, T. M. (1991). *Behavior management: A practical approach for educators.* New York: Merrill.

AUTHOR INDEX

SUBJECT INDEX